Society and Culture in India

Society and Culture in India

Their Dynamics through the Ages

INDRA DEVA
SHRIRAMA

RAWAT PUBLICATIONS
Jaipur • New Delhi • Bangalore • Guwahati • Kolkata

ISBN 978-81-7033-516-0

Reprinted, 2018

Published by
Prem Rawat for **Rawat Publications**
Satyam Apts., Sector 3, Jawahar Nagar, Jaipur - 302 004 (India)
Phone: 0141 265 1748 / 7006 Fax: 0141 265 1748
E-mail : info@rawatbooks.com
Website: rawatbooks.com

New Delhi Office
4858/24, Ansari Road, Daryaganj, New Delhi 110 002
Phone: 011-23263290

Also at *Bangalore, Guwahati* and *Kolkata*

Typeset by Rawat Computers, Jaipur
Printed at Nice Printing Press, New Delhi.

Dedicated

to those

Scholarly Giants

climbing on whose shoulders alone
would open up a time perspective
wide enough to perceive the
shaping of social structure and culture

Max Muller *P.V. Kane* *Rahul Sankrityayana*
and his colleagues

Contents

Preface

This book is a product of sustained endeavour towards a genuine sociological understanding of Indian social structure and culture. It has been made possible by close collaboration between a sociologist and a Sanskrit scholar over the last thirty years.

The pattern, processes and factors of social change, latent as well as manifest functions of beliefs and rituals, certain unknown aspects of culture contact, sociology of religion, social stratification, and the relationship of ideas and even metaphysical systems with factors of social existence, i.e., sociology of knowledge have been critically brought out through systematic analysis of Sanskrit and other texts right from the Ṛgveda to the later Smṛtis and their commentaries. It is not a paraphrasing of works belonging to different eras, as has generally been the practice so far. Nor is there any attempt either to justify and glorify, or to detract and condemn.

Though each chapter has a bearing on a number of sociological dimensions, one can particularly find analysis of social change in the essay on 'The Perspective of Social Change'; of social function in 'Latent Function of the Doctrine of Karma' and in the exposition of reasons for proliferation of rituals in

Hindu society; of a new dimension of culture contact in 'Culture Contact Between Ancient India and Iran'; of social stratification in 'Emergence of the Traditional Pattern of Social Stratification'; of sociology of religion in 'Religion of India'; and of sociology of knowledge in 'Correspondence between Woman and Nature in Indian Thought'. The essay on 'The Rise of Elite Tradition and Genesis of Indian Civilization' throws new light on the vexed question of the gensis of civilizations.

One of the common inadequacies of works based on interpretation of Sanskrit texts has been that in describing the nature of various social institutions, evidence drawn from works composed in diverse eras, separated from each other by long spans of time extending upto two thousand years and more, is put together as if it all pertains to the same socio-cultural system. The pictures constructed through such excercise are fictious. They fail to represent properly any real social institution because the socio-cultural system in India has undergone radical transformations in the course of many-many centuries of its existence. The Weltenschauung so richly in evidence in the Ṛgveda, for example, is a world apart from the worldview propagated in the Smṛtis.

Our endeavour has been to understand social institutions and values in the context of the specific socio-cultural systems represented by the works composed in those diverse eras. Thus, the processes and forces that shaped various social institutions and values through the ages are brought out, and we move towards a better understanding of the dynamics of the Indian socio-cultural system as a whole.

Many of the findings of our research work which are presented here have already been brought out in reputed international journals such as *Philosophy East and West*, XVI (1966) and the *Diogenes*, UNESCO, Paris, nos. 84 (1973), 93 (1976), 111 (1980), 130 (1985), 140 (1987) and 150 (1990). These research writings have been translated into many languages such as French, German, Italian, Spanish, Arabic and Hindi, and have received wide national and international recognition.

For drawing inferences, we have depended primarily on the evidence of the texts themselves. Secondary sources have been seldom relied upon. This is evident from the copious specific references to the original texts. In citing these references, the style of the widely available *Sacred Books of the East*, edited by Max Muller has been followed, so that the reader can easily verify for himself any statement based on a particular text.

Much of our concerted work in this field has been made possible by the research grants provided by the Indian Council of Social Science Research. We acknowledge our gratitude to the Council.

INDRA DEVA
SHRIRAMA

I

Methodological Approaches for the Study of Society in India

Systematic study of society is still in its infancy in India and it may be argued with some justification that the time has not yet come for taking stock of its accomplishments. On the other hand, the low level of growth itself seems to be a good reason for examining the methods followed so far. The present state of social science in India and the methodological perspectives that have emerged are inevitably related to the existent socio-cultural forces; and our attempt towards their assessment would naturally involve reference to the latter.

Stunted Growth of Social Science in India

Looking upon the state of the social sciences in India, one is struck by their protracted barrenness. The social sciences have been taught in Indian universities for a fairly long time to an increasingly large number of students. But fundamental contributions to social science have been rather rare. One may be able to recall a few contributions of a high order but, on the whole, the record remains surprisingly disappointing. This general paucity of fundamental contributions to social science is not to be explained on the basis of any inherently inferior intellect of Indians. Inadequacy of resources and facilities may explain the situation but only partially; for, many fields and methodological approaches that have been in vogue in the past do not require huge financial support and material equipment.

What then is the reason for this sterility? The reason seems to be primarily sociological. It has perhaps something to do with the historical context in which modern social sciences were brought to India and the class that pursued them.

Modern social sciences did not originate in India. They have their roots in the modern western society, and have been shaped in their spirit and content by the ethos and the processes of that society. It should not be surprising if they have, by and large, failed to grow and yield fruit when planted in a radically different social soil and cultural climate. More than the question of any fundamental difference between the cultures of India[1] and the West, it is a problem of the gap in the level of development of these societies.

When the British introduced English education in India, which included the study of modern social sciences, the country had a social structure which was basically different from the social structure of contemporary England and other advanced countries of the West. The social science in India has developed in an utterly different context. It is understandable, therefore, that even if the Indian teacher or student was able to understand and remember theories imported from the West, he could seldom contribute to their fundamental growth.

A question that suggests itself at this stage is: Why was it then that social sciences continued to be studied in India despite their irrelevance to the state of social development in the country? An adequate answer to this question is provided not so much by any detached love of learning, either on the part of Indian students or on that of the British rulers, but by the fact that education was assigned a different function, which it continued to perform. This function, as is well known, was the creation of an English educated middle class through which the

British could govern their vast empire. Macaulay said: "We at present do our best to form a class who may be interpreters between us and the millions whom we govern." Not that this class always remained content to perform the task of supporting the British empire. On the contrary, it spearheaded the Indian national movement. But when it comes to accomplishments in the field of social science, it fails to show a bright record.

The English educated middle class was seriously handicapped by time. Even when it came to its own and showed signs of being related to the social dynamics of contemporary India, it found itself too backdated to make a significant contribution to the social sciences. It seems that movements comparable to the Renaissance and the Reformation overtook sizable parts of India only in the latter half of the nineteenth century. It will be seen that these movements in Europe go as far back as the sixteenth or even the fifteenth century.

The transformation of parts of Indian society, from a traditional state to a comparatively modern one, did imply the emergence of certain movements comparable to the European renaissance, reformation and nationalism. But it would be a folly to think that the ideas underlying them were bodily lifted from the West. Influence of the West, primarily British in the context of India, surely acted as a catalyst, but the elements that reacted were mostly indigenous. For example, the reformist Arya Samaj movement played a role similar to Calvinism in promoting puritan and activistic ethics conducive to the growth of capitalism in western and central parts of northern India. But it primarily drew upon ancient Indian texts. In fact, it sought support from the most primeval texts, the *Vedas,* for its attack on medieval values and institutions; though of course the interpretation of these texts was rather stretched to suit its case. The Arya Samaj did not consider any form of Christianity acceptable.

This movement and many other reform and renaissance movements that sprouted up in the eighteenth and nineteenth century India, and played a remarkable role in its transformation towards modernism, nevertheless remained basically Indian. They engendered an attitude of resistance against western dominance in the field of ideas as well as those of politics and economy. They nourished beliefs about India's 'glorious' past that strengthened nascent nationalism. Such beliefs were often at variance with the history and other humanities and social sciences taught in schools and colleges under official patronage. These movements could therefore be expected to provide the basis for the growth of indigenous schools of social science, but they failed to do this. The reason for this failure lies not only in the absence of official support, but also in the lack of adequate strength and sophistication to compete with the more modern trends in social science that continued to be pursued under the auspices of the British government.

However, even though the Indian renaissance, reform and nationalistic movements failed to throw up any parallel system of social science, they do seem to have prevented a fuller participation by the Indian intelligentsia in the growth of social sciences that were brought to this country as a result of the British rule. Indians belonging to the new middle class, who taught and studied these social sciences, were mostly in the grip of one or the other of these nascent nationalistic movements; and they did not really believe in much of what they had to teach or study for earning their livelihood. In such circumstances, they could hardly make any creative contribution to its growth. Thus, on one hand, they were unable to give a disciplinary status and systematic form to their own ideas about society, on the other, they remained incapable of making substantial contribution to current social science. This situation largely continued till the opening decades of the twentieth century.

Another drawback to the intellectual creativity was the foreign medium. It cannot be denied that knowledge of the English language has made the vast and expanding treasures of modern learning accessible to Indians. But, at the same time, we have to recognize that English as a medium of study and research work does have certain cramping implications for creativity. In the first place, it tends to uproot the Indian intellectual from the surrounding social reality in several ways. In so far as a language implies a viewpoint, the use of English condemned the Indian intellectual to look upon his own land from the viewpoint of the foreigner. When we study Indian society through the English medium, we are inevitably trying to size up its reality through categories that do not perfectly fit in with it. Moreover, the use of English by the Indian intelligentsia tends to become a barrier to easy intercommunication with the masses. This becomes a serious drawback for the development of social sciences.

Secondly, though English is a useful instrument for the pursuit of modern knowledge, the costs of its acquisition and maintenance have been too high for an average Indian. Indeed, most of his academic effort is spent in acquiring competence in the English language and keeping it in proper trim; too little of his energy is left for making a productive use of this excellent instrument. Hence, there is a tendency to use it as an ornament. This tendency is further accentuated because the ability to write correct English and to speak it with proper accent is regarded in India as the chief criterion of judging a man's learning and status. This has been so because of the British rule, but the hangover continues even after independence.

There is another aspect of the matter which is less obvious. Persistent grappling with an almost impossible task, i.e., perfect mastery over a foreign language, has created a deep-seated feeling of inferiority in the Indian intellectual. Whenever he makes a statement he is haunted by the possibility of its being linguistically inaccurate. Often he is more worried about its grammar than its content. This constant anxiety seems to have contributed greatly to make the Indian intellectual uncertain of himself, and hence less productive.

Though the record of social science in India has so far been unsatisfactory, there are certain signs that indicate the possibility of some important breakthrough. This possibility is there not because of material facilities available in the developing countries like India, but due to the challenge these countries are facing. The traditional social structure which has been in existence for millenia is undergoing change at a tremendously fast pace. Apart from the numerous socio-cultural problems caused by the lags and tensions, the reconstruction of the whole social order on new foundations is a real challenge to any perceptive social scientist. It is not impossible that this challenge evokes a magnificent response. The social scientist in countries like India cannot be satisfied merely by dealing with trivial issues in a sophisticated jargon. He has to grapple with the basic problems of the dynamics of the social structure. The concentrated impact of modern forces and the telescoping of processes of change affords a unique opportunity of studying their pattern almost by the naked eye. If this challenge is taken up, social science in countries like India may advance beyond the point reached so far in the developed countries.[2]

Attempts to Construct an 'Indian Sociology'

The stunted growth of sociology in India, and to a certain extent the influence of nationalistic ideologies, have induced many a social scientist to call for the construction of an 'Indian Sociology'. This term, however, means a number of different things to different people. Broadly speaking, the term 'Indian Sociology' may be employed to cover one or more of the following aspects: (i) a special body of concepts and generalizations applicable to Indian society and culture; (ii) sociological principles derived from traditional Indian sources; (iii) the study of social structure and social processes in India; and (iv) sociology as it has developed in India.

Obviously, these denotations and connotations of the term 'Indian Sociology' are not necessarily exclusive of each other. In fact, two or three of these usually go together. For instance, very often, when a plea is made for the development of a body of sociological knowledge particularly relevant to India, (i) an explicit or implicit assumption is that this can be done only on the basis of principles found in the traditional Indian texts; (ii) similarly, the argument for developing sociological generalizations applicable specifically to India; and (iii) as a necessary prerequisite. The study of Indian social institutions as they have actually existed and the various prescriptions and formulations laid down in ancient texts are often dealt together in such a way that it is difficult to make out the one from the other.

The use of the term 'Indian Sociology' in the sense of a distinctive growth of the subject through the work of Indian sociologists does not seem to be very common yet. It is generally recognized that sufficient work has not yet been done to justify us to speak of Indian Sociology in the same sense in which we speak of, for example, German Sociology. The last sense of the term 'Indian Sociology' need not therefore detain us. The same could perhaps be said of the aspect (iii) above which merely implies the study of social structure and processes in India. There can be no dispute that these should be studied, and the various methods which have been employed to carry out this task will engage our attention later on. However, the use of the term to designate a body of concepts and generalizations, applicable specifically to Indian society and culture, requires some discussion.

The plea for the development of a special body of concepts and principles to cope with society and culture in India implies an emphasis on the distinctive character of Indian socio-cultural phenomena. In other words, Indian society and culture are considered so different from elsewhere (particularly from western society and culture, where modern social sciences have grown) that, according to the proponents of this viewpoint, an entirely different conceptual framework is required for any adequate understanding of the former.

The crucial issue, therefore, is: How far are Indian society and culture distinctive? It may be agreed at the outset that Indian society has some distinctiveness. It is our assessment of the nature and degree of distinctiveness, however, that will determine our views on the need and possibility of Indian Sociology. Every society shares some common features with other human societies. For instance, the basic nature of social interaction (which involves the use of symbols) is fundmentally similar in all human societies. Then, there are certain features which a society has in common with the societies of its kind. Tribal, peasant and industrial societies have certain institutional and cultural characteristics that societies of their own type only may share. Yet every society has certain attributes which may be distinctively its own. Only if Indian society has characteristics of the last kind in an overriding proportion, as compared to the attributes of the first two kinds, can we justifiably plead for the development of Indian Sociology in this sense.

The need of developing a special conceptual and theoretical frame for the study of Indian society is pressingly felt when it is found that concepts and theories developed in the West do not appropriately size up the Indian social reality. The sociologist in India frequently faces this difficulty. A very elementary example will illustrate the point. In general sociological terminology, 'family' refers only to husband, wife and minor children; but when this concept is applied to India, it seems to refer to no real social institution; for, family in India is a much wider unit. The same will be true of the concepts of religion, caste and several other notions. Similarly, the concepts of individuality, ego expression, and personality development, which are implicit in much of modern social science, are not found to have great relevance to Indian conditions.

However, without going into the merits of the arguments involved in the above illustrations, it can be said that similar arguments about the applicability of the modern social science concepts could be advanced with equal force on behalf of most rural and 'underdeveloped' societies. For instance, family in most pre-modern societies is a much bigger unit than the standard sociological concept would lead us to believe. Taking human societies as a whole, the actual family units have been much larger than the nuclear family. Indeed, some thinkers have argued that on a purely factual basis it will be more justifiable to refer to the modern western family as the 'contracted family' rather than designating the larger family units as 'extended' or 'joint'.

The Indian family is similar to families in other peasant societies not only in size but in most of its basic attributes. It is interesting to see how the characteristics of family and familism described by Sorokin, Zimmerman and Galpin (1930-32) for all rural societies, based on subsistence agriculture, fit in with the essential features of the traditional Indian family. They observe that "familism is the outstanding and fundamental trait in the gestalt of such a society" and point out that all such societies are marked by early age of marriage, the existence of family as the unit of social responsibility and the basis of social norms; the impress of the family on state and kingship; the predominance of cooperative rather than contractual relationships; the functioning of family as the unit of production, consumption and exchange; the existence of family cult and ancestor worship; and the dominance of tradition. It is not difficult to see from this how closely the Indian family resembles---in structure, spirit and function—the family in other peasant societies.

Similarly, the individualistic notions about personality are foreign not only to traditional India, but to other traditional societies as well. In other such societies too, a man is expected not to develop an individuality all his own, but to conform as much as possible to the traditional archetype appropriate to his or her status and role. Anand K. Coomaraswamy has demonstrated the essential unity of all traditional societies in such matters in a number of brilliant essays. According to Coomaraswamy and other like-minded scholars, it is only the modern industrial civilization which has deviated from the traditional path and has thereby become abnormal.

We find, thus, that even though many concepts and theoretical frameworks developed in the context of the modern western society do not fit in well with the social facts in India, this does not necessarily indicate the indispensability of an Indian Sociology. On the other hand, the basic similarities between Indian society and other peasant societies lead us to think that what is really needed is a wider conceptual framework which could take care of as many pre-modern societies as possible. Peasant societies, based on plough agriculture, have perhaps enough in common to warrant the development of such a framework.

It is not only the elite sub-stratum of the Indian tradition which shares much in common with the elite traditions in other civilization. The tradition of the unlettered folk in India shows no less similarities with the folk-cultures elsewhere. Indian folktales share fully in what appears to be a common stock of world folklore motifs. The same could be said about proverbs and riddles. Even more striking are the similarities in form and content between the popular heroic poems of the Indian folk on the one hand and the Greek, Teutonic and central Asian heroic poems on the other. The characteristics of heroic poetry analyzed by Chadwicks (1912; 1932) for ancient Greek and Teutonic heroic poems are present to an amazing extent in Indian heroic poems like the "Ālhā". C.M. Bowra's study (1952), comparing heroic poetry among a number of Asian and European people, confirms the above assertion. Neither Chadwics nor Bowra have discussed heroic poetry popular among the non-lettered Indian folk; but if one knows about Indian heroic poems he is sure to feel that these writers could have found their best illustrations from the tradition which is still vigorous in India. Not only are the plots, the characters, and the style of the Indian heroic poems similar to the heroic poetry of the societies far away in time and space, even the basic spirit of these poems is the same. Such facts lead one to think that the consciousness of Indian people is not essentially different from that of the people of comparable societies in other lands.

In spite of the above observations about the social structure of the elite and popular cultural streams in India, a feeling still lingers that Indian society has something which distinguishes it from other societies. This need not be denied. The crucial point is: how far uniqueness at this level will justify the building up of a special Indian Sociology. Moreover, it should not be forgotten that the vaguely perceived spirit of a nation or national character is subject to various interpretations and unforeseen changes. The history of ideas regarding national character substantiates this abundantly. National characteristics, once believed to be intrinsic, are known to have changed radically.

The attempt to build up an Indian Sociology through the study and analysis of traditional texts has not only been advocated but has also been put into practice. Apart from Sanskrit scholars and Indologists, many professional sociologists in India have depended extensively on traditional texts for the study of society in India. This, therefore, has to be treated as one of the established methodological approaches and deserves consideration on that basis.

Analysis of Traditional Texts

The need to base sociology in India on traditional Indian thought as found in ancient texts, is often emphasized. The plea is made not only by Indian scholars, but sometimes also by foreign sociologists. Dumont and Pocock (1957:7) observe: "The first condition for the development of a sociology of India is found in the establishment of the proper relations between it and classical Indology."

While the need for the analysis of traditional texts for enhancing our insight into Indian institutions and culture is undeniable, the methodological limitations of the work done so far in this direction need to be considered. When used as a source of sociological data, the same tests should be applied to the texts as to other documents employed for such purposes. But this has hardly been done; and the work of such eminent Indian sociologists as G.S. Ghurye and K.M. Kapadia is no exception to this. When dealing with any aspect of Indian society and culture, evidence from whatever source it is available is marshalled. Consequently, it does not relate to any one real historical era. The tendency generally is to accept the statements made in a ıcient texts on face value, without critical judgemnt.

It is obvious that objective description of social reality was not the primary purpose of these texts. Many of these texts such as the *Dharma Sūtras* and *Smṛtis* are of prescriptive nature, and others like the *Puranas* and the epics like the *Rāmāyana* and *Mahābhārata* have mythological and literary intent. Construction of any veridical picture of society on the basis of these will have many difficulties and would, at least, require a careful assessment of the divergence from the social reality which the purpose, motive and style of a work might have introduced. It must also be noted that the classical Sanskrit literature has belonged only to the uppermost strata of society and it can at best reveal their attitudes and values. *Smṛtis*, which embody the Hindu social and legal codes, explicitly state that the sacraments and many prescriptions made by them are meant only for the twice-born (upper *varṇas*). Thus, the commoners who must have constituted the bulk of population in traditional India, just as in other ancient civilizations, had no share in the making of these codes and other Sanskrit texts. Even among the upper strata, only males have been active bearers of the elite tradition. These texts do not represent the woman's viewpoint.

Perhaps, the most serious limitation of the attempts to study Indian society through the analysis of Sanskrit texts has been the neglect of historical dynamism of society and culture. It has not been clearly recognized that various texts belong to very different periods of history. Some of these may have been composed some two thousand years before Christ and some others later than one thousand A.D. During this long period of time, the Indian society and culture underwent innumerable changes. Things like beef-eating, which were common and even formed part of ritual in the Vedic times, were later on regarded as the very negations of Hinduism and were forbidden through the strongest religious sanctions. Even though there has been some continuity in the development of traditional institutions and culture, the changes are too vast to be ignored. The talk of the traditional form of some institution or element of Indian culture is often an abstraction for which there is no factual warrant.

Despite this, the tendency among most scholars, including sociologists, is to assemble quotations from sources widely divergent in historical time and to piece them together for constructing pictures of Indian institutions and culture. Obviously, such pictures are likely to be spurious patchworks.

A related problem is that while selecting texts for evidence on Indian society no attempt is made to follow any standard procedure for their selection in the absence of which these tend to become biased. There is a tendency to quote again and again some limited passages from Vedic literature while ignoring the bulk of the content of the *Vedas* and the *Sūtras*. The picture thus presented is very different from the one that would emerge if a proportionate representation was given to the material from these sources. The extent to which most works on Indian society and culture based on the analysis of traditional Sanskrit texts depend on the *Manu Smṛti* is remarkable; and the analysis of its reasons can make a good exercise in sociology of knowledge.

It may be mentioned that in most cases it is extremely difficult to determine the date of composition of the traditional Sanskrit texts. To relate them to a particular historical era is, therefore, not easy. This problem is further complicated by the fact that most of these works were reworked over several centuries. Different portions of the *Mahābhārata* may be separated by as many as eight centuries. It is also obvious that various works observe differential selectivity. The famous code of *Manu* which was perhaps the foremost work of the Brahmanical revival, makes no explicit mention of the great Buddhist and Jain movements which preceded it, and whom it sought to combat.

Despite these difficulties, the analysis of texts cannot be given up. Though Indian society and culture have been changing, there is a marked continuity through the ages. Contemporary institutions, values and attitudes cannot be understood adequately without reference to the vicissitudes which have shaped them. Ways must be found, therefore, to make the analysis of the traditional texts more objective.

The subsequent chapters of the present work endeavour to get over the shortcomings in interpretation of Sanskrit texts discussed above. Values and institutions are related to the specific socio-cultural eras to which they belong, and to the sections of society in which they have emerged. Thus, their manifest and latent functions are brought out. Viewing the changes in an adequately wide time perspective of socio-cultural dynamics reveals some of the forces and processes that have shaped them. Examining the relationship of ideas, beliefs and practices to other factors of social existence embodies explorations in the area of sociology of knowledge.[3]

A different approach to tradition is represented by the work of A.K. Saran (1956; 1961). Following A.K. Coomaraswamy (1948a; 1948b) and H. Zimmer (1952), Saran does not emphasize the uniqueness of Indian tradition; on the other hand, he believes in the transcendental unity of all traditional cultures. This methodological approach can be termed as logico-philosophical and it is highly critical of empiricism and scientism. While the logical and semantic analysis employed in this approach is illuminating on many points, it is difficult to see how the study of society can do without any method of observing social facts. Logic alone can at best yield consistent statements; but how do we know in what relationship they stand with social reality? This approach, however, has played a significant part in making young Indian sociologists keenly aware of the limitations of their methodological equipment, and has served as a warning against gross positivism.

Analysis of Oral Tradition

The fact that the elite religious and literary texts have been the preserve of the male upper-strata population has induced some sociologists to analyze (Deva, 1956; 1972; 1974; 1989) oral tradition of the unlettered folk. Folk-literature has been an integral part of the work, worship and leisure of the bulk of Indian population. It is actively shared by both men and women of even the lowest castes. Not only the rural people, but a large part of the population of the pre-industrial urban centres is active bearers of the oral tradition. This wide sharing is brought out by the selection of themes and their treatment in various *genres* of folk-literature. The attitude of different castes towards each other, including that of the lower castes towards the higher; the nature of the diverse relationships in the patriarchal joint family, the built-in tensions in them, and the resentments of the woman; operative religious and magical beliefs and practices among the folk; and even the impact of modern social forces find ample expression in the folk-literature of various regions of India. A systematic analysis of oral tradition can, therefore, yield useful hypotheses about many subtle aspects of social relationships and attitudes of the common people.

In the folk tradition most pieces are anonymous. There are few professionals, and there is no separate literary class. A few types may be performed by some particular groups and they may be rewarded for it, but the bulk of the oral tradition is widely shared by persons engaged in different walks of life. Thus, there is lesser likelihood of folk-literature getting alienated from the mainstream of life. It has often been pointed out that poets and literary men are prone to become ingrown and thus their works may fail to represent the more common feelings present in their society. This limitation would be far less applicable in the case of oral tradition.

The fact that folk-literature in peasant societies depends for its survival and growth on oral transmission makes it all the more valuable as a source of socio-cultural data. A piece, which appeals to the folk no more, is sure to fall into disuse and die out. There are no critics or publishers who can artificially prop up certain kinds of material and suppress others. No government can proscribe any piece of the popular oral tradition. The material is continually reworked knowingly and unknowingly. And, in the course of performance, new themes with an appeal to the people are constantly being added in a living oral tradition. This flexibility of the oral tradition must be a great help in keeping it in tune with the feelings of the people.

Folk tradition in India has certainly been influenced by the modern forces, but it has not yet lost its vigour. While some *genres* show signs of decline, the stream as a whole seems to have enough vitality not only to sustain itself but also to imbibe new elements. References to modern objects, events and experiences find their way in the oral tradition by the customary process of reworking of traditional items, composition of new pieces, and even through the emergence of new types.

While the value of the oral tradition as a source of socio-cultural data seems to be fairly clear, the development of adequate techniques for the analysis of the oral material poses a serious challenge. The correctness of conclusions drawn from a casual acquaintance with the oral material, which is so large and varied, would depend upon the selection of pieces that are cited as evidence. In this and also in the interpretation of the content, the bias of the research worker can creep in unless some objective techniques are evolved.

In this context, one is inevitably reminded of the developments in the techniques of content analysis. It is obvious, however, that this technique has usually been applied to communication material of a very different kind and its tools can hardly be adequate for our purpose without considerable adaptation and refinement. Content analysis, as it has developed, puts great stress on indicating frequencies (Berelson, 1954: 448-522). There would be special problems in applying this to the content of the oral tradition.

A living oral tradition is always in a continued state of flux. Its parameters are far from sharply defined so that the universe itself cannot be demarcated accurately. Its constituents too are continually reworked through the process of oral transmission, and so it is difficult to count them as discrete items. There are numerous versions of every folk-song, folk-tale, epic poem or proverb and none can be regarded as the only authentic text. It is difficult to decide how much variation makes a piece fit to be regarded as a distinct unit.

These attributes of the oral tradition raise serious questions about the applicability of quantitative techniques. Where neither the boundaries of the universe nor those of the constituent items are clear, attempt at applying statistical techniques begins to appear an excercise in futility. However, while efforts towards objectivity and precision must continue, the limitations of the quantifying analysis of the oral tradition need not cause undue despair. Most of the significant socio-cultural variables still remain unquantified and in so far as the data derived from the analysis of oral tradition has to be related to the former, its non-quantitative nature need not be a fatal handicap.

While developing techniques for an objective analysis of the oral tradition, we must balance the claims of verifiability and significance. Even if a technique is objective, in the sense that it eliminates the bias of the researcher, its ultimate value will lie in the significance of the results which it can yield. For example, a count of frequency of occurrence of a particular set of words in a given sample may be more verifiable than analysis in terms of certain significant themes. But, the latter may lead us to more meaningful results. However, in the interests of objectivity of analysis, procedures will have to be devised for selection of suitable samples, identification of units of analysis, and some general canons of interpretation.

Empirical Studies

Considering the vastness of India and the great diversity of its institutions and culture, empirical sociological studies have so far been too meagre. Even when we think of such basic institutions as the family, studies based on a systematic collection and analysis of the empiric data are extremely limited. Modern social survey techniques have gained currency in India only after the Second World War, and many factors have held back their growth.

Collection of data through standard techniques and statistical processing requires sizable financial resources that are not easily available in a country like India which is far from affluent. Most Indian universities do not, as yet, provide resources or facilities which can sustain such work. When no outside agency is available to sponsor a research project, it has to be carried out single-handed; and in such circumstances the sample investigated is too small to yield any meaningful results. This is, by and large, true of the doctoral research work carried out by individual research scholars. This work may nevertheless constitute the major part of scientific social research done so far in India.

The general level of technical competence of the social scientists who undertake large empiric research projects is also doubtful. Such projects began to be distributed on a substantial scale in the fifties with the establishment of the Research Programmes Committee of the Planning Commission. When high governmental agencies think of assigning such work, it is natural that they choose scholars of established standing.[4] But most of these scholars had built up their reputation through work of other kinds; they hardly had any personal experience of, or training in, empiric field survey methods. It is not surprising, therefore, that the twenty-one socio-economic surveys of cities in different parts of India, which were carried out in the fifties under the auspices of the above agency, failed to contribute substantially to the growth of urban sociology in India.

This situation continues to persist even now, though perhaps to a lesser degree. Most of the social scientists in the Indian universities have inadequate grounding and interest in modern statistical techniques. One begins to wonder whether such aversion to quantitative methods could ever contribute to the growth of scientific social survey research in India. Be that as it may, unless something radical is done to make possible a better combination of social science learning and modern statistical techniques, empiric survey research is not likely to attain a high level.

So far, the empiric research reports, whether they are of individual research scholars or of large projects sponsored by governmental and other agencies, usually show a low level of methodological sophistication. This is broadly true of sampling designs, construction of tools for data collection, as well as interpretation of material.

The cost of good research work being what it is, the possibility of its growth in a country like India will greatly depend upon its ability to develop a satisfactory relationship with governmental and other agencies. The line drawn between pure and applied research needs reconsideration in this context. When a study is planned well and carried out in accordance with the norms of science, it does not become impure if some of its results are utilized for the solution of practical problems. In fact, if the conclusions stand the test of application in the field, they should be treated as further verified.

With India's increased efforts towards planned socio-economic development, the social scientist is called upon more and more to assist in the tasks of policy formulation and execution. In this regard, the major emphasis has, so far, been on the economist. But, now, the assistance of the sociologist too is being sought at various levels. The chief difficulty in this connection has been that the sociologist does not, as yet, possess enough scientific knowledge of the crucial processes to render useful professional advice to the decision-maker. He, therefore, tends to depend upon his commonsense. This lack of expertise soon betrays itself, and thus, the discipline itself is devalued. The real way out of this situation seems to lie in making the decision-maker conscious of the type and magnitude of research work needed for a scientific assessment of the problems in hand. Such an approach will surely bring some disappointment in the beginning, but in the long run it is likely to be more conducive to the growth of social science.

In view of the extreme paucity of resources, empirical sociology in India can hardly afford to neglect whatever material it can lay hands on. Of course, every type of material will have to be critically evaluated for its authenticity and some of it, so to say, may have to be recycled. For example, the decennial census that has been carried out in India for over a century can provide a lot of data which has the added advantage of having been collected in a chronological sequence. Not all census campaigns were of the same level of comprehensiveness or quality. But some, like the census of 1931 which was carried out under the direction of J.H. Hutton, contain extremely valuable material for sociological interpretation. Similarly, the National Sample Surveys and the reports of various commissions of inquiry can provide some data of sociological relevence. Undoubtedly, the use of such material must involve careful scrutiny of the procedures followed in its collection, as also of any possible sources of bias therein. A better coordination of research work done by the students and teachers in a university department can also go a long way in conserving scarce resources and in furthering the reliability and significance of the results obtained.

Social-Anthropological Approach

Perhaps, due to the influence of the British rule, social anthropology found better initial opportunities to grow than sociology in pre-Independence India (Bottomore, 1962:98-106)

The use of anthropological method has resulted in the production of good monographs on many Indian tribes. For some forty years now, anthropological methods and concepts have been extensively used for the study of peasant villages as well. This has become so common that the suitability of the anthropological approach for the study of rural India is almost taken for granted (Clinard and Elder, 1965: 581-587; Bottomore, 1962: 100). Even when a plea is made for greater reliance on the sociological techniques of investigation, it is in the name of more emphasis on the study of the city and the industry, rather than that of the rural society itself.

A closer scrutiny would, however, show that the current village studies, based on the anthropological conceptual models and research techniques developed in the context of isolated and self-contained communities, fall far short of the requirements of the study of the Indian peasant society. While Robert Redfield himself endeavoured to develop in the closing years of his life a more adequate conceptual apparatus for the study of peasant society (1956), most of the village studies which deal with peasantry are still based on his earlier concept of 'little community' (1955) which refers in its pure form to the model of the primitive tribe. But in so far as the peasant society is essentially part-society shaped by continued interaction with an elite tradition, the models built for the tribal societies are hardly applicable.

In village studies, the procedure of investigation of a peasant village is based on the assumption that it is a little community. This assumption is clearly mistaken and it leads the social scientist to ignore the socio-cultural relationship which a peasant village traditionally has with other villages and non-industrial urban centres (Deva, 1969). Such a village is an integral part of a civilization. Its institutional and cultural elements cannot be understood without reference to the civilization as a whole and its historical background.

In view of this, it is surprising that single peasant villages have been studied as if they were socio-cultural wholes. The carrying-over of the model of the study of tribal society has also led to an indifference to history while dealing with the peasant villages. Peasant villages cannot be regarded ahistorical like primitive tribes. Though the peasants themselves may be predominantly unlettered, they belong to civilizations which have histories. Many facets of peasant life cannot be understood adequately without reference to this history. Such basic aspects of the life of a village as the pattern of settlement of various ethnic groups and the power structure can be properly comprehended only with reference to the historical forces that have shaped them.

The only justification for studying peasant villages on the models of 'folk society' and 'little community' can be that even though they do not fully conform to these ideal constructs, they can be placed on a continuum to indicate their exact socio-cultural position. It was this idea that prompted the development of the 'folk-urban continuum'. However, this also has a number of doubtful implications. Many criticisms have been voiced against the construct of the folk-urban continuum; but its most serious difficulty seems to be that it leads to a comparison of entities which do not belong to the same order. The ideal 'folk society' is a self-contained whole. But, a peasant village is not a whole; it is *essentially* a part of a bigger socio-cultural whole. Placing parts and wholes on the same continuum is bound to be misleading. It may also be pointed out that the construction of a continuum with two polar types, in the hope that all socio-cultural entities can be placed on it, implies an unwitting faith in unilinear evolution—a doctrine hardly acceptable to contemporary social science.[5]

Peasant socio-cultural systems have shown a remarkable stability since the beginning of historical times. They show distinctive structural and cultural characteristics which deserve attention in their own right. They cannot be treated as mere mixtures of the attributes of other socio-cultural systems or explained merely as intermediate points on a postulated continuum. Though any dependable account of the substantive features common to different peasant societies would require much more empirical data than is available so far, it can hardly be denied that despite numerous differences, peasant society can be viewed as a qualitatively distinct type of social organization.

Prospects

Building up a suitable conceptual and methodological framework for the study of peasant society seems to be one of the prerequisites of a fruitful pursuit of sociology in India. But if such an endeavour meets with some success, its benefits will not remain confined to India: for even now peasant society contains the vast majority of humankind. A more adequate study of the peasant institutions and culture is also likely to enrich social science as a whole. Knowledge about a social system, in which the bulk of humanity has lived since the beginning of history, is sure to be of immense value. It may help modern social science to grow out of its western ethnocentrism.

India today, like other countries which are placed similarly, is undergoing socio-cultural change at a tremendous pace. The speed of this change may help in making its pattern discernible. Almost all-round acceptance of the inevitability of fundamental social change in countries like India may stimulate the social scientist to take up his study seriously. If he does so, he is likely to add substantially to the theory of social change, which has languished considerably in contemporary sociology.

For a perceptive sociologist in contemporary India, association at some level in the efforts for social reconstruction is almost inevitable. It is also obvious that the problems which a country like India faces, are not skin-deep. Any serious effort to tackle them would lead one to consider the whole social structure and its dynamics. If the sociologist in India takes up this challenge at a professional level, his contribution is not likely to remain insignificant to the growth of pure social science either.[6]

Notes

1. Many sociologists—European, American as well as Indian—seem to have made too much of the supposed 'spirituality' and 'otherworldliness' of Indian culture. It is doubtful to what extent the Indian culture is more spiritual than that of other countries, including those of Europe in pre-modern times. The works of scholars like A.K. Coomaraswamy (1948) and H. Zimmer (1952) suggest that the predominant worldview in all traditional civilizations has been similar.
2. For a broader treatment of the general hypothesis that civilizations which have lagged behind may have a better chance of reaching the next higher stage than the more developed ones, see Deva (1966).
3. For the work done in this direction, also see Shrirama Indradeva (1966; 1973; 1976; 1980; 1983; 1985;1987; 1990) and Indra Deva and Shrirama (1980; 1986).
4. The establishment of the Indian Council of Social Science Research (ICSSR) in 1969 as an autonomous organization was an important step in the promotion of scientific social research. Projects sanctioned by the ICSSR are widely distributed geographically, as well as in terms of different specialities, methodological approaches and professional standing of the grantees.
5. The basic methodological inadequacy of the village studies for an understanding of the Indian rural society in the proper perspective, however, does not mean that they have contributed nothing. Mandelbaum (1970) has brought together some of the significant findings of such studies.
6. For further discussion of the challenges and oppurtunities for sociology in India, see Indra Deva (1997; 1998).

References

Berelson, B., 1954 'Content Analysis', in G. Lindzey (ed.), *Handbook of Social Psychology*, London : Addision-Wesley.

Bottomore, T.B., 1962 'Sociology in India'. *British Journal of Sociology* 13 (June) : 98-105.

Bowra, C.M., 1952 *The Heroic Age:* London : Cambridge University Press.

Chadwick, H.M., 1912 *The Heroic Age:* London : MacMillan.

Chadwick, H.M., and N.K. Chadwick, 1932 *The Growth of Literature.* Cambridge University Press.

Clinard, M.B. and J.W. Elder, 1965 'Sociology in India : A Study in the Sociology of Knowledge'. *American Sociological Review* 30 (August) : 581-587.

Coomaraswamy, A.K., 1948a *The Dance of Siva.* Bombay : Asia Publishing House.

—, 1948b *Figures of Speech or Figures of Thought.* London : Lucae.

Deva, Indra, 1956 'Modern Social Forces in India Folk Songs'. *Diogenes* No. 15, UNESCO, Paris.

—, 1966 'The Course of Social Change : A Hypothesis'. *Diogenes* No. 56, *UNESCO*, Paris.

—, 1969 'The Changing Pattern of Rural Society and Culture : Significance of the Rural-urban Nexus'. pp. 162-175 in N.K. Chaudhuri (ed.), *Trends of Socio-economic Change in India.* Simla : Indian Institute of Advanced Study.

—, 1972 'Folklore Studies : A Trend Report'. pp. 197-239 in A *Survey of Research in Sociology and Social Anthropology* (ICSSR). Bombay: Popular Prakashan.

—, 1974 'Oral Tradition and the Study of Peasant Society'. *Diogenes* no. 85, *UNESCO*, Paris.

—, 1989, *Folk Culture and Peasant Society in India*, Jaipur: Rawat.

—, 1997, 'Towards a More Meaningful Study of Ecology, Society and Culture' (Presidential Address at the XXIV All India Sociological Conference, Kolhapur), *Sociological Bulletin* 46 (1).

—, 1998, 'The Future of Independent India: What Can Sociologists Do?' (Presidential Address at the XXIV All India Sociological Conference, Hyderabad, *Sociological Bulletin* 47 (1).

Dumont, Louis and D.F. Pocock, 1957 'For a Sociology of India'. *Contributions to Indian Sociology* 1:7-22.

Indradeva, Shrirama, 1966, 'Correspondence between Woman and Nature in Indian Thought,' *Philosophy East and West* (Hawai,

U.S.A.) Vol. XVI, No. 3-4.

—, 1973, 'Genesis of Indian Civilization : The Evidence of Grhya Sutras'. *Diogenes* no. 84, *UNESCO*, Paris.

—, 1976, 'Status of Woman in Ancient India: Compulsives of the Patriarchal Order', *Diogenes* no. 93, *UNESCO*, Paris.

—, 1980, 'Cultural Interaction between Ancient India and Iran', *Diogenes* no. 111, *UNESCO*, Paris.

—, 1983, 'Folk Literature as a Means of Social Control', *Journal of Inter-Cultural Studies*, no. 9, Kufs Publications, Japan.

—, 1985, 'Shaping of the Traditional Pattern of Stratification in India: An Analysis of Processes through the Ages', *Diogenes* no. 130, *UNESCO*, Paris.

—, 1987, 'The Doctrine of Karma: Towards a Sociological Perspective', *Diogenes* no. 140, *UNESCO*, Paris.

—, 1990, 'Reassertion by Subjugated Cultures: The Case of Religion in India', *Diogenes* no. 150, *UNESCO*, Paris.

Kane, P.V., 1930-58 *A History of Dharmasastras : Ancient Medieval Religious and Civil Law* (5 Volumes). Poona : Bhandarkar Oriental Research Institute.

Mandelbaum, D.G., 1970 *Society in India* (2 Volumes). Berkeley : University of California Press.

Redfield, Robert, 1947 'The Folk Society'. *American Journal of Sociology* 52 (January) : 293-308.

—, 1955, *The Little Community : Viewpoints for the Study of a Human Whole.* Chicago : University of Chicago Press.

—, 1956, *Peasant Society and Culture.* Chicago : University of Chicago Press.

Saran, A.K., 1956 'Theoretical Anthropology and the Image of Man'. *Ethics* 46 (April) : 46-56.

—, 1961 'The Natural Sciences and the Study of Man : The Problem of their Synthesis in Contemporary Culture'. *Eastern Anthropologist* 16 (May-August) : 122-136.

Sorokin, P.A., C.C. Zimmerman, and C.J. Galpin, 1930-32 *Systematic Sourcebook in Rural Sociology*, Minneapolis : University of Minnesota Press.

Zimmer, H., 1952 *Myths and Symbols in Indian Civilization.* London : Routledge & Kegan Paul.

II

Salient Features of Indian Society and Culture

Continuity is perhaps the most remarkable feature of Indian society and culture. To be sure, India's culture and social structure have undergone tremendous changes in the course of several thousand years of its history, but their continuity has not been broken.

Militant Aryan hordes entered India around 1500 B.C. and subjugated the people of the city civilizations that thrived here, as well as the tribal inhabitants. The existence of the city civilizations is shown by the ruins discovered at Mohenjo-Dāro and Harappā and in other parts of India.

The Aryans were predominantly semi-pastoral while the people of proto-Mediterranean culture whom they overpowered lived in *pur* or cities. It appears that the clash and interaction between the cultures of the Aryans who entered the Indian sub-continent and the earlier settlers has been largely responsible for shaping the pattern of social stratification that finally led to the emergence of the four-fold Varṇa system. This stratification system perpetuated the supremacy of the Aryans and their progeny over the non-Aryans from ancient times down to the present day.

The way the dominent group, which was smaller in numbers, exploited the masses of the lower strata through the ages has hardly any parallel elsewhere. This dominant class first justified its supremacy on the basis of different, and supposedly superior, racial features. But when this became untenable due to the inevitable racial admixture, the criterion of superior racial features was substituted by exclusive observance of intricate and expensive rituals, which the lower castes were forbidden from observing. The hierarchy based on birth was further rationalised by the doctrine of Karma which propageted that birth in higher or lower caste is the inexorable consequence of one's own deeds in earlier lives. This belief was so inculcated that the people of the lower castes too fully internalized it and were convinced that their low status in society and exploitation by the higher castes was entirely justified.

Besides the system of stratification, other traditional institutions too seem to have been shaped largely by the processes of conflict and synthesis between the dominant Aryans and the earlier settlers. It is these processes that have endowed traditional religion and philosophy, the doctrine of Karma, the notion of Puruṣārtha, the Āśrama system, and even the traditional pattern of economy, their characteristics which have prevailed over so many centuries. In this, the contribution of the non-Aryan elements seems to have been much greater than that of the Aryan. Nevertheless, it is pardoxical that those very beliefs, systems and institutional patterns that belonged originally to the non-Aryan people were used ultimately as weapons of their subjugation.

One of the *jana* (people) among the ancient Indian Aryans were the Bharatas. Their valour was outstanding. The Ṛgveda refers to them. It is after their name that this country is called Bhārata.

The north-western part of the Indian sub-continent is referred to as Sapta Sindhu. The sacred text of the Iranian branch of the ancient Aryans, the Zend-Avesta, refers to it as Haft-Hindu. The ancient Iranian Aryans used '*ha*' in place of 'sa'.

Thus, the entire Indian sub-continent got the name 'Hindustan'. Similarly, the river Sindhu was called 'Indus' by the ancient Greeks, and so they referred to the entire country as India.

The Indian sub-continent stands apart from the rest of Asia because of certain geographical factors. There are mountain ranges in its north and east, though the north-western ranges have some passes. In the south the Indian sub-continent is surrounded by the Bay of Bengal, the Indian Ocean and the Arabian Sea. Because of these geographical features, it is primarily through the passes in the north-western ranges that hordes entered the Indian sub-continent from time to time. Once a people came here, they settled down and seldom left the sub-continent.

Special Characteristics of Indian Society and Culture

Antiquity

Indian culture has a very long tradition going back to ancient times. But many institutions and elements of culture which are regarded essential parts of Hindu culture did not exist in the Ṛgvedic times. The four-fold Varṇa system, the Āśrama system and the doctrine of Karma which are considered to be the cardinal components of Hinduism did not figure in the Ṛgveda. These evolved in later times. We know something regarding the pre-Aryan civilizations through the relics discovered at Mohen jo-Daro and Harappa and in some other parts of the Indian sub-continent. These civilizations thrived in river valleys. In all probability, they represented the proto-Mediterranean culture. The evidence from the Ṛgveda and other sources indicates that these people were predominently commercial.

Continuity

Indian culture and institutions have maintained their continuity over several millenia, despite many important changes that they had to undergo in the course of their long history. Though Hindu culture is vastly different from the culture and worldview of the Vedic Aryans, the strands of continuity can hardly be missed. The rise of Buddhism posed a mighty challenge to the way of life, beliefs and rituals based on the Vedas. But Brahmanical revival combated Buddhism strongly and asserted again the divine authority of the Vedas. Though the Vedic age could not be revived, links with the Vedic heritage were brought out prominently.

The continuity of Indian tradition can be easily seen in institutions, rituals and language. For instance, the Gṛhya Sūtras which were composed around the sixth century B.C., that is about two thousand five hundred years ago, lay down that the following rituals are essential for the marriage ceremony: Kanyādāna, Agni Sthāpana and Homa, Pānigrahaṇa, Lāja Homa, Agni Pariṇāyana, and Saptapadī. These rituals form an integeral part of the traditional marriage ceremony even today. It is interesting that the Gṛhya Sūtras say that in addition to these cardinal rituals, Lokācāra or the customs prevailling in the community should also be observed and in case there is any doubt about these, old women should be consulted. This too has been the practice all along.

Another interesting instance which brings out the continuity of Indian tradition is that the word *kuddāl* which occurs in the Ṛgveda, is prevalent even now in almost the same form and in the same meaning. The word *abalā* has been used in the Ṛgveda to refer with disdain to women. This word too is current even today in the same meaning.

Excessive Emphasis on Rituals

All human societies have their own rituals which are considered important by their members. However, in Hindu society, the emphasis on rituals seems to be exceptionally high. There are numerous rituals connected with *rites de passage*, calendaric fasts, festivals, and pilgrimages besides the daily worship of gods and goddesses. Millions of people from all corners of India congregate on specific occasions such as the Kumbha, without any invitation or announcement.

Apart from abundance of rituals connected with almost every aspect of life, the value attached to ritual also seems to be exceptionally high. Perceptive thinkers like Max Weber have noted this feature of Hindu society, but there has hardly been any adequate explanation of this phenomenon.

The study of the dynamics of Indian society and culture in a wide time perspective suggests that the chief sociological function of this excessive emphasis on rituals in Hindu society has been to justify the supreme position of the Dvijas, particularly the Brāhmaṇas. In the Ṛgvedic times the Aryans justified their supremacy primarily on the basis of their special physical features based on race. This continued upto the times of Patañjali who described the characteristics of the Brāhmaṇa mostly in terms of his physical features. But, in course of time, due to the compulsion of marrying women from the subjugated people, the racial features of the dominant elites were inevitably compromised. However, these elites would not have liked to give up their position of supremacy. The criteria based on racial features were, therefore, substituted by those of the observance of rituals. During the second Brāhmaṇical revival it was proclaimed that everyone is born as a Śūdra, it is only through sacraments that one becomes a Dvija. The dominant elites claimed superiority on the basis that they alone were sanctified through sacraments. And, of course, they did not permit the Śūdras to observe these, thus condemning them to a perpetually inferior status.

A related reason seems to be that only the Brāhmaṇs can act a priests at higher rituals, for which they receive substantial perquistes. The large number of rituals and high importance attached to them are thus obviously in the interest of the Brāhmaṇas. And, the Brāhmaṇas occupy the highest position in the traditional social hierarchy, and it is they who enunciate the norms of what should be done.

Belief in the Doctrine of Karma

For several millenia a pervasive belief in the doctrine of Karma has characterised Indian society and culture. All the Āstika systems of philosophy, which accept the Vedas as the ultimate divine authority, subscribe to this doctrine. But even prominent Nāstika schools of thought which do not believe in the divine authority of Vedas, like Buddhism and Jainism, nevertheless accept the essentials of this doctrine. As is well known according to doctrine of Karma this life is only one link in the infinite chain of births and rebirths. Everyone is reborn in his next birth according his deeds in past lives.

Unquestioning belief in the doctrine of Karma has had deep and widespread implications for Indian society. The belief that one's good and bad deeds are bound to be rewarded or punished tends to strengthen adherence to norms and is thus a strong support to processes of social control. Belief in the doctrine of Karma also performs the latent function of providing support to the caste system. The firm belief that one's birth in a particular caste is determined by his own deeds of earlier lives was shared by the people of the lower as well as the higher castes. It justified inequality based on birth on the basis of a metaphysical principle on which there was a very high degree of unanimity in the traditional Indian society. The people belonging to the lower castes too believed that their low status in society and the privileges of the upper castes were fully justified.

The Caste System

Prevalence of the caste system and its deep and pervasive influence on all aspects of life is a very remarkable characteristic of Indian society and culture. This is a unique system, as Hutton has amply demonstrated. Though stratification based on birth is common to most pre-modern societies, the intricate norms of marriage (connubium) and sharing of food and water (commesality) which were imposed severely by the Indian caste system and formed its integral part are surely unique. Such complex rules governing various aspects of life are found in no other society. The caste system thus is a unique feature of Indian society.

The norms of marriage enforced by the caste system were indeed complex. These included the rules of endogamy, exogamy and hypergamy. A caste was typically endogamous. No one was allowed to marry outside the caste. But, while marrying within the caste, one could not get married to a person belonging to his own exogamous sub-caste, Gotra or Pravara. Even within a caste, there were hierarchical sub-divisions. A girl could not be married to a boy belonging to a lower sub-division. She had to be given in marriage only to a boy of a higher sub-division. This is why many girls belonging to the highest sub-divisions could not be married in the traditional society. This is known as 'Kulinism'. Any violation of the caste norms of marriage was severely punished in traditional Indian society. The entire family was liable to be ex-communicated. This had disastrous implications. The girls and boys of the family could not be married. And, in traditional society, even the other castes of the village would impose sanctions against a family that had been ex-communicated from its own caste. For example, the barber and the Dhobi would refuse to serve the members of that family. Its occupational activities would also be jeopardized.

Similarly, the caste restrictions on the sharing of food and water were quite complicated and these too were strictly imposed. There was an intricate classification of food. Generally speaking, uncooked foodstuffs could be freely accepted. But this was not true of cooked food, which was subdivided in several categories. Food made entirely of milk and milk products by persons of other castes was generally considered acceptable even by the Brāhmaṇas. But, the Brāhmaṇa could not eat food made of cereals, even if it was fried. People of other castes would however take food made of cereals if it was fried (Pakkā) but not if it was only boiled (Kachachā). Even water could not be taken from the hands of people belonging to very low castes; and by Hindus from the hands of Muslims and Christians. These are only examples. Violation of the caste norms of sharing food and water invited severe punishment. It could lead to ex-communication from the caste and the community. In fact, adherence to the traditional norms of commensality was considered almost equivalent to following the 'Dharama' (Dharma). It was commonly held that by any deviation from the caste rules of sharing food and water one surely loses his 'Dharama'. Deviance from other ethical norms was not considered such a serious matter, and it could even be condoned.

Unity in Diversity of Indian Society and Culture

Unity in diversity of Indian society and culture is perhaps its most important characteristic.

Though India is marked by many differences pertaining to geographical features, racial elements, language, customs, modes of dress and eating and so on, its identity as a socio-cultural whole is clearly perceived both by Indians and outsiders. This perception has been the since ancient times. It was the great Adi Śaṅkarācārya who established four Maṭhas in all the four corners of India more than one thousand years ago. And it has been the wish even of the illiterate traditional woman to perform pilgrimage to all the four Dhāmas which are located in the extreme east, west, north and south of India. People from all parts of India congregate in their millions at specific times for events such as the Kumbha, with no need of an announcement or invitation. This has been so at least from the time of Harṣa, some fifteen hundred years ago.

India's society and culture do not just have diversity and unity, there is a unity in diversity. For instance, though all the major races of man—Austric, Mangoloid, Nordic, Mediterranean, Alpine, and Negro—are represented among the Indian people, various racial elements are so mixed that no caste or community can claim to belong purely to only one race.

Similarly, Indian culture is a product of interaction between innumerable diverse peoples and cultures. The militant Aryan hordes that entered India from the north-west and overpowered the earlier settlers, considered themselves to be infinitely superior to the latter. They looked upon the pre-Aryans and their gods and modes of worship with contempt. For instance, they referred to them with disdain as 'Siśnadevāh' or the worshipers of phallus. But as all of us know, in later times the worship of phallus as Śiva Linga has become acceptable throughout the country. The devout Hindus consider the Vedas as embodyment of divine truth, and at the same time worship the phallus (Siva Linga) with extreme devotion. This is only one example of the grand process of cultural synthesis that has been going on in India for several millenia. Innumerable gods and goddesses, customs and institutions which originally belonged to diverse tribal and other cultures have been so modified, integrated and synthesized in Indian culture that it is almost impossible to identify them as separate entities or to be sure of their origin. For instance, hardly anyone is conscious that the holiest of holy rivers the Gangā, derives its name not from any Aryan source but from the Mongol word 'Kyang', which means river.

It is widely recognized that the Śāstric or the great tradition, that is the traditional elite culture, is pan-Indic. To a certain extent this is the result of conscious eandeavour of the Indian elites through the ages. For instance, the great epic Mahābhārata seems to be an attempt to bring together diverse cultural patterns spread over this vast country in one common framework.

The induction of non-Aryan cultural elements was greatly facilitated by the second Brahmanical revival during which the Smrtis, epics and Purāṇas were composed. The rise of Buddhism had given a big jolt to the supremacy of the Brāhmaṇas and many aspects of Vedic precepts. To combat the influence of Buddhism among the people at large and to re-establish the acceptance of their supreme position the Brāhmaṇa elites had to give up those Aryan practices which were repugant to the bulk of the common people. They had also to take over and integrate with the tradition of elite culture, the customs, deities and modes of worship prevalent among the non-Aryan common folk. This process of synthesis has continued through the ages, down to the present day. Many tribal and village gods have thus become an integral part of the higher or great tradition of Hinduism.

Though the idea of the unity of the elite or great tradition being pan-Indic is widely accepted, it is often thought that the Indian folk traditions are local or parochial. The use of terms like the 'little tradition' and McKim Marriot's designating the process of give and take between the elite and folk traditions as 'universalization -- parochialization' seem to assume that folk culture is necessarily parochial. However, recent systemaic research in the field of folk culture shows that though the folk culture of various regions are articulated in local dialects, there is a wide and rich sharing of values, spirit, style and motifs among folk traditions of India.

Certain structural and cultural factors seem to have contributed greatly to the unique pattern of unity in diversity of India. One of these is undoubtedly the caste system. It has provided a remarkable framework and mechanism for a plural society. There are several thousand castes and each of them has certain practices which are all its own. And yet all of them are integrated through a common system of caste hierarchy.

Through the ages, the caste system has provided a mechanism for the integration of diverse peoples and cultures in a broad framework. Since time immemorial numerous tribes and incoming hordes have been integrated in the Hindu society as castes at various rungs of the caste hierarchy without having to give up entirely their own cultural heirtage. Various cultures were thus made parts of the larger plural society.

The spirit of accommodating diversities has permeated Indian culture. The readiness to accept new or different elements without giving up those that have been in existence has been greatly responsible for its rich diversity and resilience.

The age-old belief in levels of truth has been a basic factor which has strengthened the inclination to accept diversity.

While a faith in only one truth and only one path of virtue tends to stamp out differences, the belief in levels of truth promotes willing acceptance of diversity.

III

The Perspective of Social Change

For gaining a perspective of change in Indian society and culture one has inevitably to depend greatly on the traditional texts. Like other methods and techniques of social research, the analysis of text cannot be accepted at face value—it has to be interpreted in the context of the times in which it was composed, the section of people who composed it, and the motives that lay behind its composition. Most writers who have made use of the traditional texts, have not paid much attention to these factors. The general tendency has been to lump together the evidence drawn from various texts belonging to very different socio-cultural eras separated by long spans of time—even by two thousand years or more. Such piecing together of evidence leads to fictitious patchworks which represent no real socio-cultural system.

The earliest records preserved are the hymns of Ṛgveda. These hymns were orally transmitted through the ages. The hymns of Ṛgveda were kept in original shape meticulously by the priests. These hymns were composed to proclaim the deeds of valour of the Aryans. These hymns portray the ancient society. The Aryans had a light complexion and golden hair. In the early Ṛgvedic society classes or strata were not sharply demarkated among the Aryans. The vocations of priest and warrior were often combined and were interchangable. Brothers born of the same parents could take to different trades.

We find about twenty Ṛṣikās or women composers of hymns in the Ṛgveda. But as the Aryans settled down in India and took wives from the earlier settlers, the position of woman became low. The early Aryans were agriculturists and cattle-breeders. Their wealth consisted primarily of cows. And agriculture needs manpower. Aryans were short of labour. The blond Aryans looked down upon the earlier settlers due to their different physical features. But they needed their man-power. Therefore they made an institutionalized arrangement through which they could get a continuous supply of captive labour for thousands of years.

The earlier settlers had proto-Austroloid, proto-Monogol and proto-Mediterranean ethnic elements. These people are referred to as 'Dāsa' and 'Dasyu' and 'Pani' in the Ṛgveda. The word Dāsa is probably a variation of the Iranian word 'Dahae' which means countryman. The Iranian sound 'ha' often becomes 'sa' in Sanskrit. In northern India, the language of the victorious Aryans prevailed over that of the earlier settlers.

The language of the earlier settlers was almost completely overpowered in northern India though some of its words must have been taken over in Sanskrit. But, the culture and religion of Aryans could not survive; also because Aryans were smaller in number and had to take wives from the subjugated people.

The hymns of Ṛgveda vividly describe battle-loving, simple-hearted Aryans who composed hymns for victory in battle and plenty of cattle, gold and other worldly things. The plundering expeditions of Aryans and subjugation of the earlier settlers is vividly portrayed in these hymns.

Indra is their hero-god. He is described as a mighty blond complete with a flowing golden beard.[1] The earlier settlers were regarded as enemies by the Aryans. Aryans hated Dāsas because they were very different from them, physically as well as culturally.

In Ṛgveda, the word Dāsa is used for slaves as well as the vanquished earlier settlers. In Indian languages this word is still used in the sense of slaves. In the Ṛgveda Dāsas are described as dark-coloured (Kṛṣṇa Varṇa[2]) without nose (Anāsa[3]) and worshippers of phallus (Śiśnadeva[4]). Moreover, they are called riteless (Akarma) because they had different religious rituals (Anyavrata[5]). But, later on, the Aryans stopped killing them because they needed their labour.

The Paṇis were the other people whom the Aryans encountered and hated. Perhaps they were rich traders. Aryans wanted the riches of the Paṇis. But Paṇis did not want to part with their possessions without getting anything in exchange. Expecting something in exchange for everything appeared unreasonable to the Aryans. The only way out was to plunder the wealth of Paṇis. In such expeditions of Aryans the gods Soma and fire were of great help. The hero-god Indra was believed to provide the leadership. Soma was an intoxicating drink and it made fighting and plunder easier. Fire was frequently employed to destroy the settlements of the enemy. Paṇis were a commercial people and they lived in cities. The remains of the Indus valley civilization may well be their settlements. However, the invading Aryans were a pastoral people; and living at one place for all time may have seemed unnatural to them. They, therefore, did not occupy the cities of Paṇis but rather destroyed them.

Stealing the wealth of Paṇis appeared quite natural and reasonable to Aryans. The Aryans wished that 'Paṇis may sleep without getting awakened.'[6] Fire was employed to destroy the doors of the houses of Paṇis. The poet Vasiṣṭha says : 'The holy Fire of sacrifice opened the doors of Paṇis.'[7] Bhārdvāja gives the entire credit to fire: 'The Fire santches the wealth of Paṇis.'[8] Gotama appreciates the effectiveness of Fire and Soma. 'O Fire and Soma both of you have snatched cows with valour.'[9]

The animostity and hatred of Aryans towards non-Aryans has played an important part in shaping the Indian social structure, cultural traditions and patterns of values. The traditional stratification based on Varṇa hierarchy, the distinctive patterns of the elite and lay forms of culture, the double standards found in the traditional legal system and the final adjustment of all these are the outcome of open and unflinching ethnic discrimination.

Some poets praised some non-Aryans also because of the liberal gifts received from them. The poet Vaśa clearly says : 'I got a gift of one hundred cattle from the Dāsa Balabūtha and Tarukṣa. O Wind these people are thine, protected by Indra and protected by gods may they live happily.' Another poet Śanyu praises a Paṇi named Brbu who gave him gifts liberally : 'Among Paṇis Bṛbu occupies the top position, his heart is just like the wide basin of Gaṅgā. His thousand gifted cows run like wind.'[10] Thus, gradually, a kind of adjustment was achieved. The abundant gifts given by the Paṇis to Aryan priests were a sign and a component of this adjustment. Of course, in this adjustment the proud Aryans preserved for themselves a higher status while the Dāsas who were dark-skinned, broadnosed and the 'worshippers of phallus' were considered 'lowest of all'.[11] Later on these Dāsas were given the generic name of Śūdra.

The Paṇis were cattle-breeders and traders. For the Aryan priests they remained an easy source of wealth. Later on the Paṇis were given a place in the hierarchical system. Eventually they were given the name of Vaṇik and perhaps became a part of the general category of Vaiśyas.

Though in the Ṛgveda we find some woman poets, the position of woman was certainly lower than man. It appears that among the Dāsas, women occupied a position somewhat equal to men. They fought in the battlefield together with their menfolk. In Ṛgveda, Indra refers to Dāsa Śambara with contempt, because his army consisted of woman soldiers: 'Sambara, the Dāsa has made women his instrument, what can his vigourless or Abalā army do to mine.'[12] The word 'Abalā' became a synonym for woman, and this use of the word is still current in Indian languages.

Moreover, like all invaders, Aryans too did not probably have with them enough women. They forcibly took away the non-Aryan women. This is clear also from the fact that the work 'Vadhū' is used both for 'bride' and 'female slaves'. The poet Sorabhi, the son of Kaṇva, praises Trasdasyu, son of Purukutsa: 'Trasdasyu son of Purukutsa the great leader, the good protector, gave me fifty Vadhūs.'[13] The word 'Vadhū' means bride in Indian languages even today. We get similar evidence in the Atharvaveda also. It says : 'When a Brāhmaṇa grasps the hand of a woman, though she be married she becomes his wife.'[14]

Thus, the foundations of the Indian social structure were laid down during the Vedic era. The essential features of social institutions and attitudes can be seen taking shape in the early hymns of Ṛgveda. These hymns reveal that traders or Paṇis used to provide wealth to the priests while the sole duty of a Dāsa was to serve his master. This attitude gave birth to a two-fold system of law—one for the Aryans and the other for the non-Āryans, who were later subsumed under the category Śūdras. The status of woman too seems to be a product, at least partially, of this conquest of non-Aryans by the Aryans.

In the famous Puruṣasūkta of Ṛgveda, which is considered by scholars to be of a later origin, there is a mention of the emergence of the four strata of society. In this myth, the sacrifice of the primeaval Puruṣa is described. The Brāhmaṇa, the Rājanyas and the Vaiśya were made respectively from the mouth, the arms and the thighs of the Puruṣa. The Śūdra sprang from his feet. It is noteworthy that in this hymn the word Varṇa does not occur. In the other nine Mandals of the Ṛgveda the word Rājanya and Vaiśya are not mentioned.

In the earlier era the Aryans appear to have three fairly established strata: the poet-priests, the warriors and the laity.

These classes were not heriditary. The sons of poets fought in the battlefields. The term Viś is used for the common Aryan people. The king is called the lord of Viś or Vinśāpati. Gradually as the Aryans settled down and took to the life of agriculturists, the old militancy of the Aryans subsided. Simple sacrifices were transformed into elaborate and expensive sacrifices. In the later Saṁhitās, the Brāhmaṇa priests became a distinct class. The other two ranks also crystallized into distinct strata. Since priesthood was the most prestigious and remunerative occupation, most of the Aryans naturally aspired for this profession.

During the Ṛgvedic period, the Aryans took wives from the local population; just as the early European settlers of America subjugated Red Indians and had Red Indians women as squaws. As the non-Aryan people were integrated into the larger society, many Aryans consolidated themselves into a priestly elite class. Through this mechanism they tried to preserve their racial and cultural identity.

The poets of the Ṛgveda praised their patrons for the liberal gifts given to them. In the Brāhmana texts we find great emphasis on specific sacrificial fees. After each and every big or small ritual, a fee is specified. Naturally, the rewards of rituals depends upon the amount of the fees. The rewards were both of worldly and of other-worldly nature. Though we find the rank of priesthood in all the ancient civilizations but nowhere else were the priests able to exploit lower ranks as much as they have done in India for over two millenia. They not only enjoyed a priviledged position themselves but ensured it for their progeny also, generation after generation. The ascription of status by birth and restrictions on intermarriage and commensality strengthened this system. We find many passages asserting and justifying the exalted position of priestly elites in the later Saṁhitās and the Brāhmaṇa Granthas.

The Taittirīya Samhitā of Yajurveda declares the priestly elites 'the gods that can be seen'.[15] The Taittirīya Āranyaka justifies this assertion: 'Since Vedas contain all gods, the Brāhmaṇas who have imbibed the Vedas are the repositories of all the gods.'[16]

The Śatapatha Brāhmaṇa also speaks in a similar vain. It is emphasized in the Śatapatha Brāhmaṇa that only a priest who is a descendant of a Vedic seer should be given the sacrificial fee.[17]

For being a priest a person should have both the parents of Brāhmanical descent. We find stories in the Brāhmaṇas where persons were turned out of sacrifices because their mothers were not Brāhmaṇas. However, some of them were later admitted to this community by proving themselves to be genuine seers. In the Aitariya Brāhmaṇa we find the story of Kavasa Ailuṣa. He was accused of being the son of a female slave. He was left in a hot desert to die. There he perceived the hymns and the waters of Sarasvatī appeared before him. And he was established as a poet of Ṛgveda.[18] We find a similar story in the Tāṇḍya Brāhmaṇa also. People accused Vatsa that his mother was a Śūdrā. To clear himself he entered into fire. He came out unburnt and was declared a Brāhmaṇa.[19]

When the Brāhmaṇa texts were being composed there were conflicts and challenges. There were internal crises and foreign invasions in the Sapta-Sindhu. Then, the centre of culture shifted from Sapta-Sindhu to Kuru-Pañcāla. In the later Saṁhitās and Brāhmaṇas we find no mention of Sapta-Sindhu, whereas in the Ṛgveda itself there is elaborate description of the Sapta-Sindhu. Moreover, the Aryans were colonizing the eastern and south-eastern parts of India which is mentioned in the Śatapatha Brāhmaṇa. These colonizers were small in number as compared to the local population. To combat the non-Aryan influences the Brāhmaṇas tried hard to preserve their cultural heritage and racial purity. They also guarded jealously their own interests. In the Brāhmaṇa texts it is asserted that only those Brāhmaṇas who were the descendents of the Vedic seers are entitled to have the sacrificial fee.

Frequent foreign invasions were a real threat. The north-western part of India has been exposed to foreign invasions since ancient times. The Persian Aryans, who were close kins of Indian Aryans, repeatedly invaded India. They considered themselves superior to the Satpa-Sindhu Aryans, because of the racial mingling which the latter had undergone with proto-Austroloid people. The emphasis on ritual and ritual purity in later Samhitās and Brāhmaṇas was perhaps meant to provide a substitute for lack of racial purity. The battles between Sapta-Sindhu Aryans and Persians Aryans have found expression in myths of the Śatapatha Brāhmaṇa and the Avesta. The Assyrian myth of Deluge is also found in the Śatapatha Brāhmaṇa.

The position of woman became further low due to the increasing assertion of patriarchy. The legends in the Brāhmaṇas clearly show the low status accorded to woman. Woman was declared 'Avadhyā' or one not to be killed. A myth about Śrī in the Śatapatha Brāhmaṇa says : 'Surely, that Śrī is a woman, and people do not kill a woman, but rather take (anything) from her (leaving her) alive.'[20] Though woman was not to be killed she was to be dealt with by a strong hand. The Śatapatha Brāhmaṇa says that (gods used to) smite their wives and unman them, and 'thus smitten and unmaned, they neither own any self nor do they own any heritage'.[21] At another place in the Śatapatha Brāhmaṇa it is said : 'Therefore even to this day women are given to vain things; for it was on this wise that Vak turned thereto, and other women do as she did.'[22] During Varuṇapraghāsa sacrifices, the husband makes the wife confess the name of her paramour during a ceremony as if every woman has a paramour. It is asserted that 'whatever (connection) she confessess not, that indeed will turn out injurious to her relatives'.[23]

Like all ancient patriarchal societies, the society portrayed in the later Saṁhitās and the Brāhmaṇa Granthas accorded an important place to the son. In the Aitareya Brāhmáṇa it is said that 'the birth of a daughter would make him miserable if the birth of son were not to bring some heavenly light in the dark life of parents'.[24]

In the era of later Samhitās and Brāhmaṇas many elaborate and expensive sacrifices were performed by the priestly elites for the kings and nobles. In due course the Kṣatriyas revolted against these expensive sacrifices.

In fact, the Āranyakas and Upaniṣads are an expression of this revolt against the ritualistic way of life. These Āranyakas and Upaniṣads openly declared that rituals do not lead to real knowledge. The liberal attitude of Upaniṣads encouraged persons belonging even the downtrodden sections of society like women and Śūdras to participate in the highest metaphysical discussions. Unlike the later Saṁhitās and the Brāhmaṇas, the Upaniṣads are not the preserve of the Brāhmaṇa class. The Kṣatriyas took the lead in their composition. In contrast to the later Samhitās and the Brāhmaṇas, the language and content of the Upaniṣads are simple and easy to understand. The Upaniṣads constitute the first attempts towards philosophical speculation of a high order. They provided the rock-bed to the metaphysical schools that developed later.

The knowledge of the Upaniṣads became the fashion of that era. Many persons of the Brāhmaṇa class approached kings and nobles for this transcendental knowledge. In one well known instance a king went to a mere cartman to have this knowledge. Raikva, the cartman parted with his knowledge only when the king presented to him his daughter together with other wealth.[25] Similarly in the court of Janaka, the king of Videhas, Gārgī asks such awkward questions about the creation of the universe that seer Yājnavalkya loses his temper.[26] At another place in the same Upaniṣad we find that Maitreyi, the wife of Yājnavalkya prefers the knowledge of self to worldly wealth.[27]

The story of Satyakāma Jābāla reflects the declining importance of family and caste. Satyakāma, the son of a maid servant does not know the name of his father because his mother served many persons in her youth. He tells this to the teacher. The teacher accepted him as his desciple because he had not 'severed from the truth'.[28]

Many Brāhmaṇa teachers approached kings to learn about the nature of the Ultimate Reality. Gautam went to the king of Pāñcālas for the sake of knowledge. Uddālaka Āruni sent five theologians to king Aśvapati Kaikeya to learn the knowledge of Self.[29]

In the Upaniṣads we find the concept of rebirth for the first time. This concept of rebirth is contrary to the Aryan concept of heaven. Perhaps it has a non-Aryan origin. The introduction of the ideas of transmigration of soul and rebirth later on developed into a systematic theory of Karma which supported the Varṇa hierarchy for many centuries.

The Upaniṣads were a great challenge to the supreme position of the Brāhmaṇas and the Varṇa hierarchy. To quell the Upaniṣadic movement and to revitalize the Brahmanical culture a Brahmanical revival came into being.

The Brahmanical lore was revived and was consolidated in the Sūtras. It was capsuled and preserved in aphorisms. These aphorisms are easy to remember.

Like all revivals this revival also could not have revived a bygone age but it did help to weaken the state of things in the immediate past. It performed the latent function of getting rid of the Upaniṣadic influence which promoted claims of equality by Śūdras and women. This it sought to do in the name of the ancient Aryan lore. This revivalist movement aimed at establishing the Varṇa hierarchy—the backbone of Indian society.

Through the Sūtras we can have a glimpse of the daily life of the Indo-Aryan householder. Many ancient rituals and customs have found mention in Sūtras. Many of these Sūtras portray the society of that antiquated past when Aryans had not entered the Indian sub-continent. However, their main function was to establish and strengthen a social system in which the priestly elites could enjoy the highest position again.

In the Sūtras, for the first time, all the sacraments were introduced and the procedure of performing various sacrifices is laid down. Sūtras also prescribe specific hymns of specified Vedas to accompany particular rites. In this way the Sūtras fall into particular Vedic schools.

The Sūtra literature is also referred to as Kalpa Sūtras. Kalpa Sūtras cover the three catagories of Sūtra literature. These are the Śrauta Sūtras, the Gṛhya Sūtras and the Dharma Sūtras. There is a fourth catagory also which is complementary to the Śrauta Sūtras. This fourth catagory comprises the Śulva Sūtras. We do not get the complete sets comprising all the four catagories of all the four Saṁhitās. The only exception is the Kṛṣṇa Yajurveda Saṁhitā, where we get the complete set of Sūtras of Baudhayana and Apastamba schools.

The Śrauta Sūtras are the authoritative texts of the Indian sacrifical system. In the Śulva Sūtras, we find the rules pertaining to alter-making. Gṛhya Sūtras prescribe the rules of everyday life of the Aryan householder. Dharma Sūtras contain the code of law of ancient Aryans.

In the Upaniṣads there is evidence of marriage between persons belonging to different Varṇas. Racial purity of the priestly elites had been diluted so much that it had to be substituted by the scruples of ritual purity. The primary function of this assertion of ritual purity was to impress the superiority of the priestly elites over the masses. In Gṛhya Sūtras various sacraments or Saṁskāras are prescribed for the Aryans. Besides *rites de passage* we find a number of other rituals also. These sacraments should be performed from conception to death to mark the turning points in a man's life.

The Gṛhya Sūtras contain the rituals, customs and beliefs of antiquated Vedic past. In the Gṛhya Sūtras we do not find the Ṛgvedic militancy. They embody the folklore of the early Aryans of the times in which they were colonizing the Indian subcontinent. The long prayers contain the fears of the immigrant Aryans---fear due to danger from animals, from evil spirits, diseases and premature deaths. These prayers also reflect the elemental emotions of pain and pleasure, love and conflict.

The position of equality enjoyed by Śūdras and women with the elites of the Upaniṣdic era was no more for them. Just like in Ṛgveda, in the Gṛhya Sūtras also the Śūdras are called Kṛṣṇa Varṇa. The householder of Gṛhya Sūtras wants many sons. There are many rituals to ensure the birth of a son. But we do not find any ritual for the birth of a daughter. The Upanayana or the initiation, which is the most important sacrement, is to be performed only for boys. It is called second birth. Usually, the initiation should be performed between the eighth and the sixteenth year for a Brāhmaṇa boy, a few years later for Kṣatriya, and still later for the Vaiśya boys. The teacher or Ācarya who performs the initiation is considered the father of the boy, and the sacred hymn Sāvitrī his mother. Through these rites the boy becomes a Dvija or twice-born.

A peculiar practice, probably of antiquated past, is found in the Dharma Sūtra of Baudhāyana. It is that of the carrying an earthen water pot for toilet as well as for washing and use in ritual. Baudhāyana says : 'He who desires his own welfare shall use it (the earthen water pot) without hesitation for purifying (his person), for drinking and for performing his twilight devotions'. Baudhāyana justifies and describes this practice thus : 'Let him do it with a believing heart; a wise man must not corrupt his mind. The Self-Existent (Brahman) came into existence with a water-vessel. Therefore let him perform (this rites) with a water vessel.'

'Let him hold in right hand when he voids urine and excrements, in the left when he sips water. That is (a) settled (rule) for all good man.'

'For as the sacrificial cup *camasa*[30] is declared to be pure, on account of its contact with the Soma juice, even so the water vessel is constantly pure through its contact with water.'[31]

It appears that during the Sūtra era this custom had already become controversial. Later on such use of the earthen pot is described in some Smṛtis and Purāṇas as one of the practices prohibited in Kali age or as a 'Kalivarjya'.

The Brahmanical elites tried to rivive the Vedic orthodoxy in the Sūtra literature. Soon these social norms were challenged by Budhism. Some scriptures are called 'Sutta', or Sūtras in Sanskrit. The word 'Dharma' became 'Dhamma' of Buddhism. This similarity of terms suggests that the two religions coexisted for a considerable period of time. Buddha attacked at the very roots of Vedic social structure, the Varṇa hierarchy and the superior position of Brahmanical elites. Whereas the Upaniṣadic challenge was covert, the Buddhist challenge was overt. The Upaniṣads revolted against ritualism; but they did not openly challenge the validity of the Varṇa hierarchy. Though women and Śūdras participated in the metaphysical disscussions, and even a king offered his daughter's hand to a cartman for the knowledge of the Ultimate Reality, nowhere is it said that such distinctions among human beings are unjustified. It was because of this that the Upaniṣads could be included as a part of the Vedas and they are tradionally referred to as Vedānga. But the attack by Buddhism was direct. Buddha boldly and candidly proclaims:

'No Brāhmaṇa is as such by birth;
No outcaste is as such by birth;
An outcaste is such by his deeds,
A Brāhmaṇa is such by his deeds.'[32]

We find an interesting account of a discussion between Buddha and a young Brāhmaṇa, Āssalāyana, in the Majjhima Nikaya. Persuadded by the Brāhmaṇas he went to Buddha and said: 'Brāhmaṇas maintain that only they are the highest class and the others are lower. They are white, the others black; only they are pure and not the other. Only they are true sons of Brahma, born from his mouth, born of Brahma, creation of Brahma, heirs of Brahma. Now what does the worthy Gautama say to that?'

'Do the Brāhmaṇas really maintain this, Assalāyana, when they are born of women just like anyone else, of Brāhmaṇa woman who have their periods and who conceive, give birth and nurse their children just like any other women.'[33]

Though Buddha criticized the four-fold Varṇa hierarchy, we do find mention of the four Varṇas in Buddhist literature and Jātaka stories. But in the Buddhist texts Kṣatriyas are given precedence over Brāhmaṇas. Another interesting thing is that in the Jātaka stories we find some twice-born people, Brāhmaṇas and Kṣatriyas, following the occupations of the lowest Varṇa, that is of Śūdra, without the loss of caste.

It seems that the Buddhist attitude of equality among human beings and freedom to choose occupation according to individual apptitude, promoted industrial and business activity during the Buddhist era. We find mention of eighteen types of guilds of artisans and workers. There were heads of guilds of artizans and workers.The heads of guilds were members of the royal court. Naturally they could guard well the interests of the artizens. The traders used to sell these products in distant places. Thus there grew a prosperous and influencial commercial class. In the Dīgha Nikāya we find norms and values which are strikingly similar to those of the rising puritanical middle class which ushered in capitalism in modern times. The Dīgha Nikāya forbids people from addiction to drinking, roaming in the streets at improper times, frequenting fairs, gambling, keeping bad company and idleness. It points out that the idle man does not earn new wealth but fritters away what he has already earned. It also advises young men to keep away from the company of a grasping man, a smooth spoken man, a man who only says what you want to hear, and a man who helps you to waste your money. We also find a positive suggestion: 'But there are four types who should be looked upon as friends true of heart: a man who seeks to help you; a man who is the same in wealth and woe; a man who gives good advice and a man who is sympathetic.' Such suggestions are conducive to the growth of capital. However, the Dīgha Nikāya does not advise excessive profiteering. It rather advises traders to make profit bit by bit like a bee, so that the purchasing power of the customer would remain intact. It says:

'Making money like the bee,
Who does not hurt the flower;
Such a man makes his pile,
As an anthill gradually.
The man grown wealthy thus,
Can help his family,
And firmly bind his friends.
To himself he should divide,
His money in four parts;
With one part he should live,
With two(parts) expand his trade,
And the fourth he should save
Against a rainy day.'[34]

In this verse the norms and values of the rising middle class are well portrayed. Such norms and values promote industry and business. Formation of capital together with hard work is the key to industrial development. It is interesting to note that this work ethices is quite similar to the Clvinist ethics. As is well known, Max Weber has given much importance to the puritanical Protestant ethics for the rise of capitalism.

The Brahmanical revival basically served the function of combating Buddhism. It was quite clear to the Brahmanical elites that the mass of people would not favour the revival of Vedic norms in their original form. The bulk of the people were not Brāhmaṇas. They were predominantly of the non-Aryan stock. To win them over it was imperative to synthesize various non-Aryan traditions with the Brahmanical culture. In this process of consolidation of the epics, the Māhābhārata and the Rāmāyaṇa, and the Purāṇas played a crucial role. Non-Aryan myths and popular heroic poetry were liberally taken over and integrated with the Brahmanical culture.

In the epics we find myths, legends and Gāthās. The heroes of the epics, though they often were dark complexioned, were portryed as saviours of the Brāhmaṇas and Dharma. As a matter of fact the epics are the first step towards the formation of that religion which was later on called Hinduism. In order to

Brahmanize the epics, their authorship was attibuted to Vedic seers. These are Vyasa Pārāśarya of Mahābhārata and Vālmīki of Rāmāyana. Aryan gods were either rejected and forgotten or the non-Aryan gods were superimposed over them. Mitra and Varuṇa were totally forgotten; while Rudra was superimposed over the Phallus god Śiva. Thus, many pre-Aryan norms and values found their way into the epics. The Manu Smṛti tried to resurrect the Vedic religion in a relatively pure form,though it had to adopt an ambivalent attitute on many matters. But in the Purāṇas the non-Aryan gods and myths have found cupious expression.

We find derogatory remarks about Buddha and the Buddhists in the epics. It is said in the Mahābhārata that during the Kali age I (god Visnu), taking birth as Buddha, the son of Śuddhodana, dressed in yellow-garment would confuse people. The Śūdras would wear yellow garments. The priests would neither study nor perform sacrifice. Śruti and Smṛtis will be forgotten.[35] In a similar way the Rāmāyaṇa calls Buddha an atheist and a thief.[36]

The Buddhist teachings were so popular among the masses that even the priestly elites had to incorporate them in the Mahābhārata. In the Vanaparva we find, 'Truthfulness, self-restraint, penance, charity, non-violence, and adherence to duty are the means to get to the highest reality; but neither caste nor family.'[37] Similarly, in Śantiparva it is said: 'Truthfulness, charity, being without hatred and wickedness, humility, kindness and penance—one who has these is a Brāhmaṇa. If these qualities do not exist in a Brāhmaṇa and are found in a Śūdra, then the Śūdra is not a Śūdra and the Brāhmaṇa is not a Brāhmaṇa.'[38]

During the rivivalist era the culture of pre-Aryans dominated the Aryan culture. In the Mahābhārata we find the legend of the defeat of Ṛgvedic all-powerful hero-god Indra by the cowhered god Kṛṣṇa. Kṛṣṇa instigated people not to offer sacrifices to Indra. Indra brought rains for seven nights while Kṛṣṇa held up a mountain on one finger and gave shelter to the people. Kṛṣṇa was victorious. Viṣṇu, the Ṛgvedic god, a form of sun-god was superimposed on Kṛṣṇa, and Kṛṣṇa is accepted as an incarnation of Viṣṇu. The Ṛgvedic goddess Śri was called Lakṣamī and became the wife of Viṣṇu.

The Ṛgvedic god Rudra merged with the pre-Aryan phallic god and is called Śiva. Different mother goddesses were unified and were concieved as the wives of the Lord Śiva. Kumāra who is protrayed as a demon in the Gṛhya Sūtras, who used to cause epilepsy among infants was Brahmanized and was called Subrahmaṇyam or Skanda, the god of youthful power and bravery. He was recognized as the first born son of Śiva. Similarly, the four Vināyakas who were described as demons in the Gṛhya Sūtras were unified into one god and given the Aryan name of Gaṇeśa, and got accepted as the second son of Śiva. We find the mention of Pūjā or idolworship of these gods in the Mahābhārata, and also the promise of rewards[39] for performing them.

The celebrated poet of Ṛgveda, Visvāmitra is described as a king in the Mahābhārata while Vasiṣtha who is of ambiguous origin has been accorded an exalted status.

The Yavanas or Greeks, Śaka or Scythians, Pahlava or Parthians are described as Dasyu-like people in Mahābhārata.[40] The derogatory epithet Dasyu indicates the suspicion that existed towards them for being outsiders and intruders.

Like the Mahābhārata, the Rāmāyaṇa too appears to be based on heroic folk-poetry. It was also taken over by the priestly elites. Many scholars think that the original story of Rāmāyaṇa belonged to the pre-Aryan Assyrians who were the earlier settlers of India. The Rāmāyaṇa, unlike the Mahābhārata, focuses its attention on its prime hero and heroine. Rāvaṇa, the demon abducts Sītā who is recovered by her husband after a tough battle with the help of bears and monkeys.[41]

The Rāmāyaṇa greatly influenced the people of the Indian

sub-continent and became popular even beyond it. Even today in the minds of Indian people Rama represents the ideal man and Sītā the ideal wife. Perhaps the story of Rāma has such a persistant popularity and hold on the minds of people because it glorifies the value of unquestioning and unfliching obedience to the patriarch, which is the cardinal virtue of the patriarchal family which is corner stone of the whole social structure of a pleasent civilization. Rāma obeyed his father eventhough he had to leave his throne and had to go to the jungle for fourteen years.

In the myths, the culture of the oppressed people often finds expression. Rāma, the dark complexioned hero, marries Sītā. In the Ṛgveda Sītā is the field-furrow. In the Gṛhya Sūtras she attained divinity. Probably, the pre-Aryan tribes have been represented as bears and monkeys. Rāvaṇa who was a Brāhmaṇa of high birth is portrayed as the abuductor demon. This epic probably expresses the reminiscences of the atrocities of the Aryans in antiquated past.

The Varṇa hierarchy which made for the division of society on the basis of birth was disturbed due to the Buddhist influence. The racial factor which was the basis of Varṇa hierarchy was now futher diluted. Various foreign hordes which entered the Indian sub-continent and settled down here were racially far more pure than even the Brāhmaṇas. Perceiving this, the priestly elites substituted the criterion of racial purity by that of ritual purity. Another threat was from the pre-Aryan dark complexioned masses who constituted the majority in the society. In the earlier phase of the revivalist era in which the epics, particularly the Mahābhārata came into being, pre-Aryan norms and values overshadowed the Aryan culture.

The challenges were very strong and it was a question of survival. The Aryan norms and values were codified in the Manu Smṛti. The authorship of Manu Smṛti was attributed to the primeval father Manu. In the Manu Smṛti it is said that 'all doctrines, which are not based on Vedas, produce no reward after death and are founded on darkness. They spring up and perish, are worthless and false, because they are of recent age'[42]. Manu ordains that 'such heretics should never be honoured or greeted'[43]. Through such dicta Manu rejected Buddhism and other non-Vedic religions and tried to establish Aryan supremacy and Varṇa hierarchy.

Many warrior tribes which entered India are declared by Manu as 'originally Kṣatriyas, now reduced to the position of Śūdra because of omission of the sacred rites and of their not consulting Brāhmaṇas'[44]. The law-giver enumerates certain tribes: Paundrakas, the Codas, the Dravidas, the Kāmbojas, the Yavanas, the Śakas, the Pāradas, the Pahlavas, the Cīna, the Kirāta and the Daradas. But in the very next verse, probably following the Mahābhārata, it is declared that all those tribes in this world which are excluded from (the community of) those born from the mouth, the arms, the thighs, and the feet (of Brahman) are called Dasyus, whether they speak the language of the Mlecchas or that of Aryans.'[45]

Following Āpastamba, Gautama and Baudhāyana, Manu says: 'The place where too many Śūdras live or where Śūdra king rules or which has become subject to heretics is not worth living.'[46] It appears that even at that time many non-orthodox-rulers existed whom the priestly elites may have wished to patronise. But following the Dharma Sūtras, Manu forbade this.

Many old Aryan customs had become hateful to the people. Therefore it was quite clear to the law-giver that complete revival of the ancient Aryan norms was not possible. The Manu Smṛti provides : 'One should abandon what was Dharma, if it has become hateful to the people.'[47] In the Manu Smṛti we find many provisions which are first ordained but in the very next verse rejected. These include Niyoga, marrying a Śūdra wife and meat-eating. Manu calls Niyoga a 'beastly act'.[48] It appears that this ancient custom had become hateful to people. Prohibiting marriage with Śūdra women was necessary for the restoration of Varṇa hierarchy. Due to Buddhist influence

Manu forbids meat eating. But in the Vedas and Sūtras we find that people enjoyed eating even beef. Therefore, in Madhuparka, sacrifices, and Shraddhas, Manu recommends flesh offerings.

We find the inclusion of some non-Vedic gods among the Vedic gods. These are Bhadrakālī, Kubera and Hara. Manu says that an offering to Bhadrakālī should be given 'near the foot of the bed,' Kubera, who is mentioned as a demon in the Gṛhya Sūtras, and Hara or Śiva, are mentioned among Vedic gods. Manu considers idol-breaking a crime though he does not recomment idol worship. Probably, honouring the popular sentiments, Manu proclaims it to be a crime.

The rules about racial purity were replaced by ritual purity. Manu prescribes that when 'a person has the appearance of an Aryan he should not be taken as one; he should be judged by his acts'.

Manu revived the Varṇa hierarchy together with its divine myth and gave a strong blow to the theory of equality forwarded by Buddhism, and thus provided the rockbed to the social order which evolved as Hinduism in later times. The racial factor which was the basis of Varṇa or colour doctrine had to be rejected because of the light-skinned foreign hordes who were racially purer than many Brāhmaṇas. The Manu Smṛti, therefore, insists upon ritual purity. Still another threat was from the vast population of the earlier settlers whose religion, culture and norms were quite different from the Aryans. It was quite natural for the priestly elites to take extra care so that their sacred taxts might not be 'contaminated' by the non-Aryan norms and beliefs. Of course, all the Vedic norms and customs could not be revived. Those Vedic customs which were disapproved by the people had to be altered or rejected while many rules of non-Aryan origin were included into the Aryan law. An eminent example of this is the commercial law.

We come across several contradictions and repetitions. Manu prescribes a rule, and in the very next verse he countradicts it. He wanted to curb the liberties which people, especially women and Śūdras, were enjoying. But at the same time finding that this might not be wholly acceptable to the people, he makes some additional statements which are hardly consistent with the former. However, he did lay the foundations of Varṇa-hierarchy, which was legitimized on the authority of Vedas. His dispenstion seems to be particularly harsh on those peoples who had supported Buddhism. Those castes and tribes, whether of Aryan or non-Aryan origin, which failed to accept the supremacy of the priestly elites were either completely ignored or severly denigrated. Many of them were put down either as castes that had sprung out of hypogamous mixed unions or denoted as Vrātyas or those who remained without sacraments. In such dispensation, Manu included even those militant hordes which invaded India from time to time, besides many native military tribes and groups, and traders and artizans, who were enjoying a high position in the Buddhist and pre-Buddhist times. However, for some tribes and people he made a concession. He said that earlier they belonged to the military class but due to lack of contact with the priestly elites they had degenerated. He put each and every social group either indigenous or foreigner at its 'right' place. The Brāhmaṇas preserved the highest status for themselves. The position of teacher, priest, judge, minister, and assessors were reserved only for Brāhmaṇas. Thus, he was able to establish the Brāhmaṇa priestly elites as the priviledged class of society, whom all other classes should serve and worship.

Though racial purity could not be restored, through its substitution by stringent norms of ritual purity and sacraments which involved acceptance of the supremacy of the Brahmanical preisthood, and through assigning status to various existing groups on the mythical basis of origin by hypogamous and hypergamous unions, the foundations of a social order were laid which has lasted till recent times.

Notes

1. Ṛgveda, X. 96. 8.
2. Ṛgveda, III. 34.9.
3. Ṛgveda, V. 29.10.
4. Ṛgveda, VII. 21.5.
5. Ṛgveda, IV. 16.13.
6. Ṛgveda, I.124.10.
7. Ṛgveda, VII.9.2.
8. Ṛgveda, VI.13.3.
9. Ṛgveda, I.93.4.
10. Ṛgveda, VI.45.31-32.
11. Ṛgveda, II.12.4.
12. Ṛgveda, V.39.3.
13. Ṛgveda, VIII.19.36.
14. Atharvaveda, V.17.8-9.
15. Taittirīya Saṁhitā, I. 7.3.1.
16. Taittirīya Āranyaka, II.15.
17. Śatapatha Brāhmaṇa, XII.4.4.6.
18. Aitareya Brāhmaṇa, II.31. Kavasa Ailusaisa poet of Ṛgveda, X. 30-34.
19. Tāndya Mahā Brāhmaṇa, XIV. 6.6.
20. Śatapatha Brāhmaṇa, XI.43.
21. Śatapatha Brāhmaṇa, IV. 4.2.13.
22. Śatapatha Brāhmaṇa, III. 2.7.
23. Śatapatha Brāhmaṇa, II. 5.2.20.
24. Aitareya Brāhmaṇa, VII.3.13.
25. Chandogya Upaniṣad, IV. 1-11.
26. Bṛahadāranyaka Upaniṣad, III. 6.1.
27. Bṛahadāranyaka Upaniṣad, II. 4.1-12.
28. Chāndogya Upaniṣad, IV.4.1-5.
29. Chāndogya a, V. 3.7. 2; Brahadāranyaka Upaniṣad, VI.2.

30. While performing the Soma Yāga all the participents drink Soma by the same cup (Camasa).
31. Baudhānya Dharma Sūtra, I.4.7.1-4.
32. Sutta Nipāta verse 136.
33. Majjhma Nikāya, II. 147. ff.
34. Dīgha Nikaya, 3.180.ff.
35. Mahābhārata, 12.48.2.
36. Rāmāyana, Ayodhya Kāṇḍa, 109.34.
37. Mahābhārata, Vanaparva, 181.42-43.
38. Mahābhārata, Śantiparva, 188.10.
39. Mahābhārata, Anuśāsana Parva, 98.
40. Mahābhārata, Śantiparva, 65.13-15.
41. The Pahalvi texts of Parasis assert that when the Aryans married the women of local tribes in Sapta-Sindhu or Hafta-Hindu, monkeys and bears were born to them. For a more detailed discussion of this aspect, see Shrirama Indradeva, Diogenes, no. 111, (UNESCO, Paris, 1980).
42. Manu Smṛti, XII. 95-96.
43. Manu Smṛti, IV.30.
44. Manu Smṛti, X. 43-44.
45. Manu Smṛti, X. 43-45.
46. Manu Smṛti, IV. 61.
47. Manu Smṛti, IV. 176.
48. Manu Smṛti, IX. 64-68.

IV

Emergence of the Traditional Pattern of Social Stratification

Stratification, that is, the structuring of society on the basis of differential social status of various groups, is a common feature of human societies. But, the traditional pattern of social stratification in India has certain characteristics which are rather unique, and these have attracted and intrigued many scholars all over the world. The structural and cultural characteristics of the traditional pattern of stratification in India have deep roots in the past. They have stemmed from certain peculiar ethnic constellations that came into being some three thousand years ago, and they have been given many twists and turns by numerous socio-cultural currents and cross-currents through all these millenia.

The roots of the Varṇa system (Varṇa literally mean colour) lie in the clash of races. Fair-complexioned Aryan hordes which started pouring into India through the north-west around 1500 B.C. vanquished and subjugated the dark-complexioned earlier settlers; and thus the foundations were laid for a class system based on birth. To begin with, the Aryans regarded the non-Aryans as non-human[1] and beyond the pale of human society. But, it soon became clear to the Aryans that it was more advantageous to assign them a low position within the society and exploit them on a permanent basis. This was achieved through myths and metaphysics. The primeval myth is that of the Puruṣasūkta[2] in which the four orders of society emerge from the four parts of Puruṣa—the great man or Virāṭ Puruṣa.

But the original dispensation based solely on race could not continue for all time. The Aryans like all invading hordes were short of women, and they had to marry women of the dark-complexioned earlier settlers. Thus, their racial features were compromised. At the same time new hordes were coming from the north-west intermittently, and they had a fair skin and more pronounced Nordic features than the earlier Aryan settlers who had already established themselves as the dominant elites. These ruling elites therefore had to play down the importance of physical features in determining social status. To take the place of racial characteristics, elaborate scruples of ritual purity were introduced. The in-coming hordes were declared to be low for being devoid of ritual, and the vast masses of pre-Aryan settlers were condemned to a low social status by being given no right to undertake rituals. This important function that ritual performed in establishing and sustaining the social order perhaps explains the unique and execessive elaboration and importance of ritual in India, which has intrigued many a scholar.

The metaphysical doctrine of 'Karma' has provided a powerful rationalization for inequality based on birth, and has made it acceptable to the wide masses. According to the Karma doctrine, this life is but one link in the infinite chain of births and rebirths, and each being is born in a specific position according to his own deeds in past lives. He can improve the prospects for his later births only by adhering to, and performing well, the role proper to the stratum in which he is born. Paradoxically, the doctrine of Karma—and that of Mokṣa, i.e., salvation from the cycle of births and rebirths—arose in the process of protest against Brahmanic supremacy and its extravagant ritualism.

Interesting light is thrown on the circumstances and processes which have shaped the complex features of traditional stratification of Indian society by the analysis of texts like the Ṛgveda, later Saṁhitās the Brāhmaṇa Granthas, Upaniṣads, Kalpasūtras, Buddhist works, and Smṛtis. This chapter is an attempt in that direction.

Ṛgveda: The Establishment of Aryan Supremacy

In the Ṛgveda, the word 'Varṇa' clearly refers to the colour of skin and hair of the people of two different races—the Ārya Varṇa and Kṛṣṇa Varṇa. Nowhere in the Ṛgveda is the word 'Varṇa' used for the four-fold stratification of society. Though the two classes, Brāhmaṇa and Kṣatriya, are mentioned often, the word 'Varṇa' is not used to denote them. Even, in the Puruṣasūkta, where the origin of the four classes is described, the word 'Varṇa' does not occur.

The Aryan hordes were quite conscious of their cultural and ethnic identity and looked down upon the dark complexioned (Kṛṣṇa Varṇa). The word 'Dāsa' seems to be connected with the Iranian word 'Dahae' which means 'countryman'.

In the beginning Aryans hunted and looted the non-Aryans. The poet Viśvāmitra prays to Indra to destroy the blacks through his brilliance.[3] At one place a poet says that Indra has destroyed black armies.[4] At another place we find that Indra has killed fifty thousand blacks.[5] It appears that Dāsas were a militant people. They gave a tough fight to the Aryans. A poet praises Indra for killing Dāsa Śambara, a dweller of the mountains in the fortieth autumn.[6] But, finally, Dāsas were vanquished and were either absorbed in the lower rungs of the society or driven away from their dwellings and had to take shelter in dense forest and other inhospitable regions. A poet says : 'Indra kills Dāsas and increases the might of the Aryans'.[7]

Some of the pre-Aryan people were city-dwellers and traders rather than warriors. The Aryans were militant and well-armed and they massacred these peace-loving people at will. The Aryan god-hero, Indra, is credited with demolition of ninety-nine cities of the Dāsa king Śambara : 'And Indra for the sake of a king Divodāsa demolished Śambara's ninety-nine cities.'[8]

Due to different racial features the disdain of the Aryans towards the Dāsas was as so great that they were called 'Amanuṣya' or non-human[9]. And once the Dāsas were considered non-human all inhuman behaviour towards them was justified in the eyes of the Aryans. In a hymn of Ṛgveda we find: 'You (Indra) subdued Pipru and powerful Mṛgayu for Ṛjiśvan, the son of Vidathin, you smote down fifty thousand dark ones, you shattered cities as old age shatters good looks.'[10] Fire was the most effective and powerful weapon of the Aryans. They used it liberally against the Dāsas:

> 'O Fire due to thy fear forth fled the dark races
> Scattered aboard deserting their possessions,
> O glowing Vaiśvānara, when for Puru
> You burn up and rend their cities.'[11]

Thus, the Dāsas had to flee, leaving behind their settlements in utter despair. Similarly, at another place, it is asserted that 'fire drove Dāsas and brought light to Aryans'.[12]

The Aryans acquired the vast fertile lands of north-western India. They badly needed manpower. For them, the Dāsas were the most suitable source of labour. The Dāsas were captured and compelled to work for them. The Ṛgveda says: 'Indra binds a hundred and and ten Dāsas.'[13] Many Dāsas accepted the slavery of Aryans. In a hymn of Ṛgveda it is said : 'An Aryan leads away a Dāsa at will.'[14] The Aryans hounded them from place to place : 'The dark coloured Dāsas were driven away by Indra from place to place.'[15] This hymn indicates that the settlement of Dāsas were demonished more than once. Ultimately, the Dāsas took shelter in dark caves and dense forests: 'Indra made Dāsa Varṇa low and dweller of caves.'[16] It is stated that 'Dāsas lived in darkness'[17]. The word 'Dāsa' is used for slaves even in the Ṛgveda. In later times also Dāsa has been the most common word for slave.

Paṇis: The Pre-Aryan City People

Another people mentioned in the Ṛgveda are the Paṇis. Probably, these were a commercial people, and were later absorbed in the class of traders in the four-fold Varṇa hierarchy. The Paṇis are often connected with the ancient Phoenicians. Phoenicia is the ancient name of the coastal part of Syria. These Paṇis are portrayed as rich cattle-breeders and traders. Culturally, the Paṇis seem to be akin to the civilized Mediterraneans but by the time of the Aryan invasion, in terms of race they seem to have become predominantly proto-Austroloid. This is by and large true also of the people of the Indus valley civilization who probably belong to the category of the Paṇis of the Ṛgveda. The wealth of the Paṇis greatly lured the Aryans. The Paṇis did not want to share their wealth with the Aryans. The tendency of the Paṇis to expect something in exchange for anything that they gave seemed absurd to the pastroal Aryans. Commercial values do not seem to have taken root by that time among the Aryans, and they considered them reprehensible.

In the tenth Mandal of Ṛgveda we find a whole Sūkta in which the she-dog of the hero-god Indra came to find out the hidden treasure of the Paṇis. In the dialogue, the Paṇis assert that their treasure comprising cows, horses and riches is well stored in the mountain castle, and those Paṇis who are excellent guards protect it well.[18] But, the Aryans found that concealed treasure of the Paṇis and appropriated it. 'Searching out everywhere, they have obtained the great treasure of the Paṇis' hidden in the cave.'[19] Fire was employed by the Aryans against the Paṇis also:

> 'Agni, the hero, kills his enemy;
> The poet takes away the riches of Paṇis.'[20]

Fire is praised because through its help Aryans were able to open the doors of Paṇis : 'The fire is the wisest god that opens the doors of Paṇis forcefully.'[21] It appears that before going on plundering expeditions the Aryans used to drink 'Soma'. Therefore, it was quite natural for them to praise Soma (wine) too, along with Agni (fire), for the success they achieved in plundering the Paṇis: 'O Soma and Agni, your valour is famous through which you snatched the kine and food of Paṇis.'[22]

The Paṇis did not perform the Aryan sacrifices. Therefore, they seemed foolish and faithless to the Aryans. The Paṇis spoke softly or indistinctly (in the judgement of the Aryans). They did not worship the Aryans' gods; therefore, they were declared godless. The robust Aryans found no justification for allowing Paṇis to occupy the lands in which they were settled: 'They chased the Paṇis to the east and turned the godless westwards.'[23] Some of the Paṇis gave resistance to the Aryan hordes:

'With loud voice the people invoke thee, Indra,
To aid them in the battle field.
Thou with the singers, hast pierced through the Paṇis;
The charger whom thou aidest wins the booty.'[24]

The hoarded wealth of Paṇis held great attraction for the Aryans: 'The men together found the Paṇis' hoarded wealth, the cattle, horses and kine.'[25] Sometimes Aryan avoided direct confrontation and stole the wealth of the Paṇis: 'O wealthy Dawn; may Paṇis sleep without awakening. Make us wealthy, we the rich people.'[26]

Similarly, at another place, we find: 'They go to steal the food of Paṇis.'[27] All those Paṇis who did not want to part with their wealth were looked upon as enemies by the Aryans: 'O king, you yoke the ruddy horse for Agastya's nephews and defeat all the Paṇis who do not give.'[28] Soma helped in finding out the wealth of Paṇis. 'O Soma you found out the wealth of Paṇis.'[29] After consuming Soma, plundering was easier:

'O Soma you looted the wealth consisting of cows, (make your presence felt by) making noise in the sacrifice.'[30]

Similarly:

'O Soma our crushing stones aspire,
for your friendship.
Destroy the greedy Paṇi for he is a wolf.'[31]

The avariciousness of the Paṇis seemed reprehensible to the Aryans. They exhort their god Indra not to acquire this vice of the Paṇis:

> 'O noble elderly Indra, while gathering great riches, do not be a Paṇi to us.'[32]

In the course of time, the Aryans settled down on the land and developed cordial relations with the Paṇis. A poet prays to the god Pūsan: 'O Pūṣa, one who does not want to give make him liberal and soften the heart of the Paṇi.'[33] And we find some hymns in praise of Bṛbu, a leader of Paṇis:

> 'Among Paṇis, Bṛbu is the greatest;
> His heart is as large as the plains of Gaṅgā;
> He who is ready to give immediately;
> His thousand noble gifts of cows are running like wind,
> Therefore all our poets praise the noble prince, the giver of thousands.'[34]

In due course it seems that the Paṇis were absorbed among the Viś or Aryan's countrymen. The commercial terminology in Sanskrit owes a great deal to the Paṇis. Among such terms are *āpaṇa* or market, *paṇaṇa* or to sell, *paṇya* or commodity, *paṇa* or coin, and *vaṇik* or the trader. In the word *vaṇik* the sound of *pa* has changed to *va*, which is not uncommon in the evolution of languages. It is common to add the letter *ka* for making diminutives in the Avesta as well as in the Sanskrit language. The word *vāṇijya* or trade is derived from the word *vaṇik.*

In the Indo-Aryan social structure, this whole class was given the third position—lower than the priests and warriors. In the Puruṣasūkta, this class is called Vaiśya or 'the sons of Viś'. In the Ṛgveda, the word Viś is used for people. In the Zend-Avestā, the word Viś means many families or a village.

We also find Dāsas named Bababūtha and Tarukṣa who made gifts to an Aryan poet:

'I received a hundred (cows) from Dāsa Bababutha and Tarukṣa,

O Vayu these are thy people protected by Indra, protected by gods they rejoice.'[35]

Priests, Warriors, and Commoners

In the Ṛgveda we find a society in which any individual of Aryan origin had the right to choose his profession according to his ability and achievements. He could become a priest or a warrior, or an ordinary man. The word 'Brahma' means hymn and also the power inherent in the hymn. Thus Brāhmaṇa is one who is the repository of hymns. Like other ancient civilizations, in the ancient Ṛgvedic civilization too, priesthood was considered the highest profession. A priest had precedence even over the king. But becoming a successful priest was not easy. The priest was expected to compose such hymns which would lull wealthy enemies to sleep and swollen rivers to lower their level so that armies would cross them without difficulty. But, he had also to be a master strategist and an excellent warrior himself. Naturally, there was a competition among various priests for the patronage of powerful kings. King Sūdāsa replaced Vasistha by Viśvāmitra as his priest. Many of the composers of hymns seem to be priests of one king or another. Some of their sons became composers of hymns while some others found the profession of warrior more suitable. A poet vividly describes that everybody has to do some work or the other to earn his livelihood:

'I am a poet, my father is a physician,
My mother grinds corn with stone;
Striving for wealth,
We follow different occupations.'[36]

Since the professions of priest and warrior were considered nobler it is not surprising that many people aspired to these. A poet prays to Lord Indra :

'O Indra, fond of Soma, make me a guardian of people;
Or either make me a king;

Would you make me a Ṛṣi drunk with Soma?
Would you not impart to me wealth that lasts forever.'[37]

It appears that only those persons among the Aryans who were able to compose hymns were called Brāhmaṇas:

'Brāhmaṇas, the drinkers of Soma,
Making hymns set their voices at a high pitch.'[38]

Composing hymns was not an easy task. Superficial knowledge of language was not considered enough to become a good poet. A poet compares speech with a fond wife who exposes her charms only to her husband:

'A man though knows speech, does not know her;
Though he hears her yet not hears,
Like a fond well-groomed wife,
She exposes her beauty to her master.'[39]

Not everyone could be a composer of hymns. The difficult process of composing a hymn is well described by a poet:

'The heart woven with mental brilliance,
When friendly Brāhmaṇas sacrifice together,
Through their attainment they leave far behind,
Those who count themselves as Brāhmaṇas but are preparers of libations,
Using Vāk in a wrongful manner they spin out bad threads in ignorance, and
Have to take ploughshares and engage in (agricultural) operations.'[40]

Thus, if a person could neither compose hymns nor become a warrior, the only profession left for him was that of the agriculturist. The profession of an agriculturist is considered lower than that of priest and warrior. These norms of considering as low an agriculturist, and all those who earn their living by physical labour, have been inherited by the later tradition. The whole structure of the Varṇa hierarchy is based on such norms.

Entry into the rank of warrior was also quite difficult. One who failed to be a good poet could hardly be a success on the battlefield:

> 'Wandering in illusion gainlessly,
> The speech heard by him bears neither blossom nor fruit.
> Dull in friendship he is called a laggard;
> Nobody expects him to perform deeds of valour.'[41]

From this description it becomes quite clear that the heroes of war often composed the hymns themselves.

Viś was the third rank. Nowhere in the Ṛgveda do we find a hymn in which a poet aspires to be a Viś or a common man. Obviously those who could not get entry into the two higher professions remained Viś. The Viś are described as those who give taxes to the king.[42] They were cattle breeders and agriculturists. Perhaps agriculture became a common occupation later than that of tending cattle. The poet compares the earth with a cow from whom he milks a rich harvest year after year.

> 'May Indra press furrow down,
> May Puṣan guide its course aright,
> May she be rich in milk
> For milking year by year.'[43]

The Four-fold Hierachy : Organismic Analogy

In the Ṛgveda we do not find the mention of the Śūdra except in the Puruṣasūkta, which is considered to be of a later origin. The Puruṣasūkta contains a myth about the origin of the four-fold social structure. Here all the four ranks are mentioned together. In this hymns it is asserted that all the four ranks originated from the great sacrificed Puruṣa. The occupations of the four ranks are related symbolically to the parts of the body of the Puruṣa. Obviously, this is an organismic analogy between man and society, legitimizing the varying ranks and functions of different groups. So far as Ṛgveda, the oldest scripture, is concerned, the words Rajanya, Vaiśya and Śūdra occur only in the Puruṣasūkta:

'The Brāhmaṇa was his mouth,
The Rājanya was made of his two arms;
His thighs became the Vaiśya,
From his feet was produced the Śūdra.'[44]

The Brāhamana has been called the mouth of the Puruṣa and is placed highest in society. His special function pertains to speech. Being a priest, invoking gods is his privilege. The second rank, Rājanya, is born of the arms of Puruṣa and has the privilege of wielding arms. The thighs of the Puruṣa became Vaiśya. The occupation of Vaiśya is agriculture and trade. From feet was produced the Śūdra. Just as the feet are the lowest in the body, Śūdras are the lowest in society.

The Puruṣasūkta appears to be the composition of an era when the Aryans had already settled down in the Indian subcontinent. The Viś or the commoners among Aryans required agricultural labour. They employed Dāsas. Gradually, the Dāsas were given the generic name of Śūdra. Both these words are of Iranian origin. The word 'Dāsa' is the transformed version of the Iranian word 'Dahae' or common man. The word 'Śūdra' seems to have some connection with the word 'Kurda', the name of a pre-Aryan Iranian tribe still living in Iran.

In the Ṛgveda itself we find the tendency of considering the profession of priest and warrior higher, and the profession of the agriculturist lower. The people who were employed as agricultural labourers or slaves had naturally to occupy the lowest position in society.

The composition of the Puruṣasūkta and its inclusion in the Ṛgveda was probably the first attempt to systematize, justify and legitinize the exploitation of the non-Aryan masses by Aryans. The easiest way was to find some supernatural basis. This tendency of imputing divine sanction is a characteristic of the period of later Samhitās and Brāhmaṇas. We do not find this tendency in the earlier parts of the Ṛgveda. In those parts of the Ṛgveda, the non-Aryans were considered Amanuṣya or non-humans and not the descendents of Manu, the primogenitor. Their subjugation was considered natural. The Viś or the agriculturists employed the non-Aryan labour. In an agriculturist society, labour force is always needed. Later, through their shrewd farsightendness, the Aryan elite made an institutionalized arrangement which made cheap labour available as a matter of course. Śūdras formed the lowest class of Aryan society. The inclusion of this hymn in the Ṛgveda sanctioned this arrangement as natural and god-given. The society was conceived as an organic whole and all the classes formed its parts. Afterwards, in order to preserve the privileges enjoyed by the upper classes, and to avoid further racial admixture, it was necessary to give a more clear-cut character to various classes. Considerations of birth replaced those of individual achievement.

In the Avestā, the land of seven rivers is mentioned as one of the settlements of Aryans. In this land, the leader of Aryan migration, Yim, married a 'demoness' and gave his sister, Yimuk, to a demon. The issues born of these unions have been referred to as 'abnormal' in the Avestā, and 'monkeys and bears' in the Pahlavī texts. These descriptions allude to the racial admixture which took place in that early era. To avoid deformity, Yim married his sister Yimuk and thus preserved racial purity. From this myth it is quite clear that during the earliest era of settlement the Aryans married indigenous women; but when the children born of such unions had dark complexions, snub noses and other non-Aryan features, such marriages were avoided. In ancient Iran where the racial features of victorious Aryans and the subjugated people were not so different, ranks did not crystallize into endogamous groups as happened in India. In Iran, the rank of priest was hereditary but not endogamous. In India, too, caste became hereditary first. Marriage in direct order was permissible. But, in the course of time, caste crystallized into endogamous as well as hereditary groups.

Later Samhitās and Brāhmaṇas: Low Status of the Śūdra Institutionalized

In the later Samhitās hypergamy is permissible. Thus, the Aryans or men of the upper Varṇas could have Śūdra wives. It can also be seen in the Traittirīya Saṁhitā that the Aryans used to establish illicit relations with Śūdra women: 'If a Śūdra woman has an Aryan paramour she does not expect wealth for maintenance.'[45] A Śūdra could never think of marrying an Aryan woman legally. The later Saṁhitās and Brāhmaṇas give a number of justifications for the low status of Śūdras. In the Taittirīya Saṁhitā of the black Yajurveda, we find: 'Among men, Śūdra has the same position as the horse has among animals. These two, the horse and the Śūdra, are conveyances of the beings (Aryans); therefore the Śūdras could not participate in a sacrifice.'[46]

On the basis of the Puruṣasūkta, the Tāṇḍyamahā Brāhmaṇa propounds : 'Therefore, even if a Śūdra has a lot of cattle, he is not entitled to perform a sacrifice, as he is without god, no god was created after him, since he was created from the feet, he should not do anything but wash the feet (of the three higher Varṇas).'[47]

The Aitareya Brāhmaṇa puts forth another mythical justification : 'He created the Brāhmaṇa with Gāyatrī, the Rājanya with Triṣṭubh and the Vaiśya with Jagati, but he did not create the Śūdra with any metre.'[48] In the Śatapatha Brāhmaṇa, a Śūdra is simply declared as 'toil'.[49]

At another place, Śūdra, woman, dog and crow are called the untruth itself, that is, the personification of falsehood, and it is suggested that a teacher while teaching should not look at them.[50] The Aitareya Brāhmaṇa ordains that the Śūdra is to be ordered about by the others (three Varṇas), he can be made to rise at will, he can be executed at will.[51] Thus, the Śūdras were given the lowest position in the society. The elite of the society maintained a strict vigil to ensure that though the Śūdras had been assigned a place in society they should not be considered as belonging to the Aryans. Their inclusion in the four-fold hierarchy was meant only for the service that they performed for the higher Varṇas. They could in no way be counted as among them. To serve the three higher Varṇas was the sole duty of the Śūdra class. This relationship is asserted again and again in all the works of the later periods also.

Change in the Role of the Priest

By the time of later Samhitas and Brāhmaṇas, the doctrine of four Varṇas was broadly accepted by all the members of the society as god-given. We can perceive the change of the ethos in this period from the time when the hymns of Ṛgveda were composed. In the later Saṁhitās the struggle with non-Aryans no more existed. The non-Aryans, now the Śūdras, accepted the superiority of the Aryans and considered serving the latter as their sacred duty. Consequently, the old militant spirit of the Aryans declined. For acquiring the comforts of life, they had to fight no more. Since priestood was the most remunerative and respected occupation, the bulk of the Aryan people became Brāhmaṇas or priests. The simple sacrifices were made elaborate and expensive.

The priest now was neither a military strategist nor a poet; his sole job was to preserve the hymns and employ them in various complicated sacrifices which were to be performed for the fulfilment of different wishes. The character of the gods, too, changed. The militant gods lost their heroic spirit and vigour. The Aryans had by now settled down in the Indo-Gangetic plains. For the settled agricultural way of life such gods were no more needed. The gods now were expected to fulfil their mundane wishes and solve their day-to-day problems. The centre of civilization shifted further east. The land of seven rivers finds mention no more. Now, the land of Kuru and Pāñcāla became the seat of the Aryan culture. The river Sarasvatī in the west and the river Dṛasadvatī in the east formed its boundary. Broadly speaking, this land comprised the modern states of Haryana and Uttar Pradesh. The secure and comfortable life of the plains made the priests self-assured and complacent.

The priestly elites preserved the highest position for themselves. There are many assertions in the later Saṁhitās that are meant to establish their supreme position. It appears that the priestly elites themselves were not quite sure of their superiority. Therefore, it was necessary for them to assert it again and again. In all the texts of the later Vedic era we find glorification of priestly elites. The Taittirīya Saṁhitā declared them 'the gods on earth'.[52]

The sacrament of initiation, Yajn̄opavīta, played an important part in rationalizing and strengthening the system of Varṇa. The first three Varṇas acquired a privileged position for themselves. Though studentship is mentioned in the Ṛgveda, we do not find any mention of initiation rites. In the Atharvaveda, for the first time, we get the description of initiation. The poet conceives the sun as the child who is to be initiated into studentship by his teacher. This seems to be a forced analogy and there remain a number of incongruities. In this hymn studentship is called a second birth.

Gradually, the sacrament of initiation became much more elaborate. Taittirīya Āraṇyaka prescribes that a Brāhmaṇa should wear a Yajn̄opavīta of antilope skin or of cloth. It asserts that the sacrifice which is performed while wearing a Yajn̄opavīta is spread out, or becomes successful, whereas the sacrifices of him who does not wear a Yajn̄opavīta would not spread.[53] And in due course Yajn̄opavīta became the most essential part of intiation. In the Dharma Sūtras we find that the sacred cord is introduced as an option. The Āpastamba Dharma Sūtra prescribes that a householder should always wear an upper garment, or in its place he may wear the sacred thread.[54]

In the Śatapatha Brāhmaṇa, the Brāhmaṇa and Kṣatriya Varṇas are identified with the twin gods Mitra and Varuna : 'Mitra is priesthood and Varuna is nobility; and the priesthood is the conceiver, and then nobility is the doer'. It is asserted that Mitra or the priest could stand without Varuna, the nobility; but not Varuna the nobility without Mitra, the priest. It is concluded, 'therefore a Kṣatriya who wants to do something should seek guidance from a Brāhmaṇa, for he verily succeeds only when he is guided by a Brāhmaṇa'[55]

Upaniṣads: Revolt against Ritualism and Brahmanic Supremacy

Gradually, the three Varṇas other than the Brāhmaṇa developed a kind of apathy for the ritualistic way of life, and a new school of thought appeared in Āraṇyakas and Upaniṣads. In these texts it is asserted that expensive, cumbersome and prolonged sacrifices do not lead to real knowledge. It was a challenge against the supremacy of the Brāhmaṇas, and signified loss of faith in sacerdotal science inherent in it. People began to doubt the efficacy of these sacrifices. Another interesting feature of the Upaniṣads is that, contrary to the tradition, the newer thought was marked by contributions primarily from Kṣatriyas, lower Varṇas and women.

The Upaniṣadic thought is quite different in its spirit from the Vedas. As a matter of fact, there was implicit in it a revolt against the Varṇa hierarchy. The teachings of the Upaniṣads are in a simple language; therefore they earned great popularity among the people. The younger generation of the priestly class took active interest in it. In this era, the importance of family and Varṇa also diminished. The Upaniṣads contain the seeds of the systems of metaphysics which evolved later on. We come across many instances where Brāhmaṇa teachers went to learn the ultimate truth from Kṣatriyas. 'Brahma' which means only prayer in the Ṛgveda assumed a new mystical meaning in Upaniṣads. Now this term stood for the Ultimate Reality.

In this era, the supremacy of the Brāhmaṇas was challenged in various overt and covert ways. In the Chāndogya Upaniṣad we find a story in which a procession of white dogs is pictured like Brāhmaṇas. These white dogs, one after another, each holding the tail of the preceding dog in his mouth like priests when they go to sing the Vahisapavamana hymn (in this ceremony priests have to walk in a procession, each priest holding the gown of the preceding priest). When all the dogs settled down, they began to recite, 'Om, let us eat; Om, let us drink; Om, may the divine Varuna, Prajapati, Sāvitrī bring us food, Lord of food bring hither food, bring it, Om'.[56]

Many established teachers (Brāhmaṇas) approached kings (Kṣatriyas) to acquire the ultimate knowledge. Prāvahana Jaivali, king of Pāñcāla, instructed Gautma and claimed that 'Brāhmaṇas do not have this knowledge, only the Kṣatriyas possess it'[57]. We find glorification of Kṣatriyas in the Bṛhadāṇyaka Upaniṣad also : 'The Brāhmaṇa being not strong enough, the most excellent power or Kṣatriya was created. Therefore (at the Rajasuya sacrifice the) Brāhmaṇa sits down below the Kṣatriya. He confers that glory on the Kṣatriya alone.'[58] At another place we find that 'five great householders and theologians approached king Aśvapati of Kekaya carrying fuel in their hands like students to get the knowledge of self'[59].

Even the kings sometimes approached persons of lower classes to get knowledge of self. Jānśruti Pautrayaṇa approached a cartman named Raikva for instruction.

Before the Upaniṣads were composed, a great deal of racial admixture must have taken place. In the Vedic tradition persons of dark complexion are considered as non-humans or 'Amanuṣya'. Due to the strong patriarchal values, the birth of a daughter was also considered a misfortune. In the Upaniṣads we perceive a peculiar general ethos, which is totally absent in the literature composed both before and after Upaniṣads. In the Upaniṣadic literature dark complexion is not considered necessarily bad. The Brahadāranyaka Upaniṣad mentions rituals for having a dark-complexioned son together with that for a blond son. We find ritual even for the birth of a daughter, which is very uncommon in the Indian elite tradition.[60]

The Upaniṣads mark a new epoch in the history of Indian thought. The ideas found in the Upaniṣads are in marked contrast to the traditional way of thinking which always looks back to the golden past. The Upaniṣads are refreshingly forward-looking. Instead of expecting people to stick to the beaten path of the past, they exhort them to move on and on. They expect the new generation to be better than the older ones. In the Bṛhadāranyaka Upaniṣad, the father blesses his new-born son to be more ascensive than his father, than his grandfather.

In the Upaniṣads, for the first time, the concept of rebirth is introduced. As a matter of fact it is not in consonance with the Aryan tradition. In the Ṛgveda, as well as the Avestā, the dead go to live with their forefathers in heaven. The idea of souls taking another birth is found in a rudimentary form in Austric tribal cultures. This idea of transmigration of the soul was developed in the classical Indian systems of metaphysics specially in Sāṁkhya, Yoga and Vedanta. It crystallized into the theory of Karma, which rationalized and provided the rockbed to the system of Varṇa hierarchy for thousands of years.

The Upaniṣads marked a revolt against Brāhmānic supremacy. This wave of liberalization must have lead to the adoption of ideas from non-Aryan sources; and the notion of transmigration of the soul and rebirth seems to be one of these. However, it is ironic that this very idea was turned into the most effective instrument to justify inequality based on birth. The doctrine is that one is born as a Brāhmaṇa or a Śudra entirely on the basis of his own deeds in the earlier lives; in his present life he should pursue steadfastly the duties of his own Varṇa in order to better his prospects in subsequent lives. Not only was this doctrine propagated by the Brāhmaṇas as self-evident truth, but it was accepted and internalized by the most underprivileged and exploited sections also. The doctrine provided a perfect justification for gross inequality based on birth.

Sūtras: The Reassertion of Varṇa Hierarchy

During the Upaniṣadic era, the Varṇa hierarchy and the strong patriarchal order that constituted the foundation of the ancient Indian social structure were badly undermined. The Gṛhya Sūtras seem to mark a systematic and concerted effort on the part of the priestly elites to re-establish their supremacy and resuscitate the social order in which they would have an unrivalled position. The hierarchy could no more be established on the basis of race as there had already been a great deal of racial admixture. Because of this, it seems that criteria of ritual purity were introduced by the Gṛhya Sūtras to take the place of racial purity.

In the Gṛhya Sūtras, for the first time, a number of Saṁskāras or sacraments were explicitly codified. These Saṁskāras are to begin before the birth of a child and this process lasts for many years even after the death of an individual. It is expected that each individual offers oblations to his father, grandfather and great-grandfather. A professional priest has to officiate at these sacraments. All the individuals of the higher Varṇas who wanted to establish themselves as respectable members of the elite had to get these sacraments performed. Non-performance of these sacraments could result even in excommunication from the community.

During the era of Aryan invasion and colonization, the victorious Aryans had to marry women belonging to the subjugated people. But there is no evidence that they gave their own women in marriage to the non-Aryans. Thus, a sort of hypergamy was established. However, during the Upaniṣadic period, some kings gave their daughters in marriage to persons belonging to a lower order in gratitude for the esoteric knowledge received from them. It seems that the Brahmanical revival marked by the Sūtras sought to revive the earlier trend. The Gṛhya Sūtras laid down that marriages should be hypergamous, that is, in the direct order of Varṇas.

So far as the Varṇa of the progeny is concerned, there seem to be two types of traditions which are divergent. According to one, the progeny belong to the Varṇa of their father and not of the Varṇa of the mother. This seems to be the earlier practice when the Ayans had no option but to marry women from amongst the non-Aryan people. The other set of norms, which is already in evidence in the Sūtras, and is vigorously asserted in the Smṛtis, insists that both the parents should belong to the same Varṇa.

This is in sharp contrast to the practice of bestowing sonhood on the children acquired in various ways. The Gautama Dharma Sūtra recognized twelve types of sons which include besides the real son even the sons who had no biological relationship with the father or the mother. Even those whose parents are unknown have been included. The sons of all these types were given the lineage name which would imply also their inclusion in the Varṇa of their social father. It would be reasonable to surmise that such a son had to be of a fair complexion.

The Dharma Sūtras introduced many new rules about not taking food from the house of persons of lower Varṇas. In the early Vedic texts, we do not find such rules. The Baudhāyana Dharma Sūtra, which because of its archaic language seems to be the earliest among the Dharma Sūtras, does not contain any rules about taking food in the house of lower Varnas. Gautama introduced such restrictions in a liberal way. It is interesting to note that Gautama allows a Brāhmaṇa student to take food from the house of all the three higher Varṇas[61] but after completing his studentship he should not take food from the house of Kṣatriya and Vaiśya Varṇas. He was expected to take food only at the house of a Brāhmaṇa householder. Āpastamba further propounds that even among Brāhmaṇa householders, he should eat only in the house of a true Brāhmaṇa.[62]

It appears that the society was not prepared for the imposition of such rigid norms and many among the elites took objection to this. Āpastamba refers to the opinions of 'some' who allow a Brāhmaṇa to take food in the houses of Kṣatriya and Vaiśya householders. In times of distress a Brāhmaṇa could eat the food prepared in the house of a Śūdra who was under his protection for the sake of spiritual merit. Gautama says that during distress a Brāhmaṇa may take food from a Śūdra.[63]

In the Upaniṣadic era Kṣatriyas enjoyed a position at least equal if not higher to that of Brāhmaṇas. But in the Dharma Sūtras, the priestly elites made it a point to assign a lower position to Kṣatriyas. It is provided that even a king should make way for a Brāhmaṇa on the road. The gap between the two higher Varṇas definitely widened. A Brāhmaṇa of ten years and a Kṣatriya of a hundred years stand to each other in the relation of father and son; of the two the Brāhmaṇa is the father.[64]

Śūdras constituted the fourth Varṇa. Āpastamba and Vasiṣṭha refer to the Śūdras and outcaste as burial grounds.[65] Āpastamba, Gautama and Vasiṣṭha provide that serving the three higher Varṇas is his sole occupation. The higher the Varṇa he serves the greater the merit he earns.[66] Gautama provided that for serving the three higher Varṇas he would get remnants of their food, cast-off shoes, umbrellas, garments and mats. When a Śūdra servant is unable to serve his Aryan employer due to old age or illness, the Aryan employer was expected to support him. Similarly, if the employer fell into distress, the servant was expected to look after his master. It is ordained that the savings of the servant could be used by the master.

Baudhayana and Āpastamba both provide that a Śūdra can cook in the superintendence of the first three Varṇas. The cooks should daily have their hair cut, shave their beards and cut their nails before cooking.[67]

During the Upaniṣadic era, Śūdras too participated in metaphysical discussions. In the revivalist era, the priestly elites scrupulously forbade even the listening to recitation of Vedas for Śūdra; if a Śūdra intentionally listens to the recitation of Vedas his ears shall be filled with molten lead or lac. If he recites Vedic texts his tongue shall be split into two.[68] Āpastamba and Gautama provide that if a Śūdra tries to converse with an Aryan on an equal footing, walks on the road side-by-side with him or sits on the same couch, he should be given corporal punishment. The tongue of a Śūdra, who speaks evil of a virtuous persons belonging to one of the first three Varṇas shall be cut out.[69] If a Śūdra commits homicide or theft, appropriates land, or commits similar crimes, his property shall be confiscated and he himself shall suffer capital punishment.[70] It seems that the priestly elites were quite aware that the Śūdras were as capable of learning and propagating knowledge as any member of the three higher Varṇas. They did not want to share the privileged position which they enjoyed on the grounds of possessing sacred knowledge even with the Kṣatriya and Vaisya Varṇas, and not at all with the Śūdras. All the members of the Brāhmaṇa Varṇa were expected to maintain a close vigil over the Śūdras to prevent them even from listening to a Vedic recitation. Any kind of self-assertion on the part of a Śūdra amounted to a crime according to the Dharma Sūtras.

Though it is provided in the Sūtras that a Śūdra can cook the food of a Brāhmaṇa, Āpastamba and Baudhāyana provide that food brought by an impure Śūdra must not be eaten.[71]

The value of the life of a Śūdra is assessed quite low. Āpastamba provides the same penance for killing a Śūdra as he provides for killing a crow, chameleon, a peacock, Brahmani duck, a swan, a frog, a monogoose, a musk-rat, or a dog.[72]

Buddhism : Challenge to the Brahmanical Order

It the eastern parts of India, however, there developed a parallel non-orthodox stream of thought through the emergence of Upaniṣadas and Buddhist literature. Gradually, this became a challenge to the Vedic-Brahmanical tradition—in the beginning rather covertly, but later on openly.

In these movements we find a unique synthesis of different ethno-cultural streams. Because of the complex interweaving of the varied strands, it is not easy to identify and isolate the contribution made by various cultures. Among the prominent ethno-cultural strains are the Aryan, the civilized Mediterranean, the Australoid, and the Mongoloid. In the early Rgvedic times, though there existed the notion of superiority based on race, the division of society was not as rigid and elaborate as found in the post-Rgvedic treatises. In the Buddhist literature, the people described are highly commercial, liberal, affluent and happy. It appears that in the north-eastern parts of India which became the seat of Upaniṣads and Buddhism, trade and commerce flourished extensively, and liberal ideas developed among the elite of that region. Perhaps it were these ideas that found expression in the two revolts against the Brahmanical orthodoxy. A strong plea was made for equality and fraternity in that early era of civilization, both in the monarchical and republican states of that region. The pre-eminant position of Brāhmaṇas, on the basis of birth, was challenged. This in a way was also a challenge to Aryan supremacy.

Though the Upaniṣads picture many respectable teachers as belonging to the the lower Varṇas, they do not directly criticize the Varṇa hierarchy. On the other hand, Buddha openly declared the Varṇa system unreasonable and reprehensible, as all human beings belong to a common human species, whatever be the colour of their skin. He refuted the Vedic myth of the origin of the Varṇa hierarchy and declared it to be false.

The social structure depicted in the Buddhist texts is not very different from the structure that actually existed in recent pre-modern times. We find in the Buddhist texts proud kings and warriors, Brāhmaṇas who were well versed in the three Vedas, Vaiśyas or rich Śreṣthis who liberally made gifts to the new religion, and skilful craftsmen.

In the Buddhist texts, the supremacy of the Brāhmaṇas was openly challenged. The Buddha declared that one cannot be considered superior just because of birth or lineage. He declares:

> 'By mere birth no one becomes a Brāhmaṇa,
> By mere birth no one becomes an outcaste.
> By deeds one becomes a Brāhmaṇa,
> By deeds one becomes an outcaste.'[73]

During a discussion with a young Brāhmaṇa, Buddha systematically argued that all Varṇas, whether white or black, belong to one human race.

In the Buddhist literature we can witness the earlier phases of industrial and commercial society in India. Various beautiful things were produced by artisans. The artisans were organized into strong guilds. There were traders who used to take long sea voyages to sell silks, muslins, brocades, drugs, ivory and ivory work, perfumes, jewellery and gold.[74] Thus came into existence a rich, liberal middle class mainly comprising artisans and Vaiśyas. It is remarkable that in the Buddhist texts we find norms and values of the rising puritanical middle class. These values promoted activist norms and the formation of capital. The advice given to traders in the Dīgha Nikāya brings out the commercial spirit of the Buddhist era:

'Making money like the bee,
Who does not hurt the flower;
Such a man makes his pile,
As an ant-hill gradually;
The man grown wealthy,
Thus, can help his family,
And firmly binds his friends to himself
He should divide his money into four parts
On one part he should live,
With two expand his trade
And the fourth he should save
Against a rainy day.'[75]

These values promoted accumulation of capital which was necessary for industry and commerce.

It appears that the revolt of Buddhism against the Brahmanical system of stratification which is based on birth has much to do with the rise of the commercial class in the times of the Buddha.

Smṛtis and the Brahmanical Revival

Buddhism was the greatest challenge to the priestly elites for it gained great popularity among the masses. Many kings and Śreṣṭhis found Buddhism more suitable and they contributed to its spread in India and abroad. The religion of the pre-Aryans, too, reasserted itself among the people. The priestly elites were quite conscious of all these forces. It was clear to them that the ancient Vedic religion could not be revived in its earlier form. Many old Aryan practices had therefore to be rejected, and non-Aryan customs found entry into the revived religion. For restoring the Varṇa hierarchy, the backbone of the traditional Indian social structure, the Smṛtis came into existence. During the first revival of the Sūtra period, many ancient Indo-European rituals and customs were consolidated into aphorisms or Sūtras. We do not find much about the saṅskāras (Indian *rites de passage*) in the Ṛgveda. The saṅskāras were introduced in an effective manner primarily by the Sūtras. It seems that when racial purity became diluted, ritual purity was substituted for it. And ritual purity itself became the hallmark of higher Varṇa. It was all the more necessary because during the Buddhist era marriages in the lower Varṇas were no more prohibited. In the Jātakas we find many such marriages.

Since the Smṛtis belong to the revivalist era, all the authors of Smṛtis adopted the names of Vedic seers to get authority for what they said. The Manu Smṛti is the first attempt of the priestly elites in this direction. Therefore, it was perhaps natural to attribute this Smṛti to the primogenitor, Manu. Armed with the ancient myth of creation and various sacraments, together with the doctrine of Karma, Manu tried to revive the bygone golden age by re-establishing the ancient system of Varṇa hierarchy. In this process women and Śūdras were the greatest losers. The social justice they had got during the Buddhist period was taken away with a vengeance. Manu tried to assign each and every ethnic group, whether Indian or foreign, a specific place in the Varṇa system according to his own criteria. Manu generally followed the guidelines laid down by the Dharma Sūtras. Yājñavalkya, Bṛhaspati, Nārada and Kātyāyana followed the institutes of Manu.

Broadly speaking, those ethnic groups and lineages which were to be given a higher place in the social hierarchy were described to be offsprings of hypergamous unions between two Varṇas, and those that were to be assigned a low status were declared to be the progeny of hypogamous unions. The social entities of various kinds (tribes, craftsmen of different types and even hordes which came from outside) were assigned a high or low position in the social hierarchy in this way. Through the myths of the origin of various castes as a result of hypergamous and hypogamous unions between men and women of different Varnas, a way was found to explain the existence of a multiplicity of castes (not just four Varṇas) and each was assigned a specific status in the system of stratification.

The Manu Smṛti reflects the strong resentment of the Brahmanical elites against the Buddhist levelling influence. It has been categorically asserted that the dominance of priestly elites and the hierarchy based on Varṇa must be re-established not only through religious prescriptions but by the full might of the king and the state. The use of arms to restore their supremacy is openly commended. Manu calls 'punishment, the son of the creator'. The king is enjoined to establish Varṇa hierarchy through the power of punishment. Other twice-born people, too, are exhorted to resort to arms if they are in any way hindered in carrying out the duties prescribed for their particular Varṇas.[76] It is obvious from these ardent exhortations and ruthless prescriptions that Manu was conscious that re-establishing the supremacy of Brāhmaṇas was no easy task---its attainment required all the power at their command, physical as well as moral.

In the Smṛti era, once again the Brāhmaṇas ensured unquestionably the supreme position for themselves. Manu declares that the Brāhmaṇa from the very birth is an eternal incarnation of the sacred law. Manu calls the Brāhmaṇa a great god just like fire, be he ignorant or learned, just as the fire does not get contaminated, so also a Brāhmaṇa, although he may follow even a low occupation, should always be honoured and should be considered a great deity.[77]

This is in marked contrast to the theory of equality proclaimed by the Buddha. Birth in a particular Varṇa was considered enough for securing all sorts of privileges. It appears that by the time Manu Smṛti was composed, norms of ritual purity had substituted those of racial purity. Manu declared that the Brāhmaṇa is the lord of all Varṇas because of his superiority of birth and observances of rituals and sacraments.[78] He says that a non-Aryan may have Aryan appearance, therefore one must judge a person by his acts, not by his physical appearance.[79]

The Śūdras are considered lowest of all Varṇas because no sacrament is prescribed for them. Following Āpastamba and Baudhāyana, Manu too justified the lower status of Śūdras. The sacrament of initiation is not permissible for the Śūdras. Initiation is like a second birth because through initation the boy becomes a full member of the Aryan society. Since the Śūdras are not entitled to have initation, they have only one birth. Manu has emphasized that their sole occupation is to serve the twice born. Brāhmaṇas belong to the highest Varṇa; serving them would be most meritorius. Manu took no cognizance of the doctrine forwarded by Buddha that the people of all the Varṇas belong to one human species as all of them are biologically similar. To justify the low position of the Śūdras, Manu refers to the ancient divine myth of the self-existent. Brāhmaṇas sprang from the mouth of the self-existent; since the mouth is the purest part of the body, the Brāhmaṇas are the lords of this whole creation.[80] The Śūdras were produced from the feet of the self-existent; the service of Brāhmaṇas alone is declared to be the excellent occupation for the Śūdras. In return, the Śūdras are entitled to receive the remnants of food, old clothes, the refuge of grain and old household furniture. Since the Śūdra has only one birth (he is not a twice-born) no sin would cause loss of Varṇa[81] to him. Bṛahaspati provides that if a Śūdra cannot serve the twice-born he may pursue the artisans' occupations and handicrafts.[82]

In any case, a Śūdra must not be allowed to posses wealth.

Obviously, if a Śūdra became rich he would no more serve Brāhmaṇas or any other twice-born. Manu explicitly declares that the existence of a wealthy Śūdra is painful for the Brāhmaṇas.[83] According to commentators, this is so because by accumulating wealth Śūdras become proud and do not want to serve. In the Buddhist era people of all the Varṇas were free to follow the occupations that they liked without attracting any social disapproval.

The fact that Manu assigns a low position to the Vaiśyas and Śūdras, does not mean that he was not aware of their functional utility. In fact he enjoins the king to ensure that the people of the Vaiśya and Śūdra Varṇas continue to perform the work prescribed for them. Because if these castes 'swerved from their duties, the world would be thrown into confustion.'[84]

The Varṇa hierarchy influenced the legal system a great deal. Since Brahmanas are placed highest in the social structure, they enjoyed the highest privileges. The life of a Brāhmaṇas is given the highest value while that of the Śūdra the lowest. These provisions are not based on any faith in equality before law for all. The traditional Indian legal system clearly discriminates between persons belonging to different Varṇas. It is particularly harsh towards the Śūdra. This system of law seems to have its roots in the ancient confrontation between the fair-complexioned Aryan hordes and the dark-skinned snub-nosed earlier settlers whom they vanquished and subjugated. In the course of time, the criteria of racial purity had to be substituted by those of ritual purity, but the attitude of disdain persisted. Though this traditional system of law may not be enforced by the state today, its norms even now underlie the patterns of behaviour and attitudes of a large portion of the people of India. The dicta of the Dharma Śūtra and Smṛtis still form the basis of traditional institutions and values.

Untouchability in India

The foundations of untouchability were laid in antiquated past.

The immigrant Aryans were very different from the non-Aryan dark people living in India. Aryans considered themselves superior and were proud of their race, language and religion. They considered non-Aryans non-humans or Amanuṣya.[85] The non-Āryans were described as Kṛṣṇa Varṇa[86] or dark skinned, Anāsā or without nose; they speak softly and worship phallus god. In the seventh Manḍal of Ṛgveda, Vasiṣṭha says: 'The worshippers of phallus should not come near Ṛta.'[87] Thus Aryans maintained a distance from the earlier settlers or Dāsas. These Dāsas were declared to have been created as the 'lowest of all'.[88]

In the Vājasaneyi Samhitā the words 'Cānḍāla' and 'Paulkasa' occur but there is no mention indicating that these were untouchables. In the Chāndogya Upaniṣad it is clearly said that 'these persons whose actions were low, will quickly attain an evil birth, the birth of a dog, or a hog or a Cānḍāla'[89].

The Gautama Dharma Sūtra for the first time tries to explain the origin of the Cānḍālas. It says that the Cānḍāla is the offspring of a Śūdra man from a Brāhmaṇa woman and is most reprehensible among those people who are born in the reverse order or Pratiloma. [90] Gautama calls Pratiloma castes Dharmahina or without religion.[91]

The Āpastamba Dharma Sūtra says that after touching a Cānḍāla one should plunge into water, on talking to him one should converse with a Brāhmaṇa, on seeing him one should look at the luminaries of sky, for example, sun or moon or stars.[92] Manu provides that Cāndālas and Śvapākas should live outside the village.[93] Manu also provides that Antyāvāsajin should be employed in a cemetary.[94] Aparārka quotes a verse of Vṛddha-Yājanavalkya in which it is provided that on touching Cānḍālas, Pukkasas, Mlecchas, Bhillas and Pārasikas and persons guilty of Mahāpātakas or grave sins, one should bath with the clothes on.[95] It is interesting to note that even Pārasīkas or Iranians were considered outcastes by the Indian elites. Samvarta quoted by Aparārka provides that on touching a fisherman, a deer-hunter, a hunter, a butcher, a bird-catcher and a washerman one must first bath and then take one's meal.[96] Atri provides that if a Dvija or a person of first three Varṇas touches a Cāṇḍāla, he should take bath; in case he touches him while taking food, he should reject that food and bath.[97] Parāśara says that if a Cāṇḍāla or a dog seize a twice-born person while taking food, he should give up the rest of the food.[98]

Nārada mentions Śvapāka, Meda and Cāṇḍāla. He calls them Mala or refuse of human society. He provides that they should always be punished with corporal punishment. A fine from them is unacceptable because their wealth is also impure. The king should therefore never fine them.[99]

Parāśara says that on talking with a Cāṇḍāla one should talk to a Brāhmaṇa, take bath, and recite the Sāvitrī once; only then he becomes pure. On touching a Cāṇḍāla one should take bath and look at luminaries, either the sun or moon or stars.[100] If a Brāhmaṇa drinks water from a well touched by a Cāṇḍāla he should take barley water prepared in the urine of cow for three days.[101]

Parāśara prescribes elaborate treatment[102] if the house is polluted by a Cāṇḍāla. If a Cāṇḍāla enters a house, the whole house should be washed with water mixed with cow-dung and earthenwares should be thrown away. The householder with all the family members and servants should bath thrice a day and take curds with cow-urine for three days, barley water with cow-urine for the next three days, milk with cow-urine for next three days. Then, he should again take all these things for one day each. Thus, in twelve days, he becomes pure. The utensils of bronze and bell-metal should be cleaned with ashes. The kusumbha, guda, cotton, salt, oil and ghee should be burnt outside the house. After that, the householder should feed twenty-one Brāhmaṇas and make a gift of twenty cows and one bull to them.[102] A similar atonement has been prescribed if a washerwoman, a shoemaker's wife, or a hunter's wife lives in the house.[103] All these castes are considered untouchable and impure and cause pollution according to Parāśara. Parāśara prescribes that a Brāhmaṇa should keep a Cāṇḍāla at the distance of sixteen cubits.[104]

Notes

1. Ṛgveda, X. 228
2. Ṛgveda, X. XC.12.
3. Ṛgveda, III. XXII. 21.
4. Ṛgveda, II. XX.7.
5. Ṛgveda, IV. XVI. 13.
6. Ṛgveda, II. XII. II.
7. Ṛgveda, I. CIII.3.
8. Ṛgveda, II. 19.6.
9. Ṛgveda, X.22.8.
10. Ṛgveda, IV. XVI. 13.
11. Ṛgveda, VII. V.8.
12. Ṛgveda, VIII. V.6.
13. Ṛgveda, II.XIII. 9.
14. Ṛgveda, V. XXXIV. 6.
15. Ṛgveda, IV. XLVII. 21.
16. Ṛgveda, II. XII.4.
17. Ṛgveda, II. XX.7.
18. Ṛgveda, X.198.
19. Ṛgveda, II. XXIV.6.
20. Ṛgveda, IV. 13.3.
21. Ṛgveda, VII. IX.2.
22. Ṛgveda, I. XCIII.4.
23. Ṛgveda, VII. VI. 3.
24. Rgveda, VI. XXXIII.2.
25. Ṛgveda, I. LXXIII.4.

26. Ṛgveda, I. CXXIV.10.
27. Ṛgveda, V. XXIV. 7.
28. Ṛgveda, X.LX.6.
29. Ṛgveda, IX. CXI. 2.
30. Ṛgveda, IX. XXII.7.
31. Ṛgveda, VI. 51.14.
32. Ṛgveda, VI. XLV. 31-33.
33. Ṛgveda, VI. 53.3.
34. Ṛgveda, XLV. 31-33.
35. Ṛgveda, VIII. XLVI. 32.
36. Ṛgveda, IX. CXIII.3.
37. Ṛgveda, III. XLIII.5.
38. Ṛgveda, VII. CIII.7-8.
39. Ṛgveda, X. LXXI. 4.
40. Ṛgveda, XLXXI.8-9.
41. Ṛgveda, X. LXI.5.
42. Ṛgveda, X. CLXXIII.6.
43. Ṛgveda, IV. LVII.78.
44. Ṛgveda, X. XC.12.
45. Taittirīya Saṁhitā, VII.4.19.3.
46. Taittirīya Saṁhitā, VII.1.1.6.
47. Taṇḍyamahā-Brāhmaṇa, VI.I.11.
48. Aitareya Brāhmaṇa, V.11.
49. Śatapatha Brāhmaṇa, V. XIII.6.2.10.
50. Śatapatha Brāhmaṇa, V.XIII.6.2.10.
51. Tāṇḍya Brāhmaṇa, V.5.14.
52. Taittirīya Saṁhita, 1.7.3.1.
53. Taittirīya Aranyaka, II.1.
54. Āpastamba Dharma Sūtra, II. 2.4. 22.-24.
55. Śatapatha Brāhmana, IV. 1.4. 1-6.
56. Chāndogya Upaniṣad, I. 12.1.5.
57. Chāndogya Upaniṣad, V. 3.7.

58. Bṛhadāranyaka Upaniṣad, 1.4.41.11.
59. Chāndogya Upaniṣad, V. 11.7.
60. Bṛhadāranyaka Upaniṣad, VI. 4.14-17.
61. Gautma Dharma Sūtra, XVII.I.
62. Āpastamba Dharma Sūtra, 1.6.18.8-10.
63. Āpastamba Dharma Sūtra, I.6. Gautama Dharma Sūtra XVII. 5.
64. Āpastamba Dharma Sūtra, II. 5.11.5- 6; 1.4.14.25.
65. Āpastamba Dharma Sūtra, I.3.9.9.
66. Āpastamba Dharma Sūtra, I.I.I. 7-8; Gautama Dharma Sūtra, X.56; Vasiṣṭha Dharma Sūtra. II.20.
67. Āpastamba Dharma Sūtra, II.10.27.15
68. Gautama Dharma Sūtra, XII.7.
69. Āpastamba Dharma Sūtra, II.10.27.14. Gautama Dharma Sūtra XII.I.
70. Āpastamba Dharma Sūtra, I. 5.16.22; Baudhāyana Dharma Sūtra, II.2.1.
71. Āpastamba Dharma Sūtra, I. 5.16.22; Baudhāyana Dharma Sūtra, II.2.1.
72. Āpastamba Dharma Sūtra, 1.9.25.13.
73. Sutta Nipāta, 135.
74. Jātaka, I. 108.
75. Digha Nikāya, 3. 180. ff.
76. Manu Smṛti, VII.14; VIII. 346.
77. Manu Smṛti, I. 98.
78. Manu Smṛti, X.3.
79. Manu Smṛti, X.57.
80. Manu Smṛti, I. 92-94.
81. Manu Smṛti, X. 123-125.
82. Bṛhaspati Smṛti, Sanskāra Kāṇḍa, I. 530.
83. Manu Smṛti, X. 129.
84. Manu Smṛti, VIII. 417-418.
85. Ṛgveda, X. 22.8.
86. Ṛgveda, IX. 41.1.

87. Ṛgveda, Vasiṣṭha VII. XXI.5.
88. Ṛgveda, II.12.4.
89. Chandogya Upaniṣad, V.10.7.
90. Gautama Dharma Sūtra, IV. 15;23.
91. Gautama Dharma Sūtra, IV. 20.
92. Āpastamba Dharma Sūtra, II.1.2.8-9.
93. Manu Smṛti, X. 51.
94. Manu Smṛti, X.39.
95. Vṛddha-Yājñavalkya quoted by Aparārka, p. 923.
96. Saṁvarta quoted by Aparārka, p. 1196.
97. Atrismṛti 267-269.
98. Parāśara Smṛti, VI. 66.
99. Nārada Smṛti, XV.13.
100. Parāśara Smṛti, VI.22.24.
101. Parāśara Smṛti, VI.26.
102. Parāśara Smṛti, VI.34-42.
103. Parāśara Smṛti, VI.44-45.
104. Parāśara Smṛti, XII. 53.

V

The Family

In the Ṛgveda we find that the Aryans liked to live in large joint families. There is a hymn in the Ṛgveda in which the priest blesses the bride with the words :

> 'Be ye not parted, dwell ye here,
> reach the full time of human life;
> With sons and grandsons sport and
> play rejoicing in your own abode.'[1]

Thus it was common for the older generation to live with the younger generation. Aryans were fond of big families. The priest prays to god Indra that the bride may become the mother of ten sons:

> 'O Bounteous Indra, make this bride
> blest in her sons and fortunate
> Vouchsafe to her ten sons and make
> her husband the eleventh male.'[2]

In the Ṛgveda and the Atharvaveda we a find a chant probably employed by a husband for secretly visiting his wife in a joint family.[3] Through this chant the husband lulls to sleep various members of the family. In this hymn, the presence of a large joint family is implicit. In the family besides the conjugal couple a number of other relatives lived jointly.[4] In another hymn of Atharvaveda a head of a joint family wishes that all members of the family live jointly loving each other.[5]

The invading Aryans were short of women, therefore they had to take wives from the non-Aryans. This is evident from the fact that the word Vadhū is used for a bride as well as a slavegirl in the Ṛgveda.[6] In the Atharvaveda we find the statement of a general principle that when a Brāhmaṇa takes the hand of a women though she be married she becomes his wife.[7] From these passages it becomes quite clear that the Aryans took wives from non-Aryans.

But as the Aryans started colonizing the vast Indian subcontinent the family had to become nuclear. The reminisences of these colonizers have found expression in the Gṛhya Sūtras. The content of Gṛhya Sūtras is folkloristic in nature. It appears that the rituals and sacraments found in the Gṛhya Sūtras belong to an antiquated past which was long before the period when they found expression in the form of aphorisms. There are a number of rites and rituals for living a life free from dangers. It appears that the householder was apprehensive of some unknown evil sprits all the time. Parhaps these reflect the apprehensions of the early colonizers who sought to settle in an unknown land among atagonistic earlier inhabitants. The fears might have lingered among the Aryan folk from early times. These have found ample expression for the first time in the revivalistic era marked by the Gṛhya Sūtras. It is possible that the inhospitable environment encountered by the immigrent Aryan hordes of the early Ṛgvedic period was too dreadful for them in the beginning. They may not have liked even to speak about their fears. On the other hand, they would rather boost the morale of each other by saying again and again that the non-Aryans were no match to them and were bound to be crushed. The Ṛgveda is replete with such statements. The suppressed fears and anxieties seem to have persisted among the Aryans for many generations and came to surface in the Gṛhya Sūtras when the real fear had subsided to manageable proportions. To avert those apprehended evil influences, the performance of rituals was essential.

The householder in the Gṛhya Sūtras is concerned primarily with the day to day problems of setting up and running a small household. The requirements of colonization of vast areas did not permit the huddling together of a large number of kinsfolk in households. In fact, the rituals prescribed in these aphorisms do not presume the presence of any other adult except the husband and the wife. Strikingly enough, it is the husband who is supposed to act as the midwife when his wife delivers; and he has also to act as the priest-cum-magician and to perform the child-birth rituals apart from running a variety of errands.

The relationship between man and woman seems to have been deeply influenced by the fact that the Aryan settler had often to take a non-Aryan indigenous woman as his wife. Perhaps this was unavoidable as there were not enough women of his stock to go round. But he considered her inferior and was suscipious of her. In the Sūtras the wife is supposed to bring some evil elements with her which can harm her husband, his forthcoming progeny, cattle, house and fame. He also doubts her integrity. Sensing these dangers, the husband performs prayers to divert these elements towards his wife's earlier lover. On the fourth day, before establishing conjugal relationship, the husband makes offerings of cooked food in the fire for Agni or the fire-god, Vāyu or the wind-god, Sūrya or the sun-god.

> 'Agni, Thou art expiation of gods,
> What substance dwells in her that brings death to her husband,
> Drive that away from her'.
> 'Sūrya, Thou art the expiation of the gods,
> What substance dwells in her that brings destruction to the cattle,
> Drive that away from her.'

Similarly, he offers oblations to Candra, the moon, and Gandharva respectively to expicate the substances which dwell in her that bring destruction to the house and fame. Each time after he has sacrificed, he pours the remainder of the oblations into the water-pot and out of that pot he spinkles her head with the words : 'The evil substance which dwells in thee that brings death to thy husband, death to thy children, death to cattle, destruction to the house, destruction to fame, that I change into one that brings death to thy paramour. Thus live with me to old age N.N.'[8]

The householder who is a cattle breeder and a farmer eagerly wants more sons. For securing many longlived sons, a number of rituals are prescribed which appear to be magical acts. The performance of so many rituals indicates that securing a living son must have been quite difficult at that time. During the marriage ritual, the husband puts a boy of good birth on both sides of his bride's lap. It is asserted that through this rite she will certainly become the mother of male children.[9] It is ordained that after marriage the couple should sleep for three nights on the ground and serve the nuptial fire in evening and morning. On the fourth day, the first pre-natal ritual, Garbhādhāna or securing conception is performed. The wife with this verse offers the oblation in the fire. She prays the gods in pairs: 'Let the two man Mitra and Varuna, let the two men Asvins both, let the man Indra and also Agni make a man grow in me. Svāhā.'[10]

The husband prays : 'May a male embryo enter the womb, as an arrow (enters) the quiver, may a man be formed here, a son after ten months.' He further says that the gods may give girls to other women, but a son must be bestowed on him. He addresses his wife:

> 'Be a well-breeding cow and produce a son from the auspicious sperm.
> Prajāpati has created him, Savitar has shaped him.
> Imparting birth of females to other (women),
> May he put here a man.'[11]

Infantile mortality must have been a great threat. To avoid this the bridegroom prays god Agni during marriage rituals to release the offspring of his wife from the fetter of death, so that he may enjoy a long and happy life together with his son and wife.

> 'May Agni come hither, the first of the gods.
> May he release the offspring of this wife from the fetter of death.
> May this king Varuṇa grant that this wife does not weep over distress (falling to her lot) through (the death of) her son. Svāhā.
> May Agni Gārhāpatya protect this woman,
> May he lead her offspring to old age.
> With fertile womb may she be the mother to living children,
> May she experience delight in her sons, Svāhā.'[12]

The husband prepares Sūtikālaya or labour room for his wife. He besemears it with various herbs in order to drive away goblins. Then, the wife enters the room. The husband performs Ksipraprasavana or the ritual for accelerating the delivery. Having placed a waterpot near her head and a *turyantī* plant near her feet, he touches her belly. He places his hand dripping with water on her head and touches her with the dripping wet hand from the head to the heart downwards with the mantras: 'As the wind blows, may it come out together with the after-birth.'[13]

When the boy is born, he performs for him the Medhājanana or production of intelligence and Āyuṣya or the rite for procuring long life, before the naval string is cut off. He makes the new born infant lick honey and *ghee* with a gold article (gold spoon or ring) thrice, with the recitation of some Vedic mantras. Then near the child's naval or his right ear he mutters:

> 'Agni is long-lived, through trees he is long-lived;
> By that long life I make thee long-lived.
> Soma is longlived, through the herbs he is longlived;
> By that long life I make thee longlived.
> The Brahman[14] is longlived, through the Brāhmaṇas he is longlived;
> By that long life I make thee longlived.

The gods are longlived, through ambrosia (Amṛta) they are longlived;
By that long life I make thee longlived.
The Ṛṣis are longlived, through their observances they are longlived;
By that long life I make thee longlived.
The fathers are longlived, through the Svadhā[15] oblations they are longlived;
By that long life I make thee longlived.'

Then, the father should seat five Brāhmaṇas in the five directions and should say to them, 'Breathe ye upon this (child)'. In case the father can not find five Brāhmaṇas he may himself do this, going round the child.[16]

All these prayers and rituals are symbolic. The forceful movements of ocean and wind are represented by the movements of the wet hand so that the infant may come out with the after-birth. In the same ritual he ensures a long life for the infant by remembering the long-lived gods. Breathing round the infant is again a part of the same magical ritual, adding more breaths into his life.

The father washes the infant with lukewarm water. He washes his wife's right breast and gives it to the child with a verse addressed to the right breast: 'O breast you swell up for his life, glory, renown, splendour and strength'. Similarly he washes and addresses the left breast.[17]

He also establishes the Sutakāgni or the fire of confinement to the southern side of the door to ward off various evil sprits. He pronounces the names of various demons and goblins and throws mustard seeds mixed with rice chaff into that fire in the morning and evening twilight, until the mother gets up from the maternity bed.[18]

It is remarkable that in the Gṛhya Sūtras it is the husband who has to act both as the midwife and the priest during his wife's delivery. This strongly suggests that an ordinary household in that period had no other adult members besides the couple. Thus, the joint family consisting of more than two generations and several married couples, which is often regarded as the characteristic institution of the traditional Indian social structure is conspicuous by its absence during this period. This is understandable. When Aryans were colonizing the vast areas they had conquered, they had to be mobile, and the large joint family did not suit these conditions. That institution acquired its pivotal position with the establishment of settled plough agriculture.

During the Buddhist period the institution of family suffered a great deal. Buddha gave entry to unmarried as well as married young men and women in his order, provided they were of full twenty years of age and free. They could get entry only if their parents or husbands allowed them. Thus, many young housewives entered the order of Buddha leaving behind young children and old persons in the household. Similarly, many young men who were householders entered the order.

In the Vinaya text, we find a reference to a young housewife who entered the order without knowing that she was pregnent and eventually delivered the child in the Vihāra. It is obvious from such references that Buddhism disrupted the normal functioning of family life.

In the Indian tradition it is usual to consider the husband as the most important person for the wife. But in the Uchañga Jātaka a woman gives preference to her brother over her husband and son. Her husband, son and brother were arrested by the king's official. After much persuasion the king grants that she may choose one out of the three for being set free. She chooses her brother saying that, 'Grant me my brother because son and husband can be easily found again but a brother can not be found. O king, the son is found in the lap and husband is found in the way but that country is not known from where a brother can be brought.'[19] Giving preference to brother over husband and son is against the essential norms of patriarchy. This may perhaps be the only example of its kind in Indian tradition. In any case such preference for brother as against husband is rare in both folk and elite traditions. Typically, the Indian woman always takes the side of her husband if she has to make a choice.

Buddhism disrupted the proper functioning of family which is the most essential institution of human society. Perhaps, the Indian family had never faced such a crisis as it did during the Buddhist era.

To combat the ravages brought about by Buddhism, Brahmanical revival came into being. Manu Smṛti was the first major product of this revival. Manu curbed the independence given to women. He declared woman dependent on man in all stages of her life, Manu also instructs the husband to keep the wife fully occupied in the accounting and expenditure of his wealth, in keeping the house clean, in fulfilment of religious duties, in the preparation of his food and in the proper upkeep of household effects.[20] Manu has thus laid down the norms for fully utilizing the services of woman for the family and made the institution of family secure and stable. Both Mahābhārata and Rāmāyana supported patriarchal joint family and the dependent status of woman.

Later Smṛtis followed the norms set by Manu. The patriarchal values were reinforced. Nārada calls the patriarch 'Prabhu' or the lord of the family.[21] Obedience to the father is regarded as the primary virtue. All family members should respect and obey him. Nārada compares father with a king and says:

> 'Three persons are independent in this world:
> A king, a teacher, and in all castes successively a householder in his household.'[22]

All the members of household are dependent on him.

Nārada provides:

> 'Wives, sons, slaves and other attendants are dependents.
> The head of the family to whom the property has descended by right of inheritance is independent with regard to it.'[23]

Nārada compares the relative importance of father and mother and concludes that father is the seed-giver therefore he is superior to mother. However, unlike Manu, Nārada considers that on failure of father, the authority lies with mother, only on failure of the mother, the eldest son has the authority.[24]

Eventhough the father is declared free in his house, he cannot make gift of his wife and son.[25] Thus Nārada puts a limit on his authority. Kātyāyana also expresses a view similar to that of Nārada.[26]

Though Nārada places mother next to the father but she is not permitted to undertake property transactions independently even after the death of her husband. While transacting she must have the permission of her son, or on his failure, of the king. In the absence of this the transaction would become invalid.[27]

In the Smṛtis the son has been given great importance in the family. A daughter has been assigned a lower position than a son. The mother of girls has been equated to a barren woman. The son serves his father in old age. He continues the family line after father's death, maintains the family and is the heir of the rituals. Daughters belong to another family where they go after marriage. Only a son can offer Piṇḍas to his forefathers and it is only he who can performs Śrāddha.[28] It is also called the redemption of Pitṛ-ṛṇa or debt of forefathers. The person who has no son can never be free from this debt. As soon as one begets a son, he secures freedom from this debt. According to Nārada:

> 'Pitaras(forefathers) wish to have son on their own account,
> Thinking, 'He will release me from
> Uttama (superior) and Adhama (inferior) Ṛṇas (debts).'[29]

Asahaya on Nārada Smṛti explains this verse. He observes that the obligation to pay the debt of ancestors extends to the fourth generation in descent. The great grandson has to discharge Uttama-ṛṇa or superior debt to offer the Pindodaka in

Śrāddha to his great-grandfather. He is also liable to pay Adhama-ṛṇas or ordinary debts contracted by him. Bṛhaspati and Kātyāana express similar opinion.[30] Apart from these essential duties a son is expected to be learned and virtuous. According to Bṛhaspati:

> What is the use of a cow which neither gives milk nor becomes pregnant?
>
> What is the good of a son being born who is neither learned nor virtuous?[31]

Smṛtis emphasize the importance of a son for the spiritual welfare of a man. A man is saved from the hell, named 'put' by the very sight of his son's face according to Bṛhaspati.[32] A sonless persons is considered miserable. He can never secure heaven or salvation.[33] Among all the sons, the eldest son has his own importance. He has been given a place next to the father. After the father's death the eldest son becomes the head of the family. He succeeds the authority and functions enjoyed earlier by his father. At this stage, various couples and their children who have so far been within the fold of the joint partiarchal family may remain attached to it, or may sometimes break away to form new partiarchal families.

But a son who is a minor cannot become the head of the family. This constitutes an exception to the general independence of the eldest son after death of his father.[34] Norms that had been laid down by the Smṛtis continued to be followed by the people upto pre-modern time. Despite the influence of various modern forces some of these norms are still pevalent.

Family Rituals : *Pañca Mahāayajñas*

These sacrifices are to be offered by all the Aryan householders every day.

The earliest reference to the five great sacrifices is found in the Śatapatha Brāhmaṇa. The Śatapatha Brāhmaṇa treats them as equivalent to great sacrificial sessions. These are referred to in this order : Bhūta Yajña, Manuṣyayajña, Pitṛyajña, Devayajña and Brahmayajña[35]. It also defines them. Day by day one should offer a Bali or a ball of food to Beings: thus he performs Bhūta Yajña or the sacrifice to beings. Day by day one should offer a cupful of water: thus he performs that Manuṣyayarjña or the sacrifice to man. Day by day one should offer with Svadhā[36] or making offering of water to the three immediately preceding departed ancestors : thus he performs that Pitṛyajña or the sacrifice to the fathers. Day by day one should offer with Svahā the log of firewood to the fire, thus he performs that the Devayajña or the sacrifice to the gods. The Brahmayajña is one's own daily study of the Vedas.[37] The Taittirīya Āranyaka presents them in a different order. Devayajña, Pitṛayajña, Bhūtayajña, Manuṣyayajña and Brahmayajña. The Taittirīya Āranyaka follows the Śatapatha Brāhmaṇa except in the case of Manuṣyayajña where the offering of a cupful water is replaced by giving food to Brāhmaṇas. And in Brahmayajña it specifies that even if one studies a single Ṛk or Yajuṣ formula or a Sāman, this becomes Brahmayajña.[38]

The Āaśvalāyana Gṛhyasūtra follows the definition of Taittirīya Āranyaka and emphasises that these Yajñas must be performed everyday.[39] Gautama and Baudhāyana also prescribe these five Yajñas.[40]

The Pañca Mahāyajñas represent the ancient Aryan concept of universe and the position of human being in it. It was considered the duty of the Aryan householder to appease various other beings of the universe who are also parts of it. There are other living beings in this world that are satiated by Bhūtayajña through the offering of Bali or a ball of food. The other human beings are satiated by offering water to them or offering food to Brāhmaṇas is the Manuṣyayarña. The three immediate preceding departed ancestors are satiated by giving water twice or offering Svadhā.[41] And in this way Pitṛyajña was performed. Similarly the householder offers a piece of wood in fire for the gods who live in the sky and satiates them. Fire is called the mouth of the gods in the Ṛgveda.[42] And thus

Devayajña is performed by offering a log in the fire. Vedas were the most cherished heritage of the Aryans. This was the most prized inheritance from their forefathers which they wanted to preserve. Reciting part of Vedas is the Brahmayajña.

Manu gives another explanation of the five great sacrifices. The Manu Smṛti seems to have been greatly influenced by Buddhism and Jainism.

According to Manu the householder had five slaughter houses as it were, namely, the hearth, the grinding-stone, the broom, the pestle and mortar, and the water-vessel. By using these he is bound by the fetters of sin. In order to expiate the offences committed by means of all these five, the great sages have prescribed for the householders the daily performance of the five great sacrifices.[43] But Manu does not explain clearly how a householder gets rid of the sin committed through the use of household implements by performing these five great sacrifices. Manu has also changed the order of the five yajña. He puts these in following order: Brahmayajña. Pitṛyajña, Devayajña, Bhūtayajña and Manuṣyajña.

Brahmayajña

The Śatapatha Brāhmaṇa says that in the Brahmayajña one should study not only the four Vedas but also study the Anuśāsanas or Vedāngas including Vidyas such as Sarpa Vidyā, Vākovākya or theological discourses, Itihāsapurāṇa or traditional history and legends and the Nārāśaṁsī Gāthās[44] or stanzas in praise of heroes. Taittirīya Āraṇyaka follows the Śatapatha Brāhmaṇa and adds in that list Kalpas or works on Srauta sacrifices.[45] It is interesting to note that while praising the study of Atharvāngniras or Atharvaveda the Śatapatha Brāhmaṇa calls them (like) the offerings of fat in the fire while Taittirīya Āranyaka calls Brāhmaṇa texts, Itihāsas, Purāṇa, Kalpas and Gāthā Narāśamsīs fat offerings. From this evidence it becomes clear that giving offerings of fat in the fire was not taboo even in the times of the Taittirīya Āranyaka. These works enumerate the renords of performing the Brahmayajña. According to Taittirīya Āranyaka Brahmayajña is to be performed in the morning at a pure spot of the village in east, north or north east, as far away from the village that thatch coverings of houses are not visible. It further says that if one is unable to go out of the village he may perform it in the village itself, even during day or night, sitting, standing or lying.[46] Gṛhyasūtras of Āśvalāyana follow the Taittirīya Āraṇyaka.[47]

Pitṛyajña

The earliest reference of Pitṛyajña is found in the Śatapatha Brāhmaṇa. In the Pitṛyajña the householder should offer a cupful of water every day to three forefathers. Once in a month the householder after offering food to Agni and Soma in the fire, should offer food to the three forefathers just preceding himself. He should put a firebrand at the farther south end of the line for preventing Asuras and Rakṣas from tampering with the food of the forefathers. Then, he should take the water-pitcher and make the forefathers wash their hands, merely saying 'N.N.wash thyself' (naming his father); 'N.N. wash thyself' (naming his grandfather) N.N. wash thyself (naming his great grandfather). According to the Śatapatha Brāhmaṇa, the householder should pour out water as he would pour out water for washing hands for a guest when he is about to take food. The householder should cut the stalks of sacrificial grass near the root. He should spread them along the line with their tops towards the south. Then he presents to the fathers the three Piṇḍas or balls of rice. The householder should say, 'N.N. this for thee', as to the householder's father; 'N.N. this is for thee', as to his grandfather; 'N.N. this is for thee' as to his great-grandfather. He then mutters, 'Here O fathers regale yourselves: like bulls come hither each to his own share.' Then, he says, 'Eat ye each his own share'. Then, the householder should turn round to the left so as to face the opposite side. He should remain in this position for a moment. Then, he should turn round to the right and mutter, 'The fathers have regaled themselves: like bulls they have come each to his own share.' He takes the water-pitcher and makes them wash themselves, merely saying 'N.N. wash theyself'; naming his father, grandfather and great grandfather. Then he pulls down the tuck of his garment six times. He mutters, 'Give us houses, O fathers.' The Piṇḍas or balls of rice should be put back in the pot containing the remaining rice. Then he smells at the rice, this is his share. The stalks of sacrificial grass should be put on the fire. The firebrand should be thrown away.[48]

The Āśvalāyana Gṛhyasūtra prescribes morning and evening offering of Svadhā or the sacrificial rice to the fathers after offering the Vaiśvadeva sacrifice. The householder should pour out the remnants to the south, with the sacrificial cord suspended over the right shoulder, muttering the words, 'Svadhā to the fathers'.[49]

Manu prescribes three ways of performing Pitṛyajña: offering the remnants of Vaiśvadeva food to the manes in a southerly direction;[50] performing Tarpana or offering water for manes;[51] and feeding one Brāhmaṇa in honour of the manes.[52]

Devayam̃a

The Śatapatha Brāhmaṇa defines Devayajña as offering a fuel stick daily to fire with Svāhā.[53] Taittirīya Āranyaka, Āpastamba Dharmasūtra, Baudhāyana Dharmasūtra and Gautama Dharmasūtra follow the Śatapatha Brāhmaṇa. The word Svāhā should be uttered after naming the gods in dative case.

According to Āśvalāyana Gṛhyasūtra the householder should make oblations in the evening and in the morning of prepared sacrificial food to the deities of the Agnihotra (Sūrya, Agni and Prajāpati) to Soma Vanaspati, to Agni and Soma, to Indra and Agni, to Heaven and Earth, to Dhanvantari, to Indra, to the Viśvedevas, to Brahman with Svāhā. Now he should offer the Balis to those same deities, to the waters, to the herbs and trees, to the house, to the domestic deities, to the deities of the ground, to Indra's men, to Yama and Yama's men, to Varuṇa and Varuṇa's men, to Soma and Soma's men—these oblations he should make to the different quarters. To Brahman and Brahman's men in the middle and the householder should offer Bali to Viśvedevas.[54] We find no mention of offering Balis to gods in the Śatapatha Brāhmaṇa, but in the Āśvalāyana and Śāṅkhāyana Gṛhyasūtra it is probably introduced as a result of non-Aryan influence. The non-Aryans used to offer food to their gods. Manu seems to have accepted the non-Aryan practice.

The Śāṅkhāyana Gṛhyasūtra also provides the Vaiśvadeva sacrifice. It is interesting to find that among Vedic gods the name of Bhadrakālī is also included. It is provided that a Bali should be offered to her at the foot of the bed.[55]

Manu follows Gṛhyasūtras. He prescribes Vaiśvedeva sacrifice to the Vedic deities, but following Śāṅkhāyana Gṛhyasūtra he provides that the householder should offer a Bali to Bhadrakālī at the foot of the bed.[56]

Bhūtayajña

Bhūtayajña is the sacrifice to beings. According to the Śatapatha Brāhmaṇa a householder should offer Bali or balls of food to beings. Āśvalāyana Gṛhyasūtra says that the householder should offer the Balis or Balls of food to the day-walking beings in the morning and to the night-walking beings in the evening. He should offer to the Rakṣas towards the north.[57] Śāṅkhāyana Gṛhyasūtra follows the Āśvalāyana Gṛhyasūtra.[58] Manu follows these Gṛhyasūtras.[59]

Manuṣyayajña

Manuṣyayajña is the sacrifice to men. Śatapatha Brāhmaṇa describes it as offering a cupful of water to men everyday.[60]

Āpastamba Dharmasūtra provides that if a Śrotriya Brāhmaṇa comes to the house, the householder should honour him according to his age. He should himself wash his feet or two Śūdras should wash his feet. He should offer him milk with eatables or at least water. He should offer him a room, a bed, a matress, a pillow with a cover etc. He should get prepared rice or barley for him.[61] The Gautama Dharmasūtra also provides that a guest should be offered a couch, a seat, lodging, and he should be attended to respectfully during his stay. Gautama says that only such person should be called a guest who lives in a different village and intends to stay for one night only. A man of lower caste cannot be the guest of a Brāhmaṇa. A Kṣatriya should be fed after the Brāhmaṇas. And the persons belonging to other castes (Vaiśya and Śūdras) should be fed with servants for mercy's sake.[62] The Manu Smṛti follows the rules of the Gautama Dharmasūtra.[63]

The influence of Varṇa hierarchy can be seen on the rules of Gautama Dharmasūtra and Manu Smṛti and the subsequent Smṛti texts. As a matter of fact till the pre-British period such norms continued to prevail throughout the Indian sub-continent.

Purṣārthas or Goals of Human Existence

There are four Puruṣārthas : Dharma, Artha, Kāma and Mokṣa. The first three Purusarthas are mentioned in the Mahābhārata[64] as Trivarga or three goals. These are : Dharma or right conduct Artha or economic interests, and Kāma or pursuit of love and pleasure. In fact it is common to mention only these three together. Mokṣa or salvation has been usually treated as a class by itself separately. The first reference to these three basic goals occurs in the Gautama Dharma Sūtra. Though the term Trivarga is not mentioned, the Gautama Dharma Sūtra says, 'Let him not remain idle during morning, midday and evening so far as Dharma, Artha and Kāma are concerned. But among these three, one should attach the highest importance to Dharma.[65] Yajñavalkya follows Gautama Dharma Sūtra.[66]

The Mahābhārata declares that 'a wise man tries to secure all the three but if all the three cannot be attained, he secures Dharma and Artha or only Dharma if he has to choose only one from among the three. The middling type of man prefers

Artha to the other two; Dharma is the source of both Artha and Kāma.' In the Śāntiparva of Mahābhārta it is declared that Dharma is the best, Artha is middling and Kāma is the lowest.[67] Manu Smṛti presents several views regarding the relative importance of these three goals and concludes that one should aspire for all the three; in case Artha or Kāma is in conflict with Dharma, they should be given up.[68]

Dharma

The word 'Dharma' has been used in various senses in the Indian tradition. It is used for Vedic and non-Vedic rituals, ethical conduct, Varna and Āśrama rules, and civil and criminal law.

As the Indian society changed, the concept of Dharma also changed. The Gautama and Apasatmba Dharma Sūtras declare that 'Veda is the source of the sacred law and the tradition and practice of those who know the Veda.'[69] Both of these Dharma Sūtras admit that ancient seers sometimes transgressed and violated Dharma but it is argued that because of the aura of their lustre, they incurred no sin. However, a person of the later age should not count these as precedents because he is too weak to emulate their actions.[70] Āpastamba says that among men of later age no Ṛṣis are born because of transgressions of Dharma.[71]

In the literature of the era of the second Brahmanical revival we find the concept of four Yugas or ages. In the Upaniṣads the words Kṛta, Dvāpara and Kali are used in the sense of throws of dice.[72] In the Mahābhārta, Kṛta and Dvāpara are used in both the senses, that is, for throws of dice as well as for different ages.[73] Mahābhārata and Manu Smṛti compare Dharma with a Vṛṣa or bull.[74] In the Kṛta age Dharma is in its perfect condition, it stands on all four feet; and it deteriorates by a quarter in each of the following ages in Treta on three feet; in Dvāpara on two; and in Kali on one foot.[75] Thus in Kali Yuga (the Dark Age) only one quarter of Dharma remains and Adharma occupies three quarters. In Kṛta men live for four hundred years free from disease and get what they wish. In the following ages beginning with the Treta their span of life decreases successively by one quater. Dharma too differs according to the Yuga. Austerities were at their highest in the Krta, sacred knowledge in Tretā, sacrifice in Dvāpara and charity alone in Kali.[76] Brahma Purāṇa and Matsya Purāṇa make an interesting remark that 'in Kṛta there was a single Varṇa but at the end of the Kali age almost all will be Śūdras.'[77]

Gautama Dharma Sūtras prescribe even for the Śūdras truthfulness, meerness and purity.[78] The Mahābhārata states that three are the best qualities for all beings, these are - absence of enmity, truthfulnes and freedom from anger.[79] Manu lays down that the following aspects of Dharma should be observed by all the Varnas, abstinence from injuring (creatures), veracity, not stealing, purity and control of the organs.[80]

Vāmanapurāṇa also speaks of tenfold Dharma, common to all the four varnas : abstinence from injuring (creatures), truth fulness, making gifts, forbearances restraint, quiescence, not demeaning oneself, purity and austerity.[81]

Artha

The literature of the second Brahmanical revival especially the Nārada and Kātyāyana Smṛtis prescribe elaborate rules of debt, deposits, partnership, etc., which indicate the existence of a highly developed commercial society. This shows that though Smṛti literature is of basically religious in nature, it is amply recognized that the smooth functioning of trade, commerce and industry is essential for the society.

We find mention of guilds in these Smṛtis. These guilds had their own conventions and established usages, and these were recognised by the courts of law.[82] The traders and artisans followed the rules of the guilds.

In the Yājñavalkya, Brahaspati and Nārada Smṛtis, we find elaborate rules for apprentices and master craftmen. The apprentice lives with the master like his son and learns the craft.[83]

By these rules it becomes quite clear that the Indian society was commercially and industrially well developed around 200 A.D. to 600 A.D.

Kāma

Kāma or sex has been given the lowest place in the Trivarga or the three ends. Āpastamba says that a person should enjoy all such pleasures which are not forbidden by Dharma. Acting in this way he earns both the worlds.[84] Manu too says that there is no sin in eating, drinking and sex, for that is the natural way of created beings, but abstention from these brings great rewards.[85] In the Bhagvat Gita Kṛṣṇa identifies himself with Kāma and says that it is not against dharma.[86]

In 400 A.D. Kāma Sūtra or Aphorisms on sex were composed by Vātsyāyana. He describes the daily routine of an urban man or Nāgaraka.

Mokṣa

The ultimate goal of man's life is believed to be Mokṣa or salvation. It is considered higher than the other three goals. It is associated with Dharma. The Aryans used to perform sacrifices to propitiate the gods so as to earn the enjoyments of heaven after death.

In the Upaniṣads the theory of Karma and the doctrine of rebirth was introduced. Upaniṣads also introduced the concept of Brahma for the first time. Brahma is the ultimate reality. When one realize Him, he becomes one with Him. The ultimate reality is devoid of all adjuncts.

Upaniṣads influenced the systems of metaphysics a great deal. Systems of metaphysics especially Sānkhya, Yoga and Vedanta adopted and moulded some of the seminal ideas of the Upaniṣads.

The devotional sects which developed later enunciate that salvation is attained through devotion to particular deities.

The main devotional sects of Hinduism are Vaiṣṇva, Śaiva

and Śākta. Viṣṇu, Śiva and Śakti are the deities of these sects. These deities are supposed to be omnipresent, omniscient and omnipotent. The devotee is expected to surrender completely to his deity. This surrender might be through the worship of the idol of his deity or by singing devotional songs or chanting names of his deity. The worship of an idol of the deity consists of bathing the idol, offering him food, water, flowers, leaves, incense, music and dancing. It is believed that by wholehearted worship of the deity the sins of the devotee are condoned by the deity and the devotee goes to the heaven of that particular deity.

Latent Function of the Three Debts (Ṛṇas)

Since very old times, it is considered to be a Brāhmaṇa's basic duty to redeem the three cardinal debts (Ṛṇas). These are : (i) Rsi Ṛṇa, which is redeemed or paid back by study through stay as a Brahmacāri (student): (ii) Deva Ṛṇa, which is redeemed through Yajñas or fire sacrifice offered to the gods; and (iii) Pitṛ Ṛṇa which is redeemed by begetting sons.

This concept of the three debts has prevailed for a very long time indeed. It has been propagated since the later Vedic times. We find the first enunciation of these three debts in the Taittirīya Sanhita of the Yajurveda and since then belief in this idea has remained intact. The Taittirīya Samhitā says: 'Every Brāhmaṇa is born with three debts. He redeems himself through Brahmacarya (studies as a student) from his debt of the Risis; through Yajñas (fire sacrifices) from the debt of the gods; and by begetting son from the debt of his ancestors. Verily, that person is redeemed who has a son, who performs Yajñas, and who lives as a Brahmacārī in the house of his teacher.'[87]

The Aitareya Brāhmaṇa, while describing the merit of begetting son says : 'One is redeemed from the debt of ancestors, attaining immortality and haven by begetting a son.'[88]

The Mahābhārata refers to four debts at one place, and to five debts at another. In the Ādi Parva of the Mahabhārata it is said that a man has four debts on him. Three of these are Vedic (i.e., enunciated in the Vedas) and the fourth is his debt towards humanity which is redeemed through good behaviour with all beings.[89] The Anuśāsana Parva of the Mahābhārata mentions five debts, by adding two debts to the three debts prescribed earlier. Of the two additional debts one is to the Brāhmaṇas and the other to the guests.[90]

Following the Taittirīya Samhita, the Manu Smṛti mentions three debts. It says : 'When a man has paid back his debts to the great Ṛṣis, ancestors and gods, he should live with detachment without engaging himself in worldly matters.'[91]

According to the Nārada Smṛti, 'the ancestor begets sons with the hope that they would redeem him from high (Uttama)and low (Adhama) debts.'[92] The three basic debts are considered to be Uttama (high) and monetary debts are regarded as Adhama (low). Similarly, the Bṛhaspati Smṛti says: 'The son gets his father free from high and low debts; therefore a son who does not carry out these duties is useless.'[93]

The fact that the belief in these basic debts has thrived for the last three thousand years suggests that it must have been performing some vital social function. In sociological parlance social function refers to the contribution that any element of culture makes to the sustenance of the culture as a whole. This contribution or function may or may not be consciously intended or recognized by the people belonging to that culture. A function that is neither recognized nor intended is called latent function.

It seems that the belief that it is a cardinal duty to pay back the three basic debts performed the latent function of preserving and carrying forward the age old traditional culture and learning, and also the propagation of the race. To pay back the Rsi Ṛṇa, one has to stay with his teacher to acquire traditional knowledge, living in austerity. Thus, the tradition of learning is maintained from one generation to another. Similarly, to pay back the Pitṛ Ṛṇa, one has to beget sons, thus propagating the race. It does seem that faith in the unescapable duty of redeeming the three debts for every Brāhmaṇa has greatly contributed to the remarkable continuity of Indian society and culture over the ages.

Notes

1. Ṛgveda, X.LXXXV.42.
2. Ṛgveda, X.LXXXXV.115
3. Ṛgveda, VII. LV. 5-8, Atharvaveda, IV. V. 3-6.
4. Even now we find many such folk-songs in which the husband and wife find it difficult to meet each other because of the presence of other family members.
5. Atharvaveda, 111.30.
6. Ṛgveda, VIII. 19.36-37.
7. Atharvaveda, V.XVII.8-9.
8. Śāṅkhāyana Gṛhya Sūtra, I.18.3; Paraskara Gṛhya Sūtra, I.11.2-4.
9. Śāṅkhāyana Gṛhya Sūtra, 1. 16.8.
10. Śāṅkhāyana Gṛhya Sūtra, 1.17.9.
11. Śāṅkhāyana Gṛhya Sūtra, I. 19.6.
12. Pārasakara Gṛhya Sūtra,I.5.11.
13. Kāṭhaka Gṛhya Sūtra, XXXIII. 1-3; Āpastamba Gṛhya Sūtra, VI.14.14, Hiranyakesin Gṛhya Sūtra, II.1.3.1.
14. The word Brāhmaṇ refers both to the Mantras and the mysterious power inherent in them.
15. Offerings made to forefathers during the Śrāddha ceremony.
16. Pāraskara Gṛhya Sūtra, XVI. 3-18.
17. Hiranyakeśī Gṛhya Sūtra, II. 1.4.3-4.
18. Ucchanga Jātaka no. 67.
19. Manu Smṛti,IX. 3.
20. Manu Smṛti, IX. 11.

21. Nārada Smṛti, XIII.15.
22. Nārada Smṛti, XIII. 32.
23. Nārada Smṛti, XIII.34.
24. Nārada Smṛti, XIII. 37.
25. Nārada Smṛti, IV.4.
26. Kātyāana Smṛti, 471, 638.
27. Nārada Smṛti, XIII. 26-27.
28. Nārada Smṛti, XII.94.
29. Nārada Smṛti, XIII.5.
30. Bṛhaspati Smṛti, XXVI.35; Kātyāyana Smṛti, 551.
31. Bṛhaspati Smṛti, XXVI. 37.
32. Bṛhaspati Smṛti, XXVI. 81.
33. Bṛhaspati Smṛti, XXVI. Saṁskara Kānda I.58.
34. Nārada Smṛti, XIII.31.
35. Śatapatha Brāhmaṇa, XI.5.6.1.
36. Śatapatha Brāhmaṇa, II.4.2.16.23; II.6.1.34.
37. Śatapatha Brāhmaṇa, XI. 5.6.2-3.
38. Taittirīya Āranyaka, II.10.
39. Āśvalāyana Gṛhya Sūtra, III. 1.1-4.
40. Gautama Dharmasūtra, V. 8-9. Baudhāyana Dharmasūtra, II. 6.1-8.
41. Śatapatha Brāhmaṇa, II. 4.2.16, 23; II.6.1.34.41.
42. Ṛgveda, II. 1.13-14.
43. Manu Smṛti,III. 63-69.
44. Śatapatha Brāhmaṇa, I. 5.6. 3-8.
45. Taittirīya Āranyaka, II.10.
46. Taittirīya Āranyaka, II. 10-13.
47. Āśvalāyana Gṛhyasūtra, III. 22. III. 3.4.
48. Śatapatha Brāhmaṇa, II, 4.2.14-24.
49. Āśvalāyana Gṛhyasūtra, I. 2.10.
50. Manu Smṛti, III.91.
51. Manu Smṛti, III.70 and283.

52. Manu Smṛti, III. 82-83.
53. Śatapatha Brāhmaṇa, XI. 5.6.2.
54. Āśvalāyana Gṛhyasūtra, I. 2.1-7.
55. Śāṅkhāyana Gṛhyasūtra, II. 14.14.
56. Manu Smṛti, III. 89.
57. Āśvalāyana Gṛhyasūtra, I. 2.7-9.
58. Śāṅkhāyana Gṛhyasūtra, II. 14.16.
59. Manu Smṛti,III. 90.
60. Śatapatha Brāhmaṇa, XI. 5.6.2.
61. Āpastamba Dharmasūtra, II. 3.6.5-16.
62. Gautama Dharmasūtra, V. 38-45.
63. Manu Smṛti, III. 107-112.
64. Mahābhārata, Udyogaparva, 142, 34- 38.
65. Gautama Dharmasūtra, IX. 46-47.
66. Yajñavalkya Smṛti, I. 115.
67. Mahābhārata, Udyogaparva, 124. 34- 38; Santiparva, 167-86.
68. Manu Smṛti,II. 224. Manu Smṛti, IV. 176.
69. Gautama Dharmasūtra, I.1-2. Āpastamba Dharma Sūtra, I. 1.1.1-3.
70. Gautama Dharmasūtra,I. 3-4.
71. Āpastamba Dharma Sūtra, I. 2.5.4.
72. Mahābhārata, Virāta Parva, 5024
73. Mahābhārata, Vanaparva, 149, 188; Santiparva, 69. 231-232.
74. Mahābhārata, Vanaparva. 190.9; Manu-Smṛti, VIII. 16.
75. Mahābhārata Śantiparva 232.23-24; Manu Smṛti, I. 81-82.
76. Mahābhārata, Śantiparva 232. 25-28, 261. 8. Manu Smṛti, I. 83-84.
77. Brahma Purāṇa, 229- 52; Matsya Purāṇa, 144. 78.
78. Gautama Dharma Sūtra, X. 51.
79. Mahābhārata, Assravasikamparva, 28.9.
80. Manu Smṛti, X. 63.
81. Vāmanapurāṇa, 14. 1- 2.
82. Nārada Smṛti, X. 1-3.
83. Yajñavalkya Smṛti, II. 184; Bṛhaspati Smṛti, XV. 7; Nārada

Smṛti, VIII. 16-20.

84. Āpastamba Dharma Sūtra, II. 8. 20. 22-23.
85. Manu Smṛti, V. 56.
86. Bhagvat Gita, VII. II.
87. Taittirīya Samhita, 6.3. 10.5.
88. Aitareya Brāhmaṇa, 33. 1.
89. Mahābhārata, Adi Parva, 120 17-20.
90. Mahābhārata, Anuśasana Parva, 37.17.
91. Manu Smṛti. 4.257.
92. Nārada Smṛti, Ṛṇadana, 5-6.
93. Bṛhaspati Smṛti, 10. 114.

VI

The Saṁskāras

The word 'Saṁskāra' is used for sacraments in the Sūtras for the first time.

Manu says that the taint derived from both parents is removed from the twice-born men by burnt oblations offered during the mother's pregnancy, by the Jātakarma or the ceremony after birth, the tonsure, and the Mauñjībandhana or the tying of the sacred girdle of Munja grass.[1].

According to Manu all the Saṁskāras should be performed on a woman also in order to sanctify the body at the proper time and in proper order, but without the recitation of sacred texts.[2]

Manu declares that only twice-borns have the right to perform the Saṁskāra.[3]

But Śankha quoted by Viśvarūpa on Yājñavalkya says that Śūdras can also have Saṁskāras without Vedic Mantras.[4]

There is difference of opinion among the writers of Dharma Śāstra about the number of Saṁskāras. The Gautama Dharmasūtra prescribes forty Saṁskāras. Among these are included various sacrifices and calendaric festivals along with the *rites de passage.* These are the Garbhādhāna or ceremony to cause conception; the Puṁsavana or ceremony to cause the birth of a male child; the Sīmntonnayana or arranging the parting of the pregnant wife's hair; the Jātakarman or the ceremony on the birth of the child; the Nāmakarana or the ceremony of naming the child; the Annapraśana or the first feeding; the Caula or tonsure of the head of the child; and the Upanayana or the initiation; the four Vratas undertaken after the study of the Vedas; the Snāna or the bath on completion of the studentship; Vivāha or marriage; the five daily Mahāyajñas for Deva, Pitṛ, Manuṣya, Bhūta and Brahman; seven kinds of Pākayajñas, namely, the Aṣṭaka, the Parvana, the funeral oblations, the Śrāvani, the Āgrāhayani, the Caitri and Asvayuji; seven Haviryajñas namely Agnāyadheya, Agnihotra, Darśapauraṇamāsa, Agrāyana, Caturmāsyas, Nirudhapaśubandha and Sautrāmaṇi; seven Soma sacrifices, Agniṣtoma, Atyagnistoma, Ukthya, Soḍasin, Vājpeya, Atirātra, and Aptoryāma.[5]

Manu does not enumerate the Samskāras, but only mentions that these are from Garbhādhāna or rite on conception to Antyeṣṭi.[6] The main Saṁskāras are the following:

Garbhādhāna

The earliest reference to this Saṁskāra is found in the Bṛhadāraṇyaka Upaniṣad. It is as follows:

'When the monthly illness seizes his wife, she should for three days not drink from a metal vessel and wear a fresh dress. Let no Śūdra man or woman touch her. At the end of the three days, when she has bathed, the husband should make her pound rice.'[7] And then towards morning after having according to the rule of the Sthālīpāka (pot boiling) performed the preparation of the Ājya (clarified butter), he sacrifices from the Sthālīpāka bit by bit, saying: 'This is for Agni, Svāhā; this is for Anumati, Svāhā; this is for the divine Sāvitrī, the true creator, Svāhā.' Having sacrificed he takes out the rest of the rice and eats it, and after having eaten he gives it to his wife. Then, he washes his hands, fills a water-jar and sprinkles her thrice with it, saying: Rise hence, O Viśvavasu, seek another blooming girl, a wife with her husband. Then he embraces her and says: 'I am Ama (breath), thou art Sā (speech); thou art Sā, I am Ama. I am the Sāman, thou art the Ṛk. I am the sky, thou art the earth. Come let us strive together, so that a male child may be begotten'.[8]

The Āśvalāyana Gṛhyasūtra says that the Upaniṣad lays down the ceremonies for the Garbhālambhana or conception of child, Puṁsvana or causing the male child and the Anvālobhana or guarding the embryo from dangers. Though Āśvalāyana does not name the Upaniṣad he probably refers to the Bṛhadāraṇyaka Upaniṣad.[9]

The Śāmkhāyana Gṛhyasūtra elaborately prescribes the Caturthikarma or rites of the fourth day. When three nights have elapsed, he makes offerings of cooked food(with the words):

> 'Agni, thou art expiation, thou art the expiation of the gods.
>
> What substance dwells in her that brings death to her husband, that drive away from her.'

Similarly, the husband makes offerings to Vāyu, and Sūrya for driving away the substances that bring 'sonlessness' and 'destruction to the cattle'. Moreover, the husband makes offerings to god Aryaman. He says:

> 'To god Aryaman the girls have made sacrifice, to Agni;
>
> May he, god Aryaman, loosen her from this, and not from that place.'

With similar prayer the husband offers oblation to Varuṇa and Pūṣan and then seventh oblation to Prajāpati with a verse from Ṛgveda (X. 121.10) and eighth to Sviṣṭakṛt.[10]

Similar provisions are found in the Pāraskara Gṛhya Sūtra.[11]

Punsavana

According to Āśvalāyana Gṛhya Sūtra, 'in the third month of

the wife's pregnancy, under the Naksatra Tiṣya, give to eat to the wife after she has fasted, in curds from a cow which has a calf of the same colour, two beans and one barley grain for each handful of curds.' He should give it thrice. Then, he should ask her 'what does thou drink ? What dost thou drink'. The wife should thrice reply Punsavana or 'Generation of a male child, Generation of a male child.'

The Āśvalāyana Gṛhya Sūtra places this Saṁskāra after Garbhālambhana.[12] But Āpastamba, Hiranyakesī and Bhāradvāja place it after Sīmantonayana. They prescribe different rites to be performed. Āpastamba provides that it should be performed when pregnancy has become visible, under the constellation Tiṣya. The husband takes a shoot with two fruits that look like testicles from a branch of a Nyagrodha tree which points eastward or northward. The husband causes a girl who has not yet attained maturity to pound the Nyagrodha shoot on an upper mill-stone with another upper mill. He makes his wife lie down on her back the the west of the fire, facing east and inserts the pounded substance with his thumb into her right nostril with the Yajuṣ (II.11.13). It is asserted that the wife would give birth to a son.[13]

Sīmantonnayana

According to Āśvalāyana Gryasūtra the Saṁskāra of Sīmantonnayana or parting of the hair should be performed in the fourth month. It should be performed in the fortnight of the increasing moon, when the moon stands in conjunction with a Nakaṣatra that has a name of masculine gender. Then, the husband establishes the fire and spreads a bull's hide to the west of it with the neck to the east and hair outside, while his wife sitting on the hide takes hold of him. The husband makes oblations with the two verses, 'May Dhatṛ give to his worshipper'[14] and again with the two verses, 'I invoke Rākā'[15] and then with three verses 'Nejamesa'[16] and 'Prajāpati, no other one than thou'.[17] The husband then three times parts her hair upwards, beginning from the front with a bunch containing an even number of unripe fruit and with a porcupine's quill that had three white spots and with three bunches of Kuśa grass with the words, 'Bhūr, bhuvah, svah, om,' or he may do it four times. He gives order to lute-players, 'Sing king Soma'. They sing 'May Soma our king bless the human race. Settled is the wheel of N.N.'—here they name the river near which they dwell. And then do whatever aged Brahmana women, whose husbands and children are alive, tell them to do. A bull is the fee for the sacrifice.[18]

Jātakarma

This sacrament is very ancient. In the Taittirīya Samhita it is provided that 'when a son is born he (father) should make offerings on twelve potsheds to Viśvānara. After giving the details of the sacrifice it is asserted that he on whose birth he offers this sacrifice becomes pure, brilliant, an eater of food, powerful, possessed of cattle.'[19] In the Śatapatha Brāhmaṇa it is provided that before cutting navel-string five Brāhmaṇas should breathe over him in all the four directions and over the child.[20] The Bṛhadaraṇyaka Upaniṣad also describes the rites on the birth of a son. When a son is born, he prepares the fire, places the son on his lap, pours Pṛṣadājya that is Dadhi or curds mixed with Ghṛta or clarified butter into a bellmental jug, he offers oblations of the Pṛṣadājya with the Mantras, 'May I, as I prosper in this my house, nourish a thousand, May fortune never fail in his race, with offspring and cattle Svāhā.

'I offer to thee in my mind the vital breaths which are in me, Svāhā.'

'Whatever in my work I have done too much or whatever I have done too little, may the wise Agni Sviṣṭakrt make this right and proper for us, Svāhā.'

Then putting his mouth near the child's right ear he says thrice: Speech, speech, speech. After that he pours together curds, honey and clarified butter, and feeds the child with a ladle of pure gold saying, 'I give thee Bhū, I give thee Bhuvah, I give thee, Svah; Bhūr, Bhuvah, Svah, I give thee all'. Then he gives him his name saying: 'Thou art Veda', but this is his secret name. Then he hands the boy to his mother and gives him her breast, saying: 'O Sarasvati that breast of thine, which inexhaustible, delightful, abundant, wealthy, generous, by which thou cherishest all blessings make that to flow here. Then he addresses the mother of the boy, 'Thou art Ilā Maitrāvaruṇī; thou strong woman has born a strong boy. Be thou blessed with strong children, thou who has blessed me with a strong child'. And they say of such a boy: 'Ah, thou art better than thy father; Ah thou art better than thy grand father'. Truly he has reached the highest point in happiness, priase, and Vedic glory who is born as the son of a Brāhmaṇa that knows this.[21] The Gṛhyasūtras follow the procedure given in Bṛhadaraṇyaka Upaniṣad.[22]

Following Gṛhyasūtras, Manu also prescribes that before the navel-string is cut, the Jātakarma Saṁskāra must be performed for a male child and while sacred formulas are being recited he must be fed with gold, honey and butter.[23]

Nāmakaraṇa

Gobhila Gṛhyasūtra prescribes that when ten nights have elapsed after the son's birth, or hundred nights or one year, the Nāmadheyakaraṇa or giving a name to the child is performed.

He who is going to perform that Saṁskāra, the father or representative of father, sits down to the west of fire, on northward-pointed Darbha grass, facing the east. Then the mother, having dressed the son in clean garment hands him, from south to north, with his face turned to the north, to the performer of the Saṁskāra. She then passes behind his back and sits down to the north of him, on northward-pointed Darbha grass. He then sacrifices to Prajāpati, to the Tithi of the child's birth, to the Nakṣatra of the child's birth and to the presiding deity of that Tithi mutters Mantra, 'Who art thou ? What person art thou?[24] touching the sense-organs at the boys head. In the passage of the

Mantra, 'Enter upon the month, that belongs to Ahaspati or the lord of days N.N.' and at the end of the Mantra he should give him a name beginning with a consonant with a semivowel in it, with a long vowel or the Visarga at the end and formed with a Kṛt suffix. It should not contain a Taddhita suffix. He should give a name with an odd number of syllables ending in 'da' to girls. And after he has told the name to the mother first, they may do what they like. In the end the Sūtrakāra provides that 'a cow constitutes the sacrificial fee'.[25] From this provision it appears that though in earlier times the father himself used to perform the Saṁskāra of his son, when the Sūtras or aphorisms were consolidated the priest had taken over from him.

Pārsakara provides that the name of a Brāhmaṇa should end in Śarman, that of a Kṣatriya in Varman that of a Vaiśya in Gupta.[26] Manu follows the Gṛhyasūtras. He says that let the father perform or cause to be performed the naming of the son on the tenth or twelfth day after birth, or on a lucky lunar day, in a lucky Muhurta, under an auspicious constellation. Manu says that the first part of a Brāhmaṇa's name should denote something auspicious, a Kṣatriya's should be connected with power and a Vaiśyas with wealth, but the name of a Śūdra expresses something contemptible. The second part of a Brāhmaṇa's name should be a word implying happiness, of a Kṣatriyas a word implying protection, of a Vaiśya's a term expressive of thriving and of a Śūdra's an expression denoting service.[27]

Karṇavedha

Karṇavedha is the piercing of the ear-lobes of the child. In this Saṁskāra the ears of the child are pierced. The piercing of the lobes of the child seems to be an ancient custom. In the Ṛgveda the poet Kakṣīvān prays all the Deities (Visvedevas) to bestow a son with gold ear-rings and jewel in the neck.[28] It appears that it is an early custom of Aryans but it had not been given the status of Saṁskāra. The Baudhayana Gṛhya Seṣasūtra provides that Karnavedha should done in the Seventh or eighth month.[29]

Bṛhaspati quoted in Saṁskāraprakāśa provides that it may be performed on the tenth or twelfth or sixteenth day from birth.[30]

Niṣkramaṇa

In the fourth month Niṣkaramaṇa or the rite of taking out the child should be performed, according to the Pāraskara Gṛhyasūtra. He (the father) makes the child look at the sun, pronouncing the verse, 'that eye'.[31] Manu says that the Niṣkramaṇa Saṁskāra should be performed in the fourth month.[32]

Annaprāśana

When the child is six months old, the father should prepare food to feed him, according to Śankhayana and Āśvalāyana Gṛhyasūtras. The father should feed the child while reciting the Mahāvyahrtis or 'Bhūr, Bhuvah, Svah.' According to the Śaṁkhayana and Āśvalāyana Gṛhyasūtras, if the father desires nourishment for the child, he should feed him goats' flesh; if he is desirous of holy lusture he should feed him flesh of partridge.[33] He should feed the child with fish if he is desirous of swiftness; such food should be prepared with boiled rice with milk, curds and honey. After that, the father should make the oblations to fire with four verses, 'Lord of food, give us food, painless and strong bring forward the giver; bestow power on us, on men and animals' (Ṛgveda, IV. 12. 4-5) and 'Him, oh Agni, lead to long life and splendour'. The father should recite over the child the hymn of Ṛgveda, IX. 66.19. and then put the child on northward pointed Kuśa grass with Ṛg. 22.15. The remnants should be eaten by the mother.[34]

Manu also provides that the Saṁskāra of Annaprāśana should be performed in the sixth month.[35]

Cūḍākarma or Caula

Cūḍākarma or Caula is the tensure of the child's head. Āśvalāyana Gṛhyasūtra ordains that the Saṁskāra should be performed in the third year or according to family usage.

The various things that are to be employed in the Saṁskāra are to be arranged in a particular way. The father should keep four vessels each of which should be filled with rice, barley, beans and sesamum seed, to the north of the fire. The mother should be seated to the west of the fire with the boy in her lap. There should be kept two new vessels, one filled with the dung of a bull and the other with Śami leaves. The father should sit to the right of the mother holding twenty-one bunches of Kuśa grass or the Brāhmaṇa priest should hold them. The father should sit to the west of the boy. There should be a razor of copper.

When Homa is performed, the tonsure of the boy's head begins. The father pours warm water with the Mantra, 'With warm water, O Vāyu, come hither' (Mantra-Brahman I. 62). The father taking of that water or fresh butter or some drops of curds anoints the boys head from left to the right with the Mantra, 'May Aditi cut thy hair, may the waters moisten thee for vigour.' Into the right part of the hair, he puts each time three Kuśa bunches with the points towards the boy himself, with the Mantra, 'Herb protect him' (Taittirīya Saṁhitā, I.2.1.1.) with the word, 'Axe, do no harm to him' (Taittirīya Saṁhitā, I.31.1.). He presses a copper razor on the Kuśa blades and cuts the hairs with the verse, 'The razor with which in the begining Sāvitrī, the knowing one, has shaved (the hair) of king Soma, and of Varuṇa, with that ye Brāhmaṇas, shave now his (hair) that he may be blessed with long life with old age'. Every time the hair is cut he gives the cut hair with their points to the east, together with Śami leaves, to the mother. She puts them sown on the bull-dung. Second time the father should cut with the Mantra, 'With what Dhātu has shaven (the head) of Brahaspati, Agni and Indra, for the sake of long life with that I shave thy (head) for the sake of long life, fame and happiness'. The cutting of hair should be done the third time with the Mantra, 'With what he may after night (is past) see the sun again and again, with that I shave thy (head) for the sake of long life, fame and happiness'. The cutting should be done fourth time with all the three Mantras together. Similarly the hair should be cut on the left side of the head. The father should wipe off the edge of the razor with (the words), 'If thou shavest, as a shaver his hair with the razor, the wounding, the well-shaped, purify his head, but do not take away his life'. The father then orders to the barber, 'with luke-warm water doing what has to be done with water, without doing harm to him, arrange (his hair) well.' The barber should arrange the hair according to the custom of his family. The Saṁskāra of the girl should be performed without Mantras.[36] Following Sūtras, Manu provides that the Cūḍakarman or tonsure (of boy) should be performed for the sake of spiritual merit by all twice- born men in the first or third year.[37]

Vidyārambha

We do not find mention of this Saṁskāra in the Sūtra literature. It appears that the early Aryans did not begin the education of children from a tender age. We do find in the Arthasastra of Kauṭilya that the prince should be taught alphabet and arithimetic after the Saṁskāra of Caula.[38]

But Aparārka (1100 A.D. to 1200 A.D.) and Smṛticandrikā (1150 A.D. 1225 A.D.) quote verses from Mārkandeya- Purāṇa in which the Saṁskāra of Vidyārambha is prescribed. It is to be performed during the fifth year of the boy on a day from 12th of the bright half of Kārtika to the 11th of the bright half of Aṣāḍha, on 4th, 9th and 14th avoiding Saturday and Tuesday. In this rite Hari or Viṣṇu, Lakṣmī, Sarasvatī, Sūtrakāra of one's branch and lore (Vidyā) of family should be worshipped. One should offer fire oblations of clarified butter to these deities. The father should honour the Brāhmaṇas by giving them Dakṣiṇā. The teacher should be seated facing the east and the boy should face the west. And blessed by the Brāhmaṇas the boy should be taught the first lesson by the teacher. The teaching should not be performed during the Anādhyāya days.[39]

As is obvious the Saṁskāra of Vidyārambha is of late origin and therefore no Vedic gods or Mantras are prescribed for this rite. This rite could not get the status of a full Saṁskāra even in later times. Probably it was introduced as a result of Muslim contact, on the pattern of their ceremony of Maktab.

Upanayana

Upanayana or initiation is the most ancient Indo-Iranian Saṁskāra. In the Atharvaveda, a whole hymn is found in which the sun is portrayed as a student. In this hymn we find all the chief characteristics of a student. These are wearing deerskin, girdle, offering fuel sticks, begging, and leading a life of hard work and restaint.[40]

In the Śatapatha Brāhmaṇa we find a dialogue between student and teacher, which is almost wholly borrowed by the Gṛhyasūtras. A brief account is being given below. The boy says to the teacher, 'I have come for Brahmacarya. Let me be a Brahmacārī'. The teacher asks, 'What is thy name'. The teacher takes his (right) hand with, 'Indra's disciple thou art; Agni is thy teacher, I am thy teacher, N.N. (addresses the boy by his name)'. Then the teacher commits him to the deities, 'To Prajāpati I commit thee, To the god Sāvitrī I commit thee, To the waters, To the plants I commit thee, To Heaven and Earth I commit thee'. Again the teacher says to him, 'Thou art a Brahmacarin. Drink water. Do thy work (in the teacher's house). Put a stick (on the fire). Do not sleep (by day)'. The teacher recites the Sāvitrī to him. Formerly it was taught after a year or after six months or after twenty-four days or after twelve days or after six days or after three days. However a Brāhmaṇa should be taught Sāvitrī at once. The teacher should recite it by Pāda or one quarter then by half verses, then whole of the verse. Being a Brahmacārin he should not eat honey.[41]

In the Gopatha Brāhmaṇa, it is provided that the student should bring fuel sticks daily for worshipping fire and beg. In case he fails to do so for seven days, his Upanayana should be performed again. The housewife should give alms every day to student so that her wealth, merit due to Isṭapurta might not be restrained. A student should not sleep on a cot, should not sing or dance, should not roam about, should not spit about, neither should go to the funeral ground.[42]

The Gṛhyasūtras are not in favour of engaging the boy in studies in early childhood. The age, dress and staff of the boy would also differ according to his Varṇa.[43]

Śāmkhāyana declares that whatever the boy wears at his initiation is taken by the teacher.[44]

The student should wash and adorn himself.

The teacher should sacrifice with his face towards the east while the student should keep his face to the west. The student should be shaved all round (his head) then the teacher should initiate him.

The proper time for initiating the boys of different Varṇas would vary according to their Varṇas. According to Āpastamba Gṛhyasūtras, spring for Brāhmaṇa, summer for Kṣatriya, and autumn for Vaiśya are the proper time for initiating the boys.[45].

According to Śāmkhāyana Gṛhyasūtra the teacher should initiate the boy standing and he should also stand. The boy should put on the skin with the Mantra,'The firm, powerful eye of Mitra, glorious splendour, strong and prosperous and chaste, flowing vesture, this skin I put on a valiant (man).'[46]

The boy should tie the girdle from left to right thrice round while repeating these words three times: 'Here has come to us protecting us from evil words, purifying our kin as a purifier, clothing herself, by (the power of) inhalation and exhalation, with strength, this friendly goddess, this blessed girdle.' The boy should make one or three or five knots according to the family custom. The teacher should adjust the sacrificial cord with the words, 'The sacrificial cord art thou. With the cord of the sacrifices I invest thee'. The teacher fills the folded hands of his own and boy's (with water) and asks him: 'What is thy name ?' 'I am N.N., Sir' says the boy declaring his name. 'Descending from the same Ṛṣis ?' asks the teacher. 'Descending from the same Ṛṣis, Sir' says the boy. Then the boy declares that 'I am a Brahmacārī'. The teacher sprinkles water with his joined hands on the joined hands of the boy with the Mantra, 'Bhūr Bhuvah Svah, 'and seizing the boy's hands with his own hands holding the right uppermost, the teacher mutters, 'By the urge of the god Savitar, with the arms of the two Aśvins, with Pūṣan's hands I initiate thee, N.N.'

Śāmkhāyana declares that to those who are desirous of a host of adherents the teacher should initicate with the Mantra, 'Thee, the lord of hosts' (Ṛgveda, II, 23,1), sick persons with the Mahāvyahrtis, warriors with the Mantra 'Come here do not come to Harm' (Ṛgveda, VIII.20.1.).

The teacher recites, 'Bhaga has seized thy hand, Savitar has seized thy hand, Pūṣan has seized thy hand, Aryaman has seized thy hand. Mitra art thou by right, Agni is thy teacher, and I N.N. both of us Agni, I give this student in charge of thee. Indra I give this student in charge of thee. Sun, I give this student in charge of you Viśvedevas, I give this student in charge to you, for the sake of long life, of blessed offsping and strength, of increase of wealth, of mastership of all Vedas, of renown, of bliss.' He further says, 'In Indra's course I move in the sun's course I move after him'—with these words he turns round from left to right, and grasping down with the span of his right hand over (the students) right shoulder he touches the place of his heart with the words, 'May I be dear to thy inviolate heart'. Having silently turned round from right to left, and then laying his hand with the fingers upwards on his (i.e. the boy's) heart, he mutters, 'Under my will I take thy heart my mind shall thy mind follow: in my word thou shalt rejoice with all thy heart, may Bṛhaspati join thee to me.'

The teacher addresses the boy with the words, 'Thou art the Brahmacārin of Kāma, N.N.' The teacher turns round as before with the same words. He touches with a span of his right hand (the boy's) right shoulder, he mutters: 'A Brahmacārī art thou. Put on fuel, Drink water. Do the service. Do not sleep in the day- time. Keep silence till the putting on the fuel'. The boy puts the fuel on the fire with the words, 'Thine Agni, is this piece of wood'. He puts the fuel silently.

The Sāvitrī should be recited to the boy after a year or after three nights or immediately. The teacher should recite a Gāyatrī (Ṛgveda, Viśvāmitra III. 62.10) to Brāhmaṇa boy; a Triṣṭubh (Ṛgveda, Hiranyastupa I. 35) to a Kṣatriya; a Jagati (Ṛgveda, Vāmadeva IV. 40 5.) to a Vaiśya. But it should be a verse sacred to Savitar. The teacher and boy should sit to the north of the fire. The teacher with his face turned eastwards and the student westwards. The teacher recites the Sāvitrī to him first quarter by quarter then hemistich by hemistich, and finally without a stop.

The teacher makes the student sip water three times with the words, 'Waters are ye by name; happy ones are ye by name; sappy ones are ye by name; undecaying ones are ye by name, fearless ones are ye by name; immortal ones are ye by name. Of you, being such may I pertake, receive me into your favour'. The teacher hands over to him the staff with the five Mantras, 'Blessing may give us' (Ṛgveda, V. 51. 11-15). The teacher leads round the fire turning his right side towards it, (the student) goes through the village to beg food. The student should beg of his mother first or of a woman who will not refuse. The student should annouce the alms to the teacher, then he may eat the food with his teacher's permission. The teacher hands over to him the staff with the five Mantras, 'Blessing may give us'(Ṛgveda, V. 51. 11-15).

The daily putting of fuel, the going for alms, the sleeping on the ground and obedience to the teacher; these are the standing duties of a student.

The study of Veda is the most important duty of the student after Upanayana. According to Sāmkhāyana the teacher should declare the Ṛṣi and deity and metre of the hymn, and then recite the hymn.

The student should perform Saṁdhyā or twilight prayer in the evening turning his face northwest until the stars appear. Then he should mutter the Mahāvyāhṛtis, the Sāvitrī and the auspicious hymns. Similarly in the morning he should perform Saṁdhyā turning his face to the east, standing until the disk of the sun appears.[47]

Manu provides that a Brahmacārī should perform Saṁdhyā standing in the morning and seated in the evening.[48]

Āpastamba Dharmsūtra provides that the student must clasp his teacher's feet when he meets the teacher after sunrise, before the Vedic study and after the Vedic study. Manu follows him.[49]

The initiation is a very important Saṁskāra. The person whose initiation is not performed becomes excommunicated from the society. Such persons are called Patitasāvitrīka—those who have lost their right of learning Sāvitrī Mantra. They are called Vrātya by the Āśvalāyana, Baudhāyana, and Āpastamba Gṛhyasūtras, and the Manu and Yājñavalkya Smṛtis.[50]

The maximum age for performing initiation is sixteen for Brāhmaṇas; twenty-two for Kṣatriyas and twenty-four for Vaiśyas. The Āpastamba Dharmasūtra prescribes that after passing these years the person should follow the rules of studenthood for two months, then his initiation should be performed. Then for one year he should bathe thrice everyday, only then he should be taught Vedas.[51] Manu prescribes three Prajāpatya penances for a person who has not been taught the Sāvitrī.[52] In the Prajāpatya penance the person should take only morning meal for three days, only evening meal for three days, subsist of alms got without asking for three days, and observe fast for three days.[53]

Those whose father and grand father have not been initiated, they are called slayer of Brahma (the Vedic hymn); with such persons social intercourse, eating and intermarriage are prohibited. In case they want to be initiated they should perform the following penance after that they can be admitted into their original Varṇa. Such persons should perform the penance (rules of studenthood) one year for every genration, then they should be initiated. For one year they have to bathe every day while reciting the seven Pavamānī Mantras beginning with 'If near or far' (Rg. IX. 67. 21-27) with the Yajuṣpavitra (Taittirīya Saṁhitā, I. 2.1.1), with the Sāmapavitra and with the Mantra called Añ ngirasa (Rg. IV. 40.5) or he may pour water while reciting Vyahṛtis (Om Bhūḥ, Bhuvaḥ, Svaḥ).

Similarly those whose great grandfather, grand father and father's initiation has not been performed are called 'burial-grounds'. Such a man would observe the same penance for twelve years. After that he can be initiated. Then, the person will have to bathe with Pavamāna and other Mantras. Then the duties of householder are given to him. Even then he shall not be taught the whole Veda but only the sacred formulas required for the domestic ceremonies.[54]

Keśānta or Godāna

This is the ceremony of shaving the beard. We find this Samskāra in the Gṛhyasūtras and Smṛtis. But later on this Samskāra went out of practice. Śāmkhāyana Gṛhyasūtra prescribes that the Godāna or Keśānta Samskāra should be performed in sixteenth or eighteenth year. Sūtrakāras prescribe that in Godāna or Keśānta Saṁskāra the precedure of Cūḍākarma should be followed with some difference.[55] According to Āśvalāyana wherever the word hair (Kesa) occurs in the Mantra the teacher should put the word 'beard' (Smaśru). The Mantra is, 'Purify his hand and his face, but do not take away his life'. He gives orders (to the barber): 'Arrange his hair, his beard, the hair of his body, and his nails, ending in the north'. Having bathed and silently stood during the rest of the day, let him break his silence in the presence of his teacher, (saying to him) 'I give an optional gift (to thee)'. An ox and a cow is the sacrificial fee. The teacher should instruct him to keep the observances for one year.[56]

Manu provides that Keśānta Saṁskāra should be performed for a Brāhmaṇa in the sixteenth year, for a Kṣatriya in the twentysecond and for a Vaiśya in twentyfourth year.[57]

Samāvartana or Snāna

According to the Āśvalāyana Gṛhyasūtra the Snāna should be performed, when the student after finishing his learning has offered something to the teacher or has received his permission, he should take a bath which signifies the end of his studentship.[58]

When the student is returning home from his teacher's house he should get the following things: a jewel to be tied round the neck, two ear-rings, a pair of garments, an umbrella, a pair of shoes, a staff, a wreath, pounded seed of the Karañja fruit for rubbing with, ointment, eye salve, a turban; all these things for himself and for the teacher. If he cannot procure these things for both, then he should get them only for the teacher. He should get a piece of wood of a tree which is sacrificially pure. If he desires enjoyment of food or prosperity, or splendour, he should take sappy wood. If he desires holy lustre he should take dry wood. If he desires both he should take a wood which is sappy and dry in its different parts. He should put the piece of wood at a high place, not on the floor. Then he should give food and cow to Brāhmaṇas. Then he should perform the ceremony of shaving the beard or Godāna Saṃskāra. He should utter the Mantras so that they refer to himself. He should rub himself with pounded Ekaklitaka. After washing himself with lukewarm water he should put on two new garments, which have not yet been washed, with the Mantra, 'You two (Mitra and Varuṇa) put on garments with great splendour' (Ṛgveda, I. 152.1). He should anoint his eyes with the words, 'The luster of stone art thou, protect my eyes'. He should fasten the two ear-rings with the words, 'The luster of stone art thou, protect my ear'. After salving his two hands with ointment a Brahamna should salve his face first, a Rājanya his two arms, a Vaiśya the belly, a woman her secret parts, persons who gain their livelihood by running, their thighs. He should put on the wreath with the words, 'Free from pain art thou free from pain may I become'. The wreath should not be called Mālā. If someone calls it Mala he should cause them to call it Sraj. He steps into the shoes with the words, 'You two are the supports of gods, protect me from all sides'. He takes umbrella with the words: 'The heaven's covering art thou'. He takes the bamboo staff with the words, 'Bamboo art thou, thou art the child of a tree, protect me from all sides'. He ties the jewel to his neck and arranges the turban on his head with the hymn beginning with 'Giving life'. Then he should, while standing, put the piece of wood on the fire. He should say, 'Memory and reporach and knowledge, faith and wisdom as the fifth what is sacrificed and what is given (as gift) and what is studied, and what is done, truth, learning, observances. O Agni the vow (of thee) together the Ṛsis that are Kṣatriyas, with the Fathers, with the kings among the Fathers, with men and with the kings among men, with shine, over-shine, after-shine, counter- shine, with gods and men, with Gāndharvas and Apasaras, with wild animals and domestic animals—the vow belonging to my own self, dwelling in my own self, that is my entire vow. O Agni I shall on all sides become this vow Svāhā. He should put fuel-sticks on fire, one for each Mantra. 'Mine, Agni be the glory' (Rg. X. 128. 1). He should pass that night at a place where they will do honour to him (by offering Madhuparka or honey-mixture). The snataka has to keep the following observances: he shall not bathe in the night-time; he shall not bathe naked; he shall not look at a naked woman except during sexual intercourse; he shall not run during rain; he shall not climb up a tree; he shall not descend into a well; he shall not swim with his arms across a river; he shall not expose himself to danger. A great being indeed is a snataka—so it is known (from the Śruti)'.[59]

Manu and Yājñavalkya follow the rules prescribed in Gṛhyasūtras.[60]

It seems that by the time these sacraments crystallized the Brahmanical elite had become very concious of the need to preserve the Aryan tradition contained in the Vedas. The persons who had undergone systematic training in the Vedic lore were therefore considered precious, and elaborate rules were made so that their lives might not be endangered in any way.

Vivāha Saṁskāra

Marriage is the most ancient and important Samskāra. Even today rites and ritual of marriage which were prescribed by the Gṛhyasūtras are strictly followed by all high-caste Hindus. The proclaimed purpose of marriage is to perform sacrifices and procreate sons. The unmarried man is considered incomplete. The Śatapatha Brāhmaṇa declares: 'The wife is indeed half of one's self; therefore as long as a man does not marry a wife, as long he does not beget a son he is not complete, but when he marries a wife and begets a son, he becomes complete.'[61] The Āpastamba Dharmasūtra forbids a husband from taking a second wife if the first wife is able to perform sacrifices and has got a son.[62] In the Mahābhārata wife is declared to be the source of Trivarga, that is Dharma or religious sacrifices, Artha or wealth, and Kāma or sex and other pleasures.[63] Manu also says that 'on wife alone depends the procreation of sons, the performance of religions rites, faithful service, highest conjugal happiness and heavenly bliss for the ancesters and oneself.'[64]

The age of the bridegroom is not mentioned specifically in the early Dharmasūtras. As marriage was performed after the Samāvartana, it was around the age of sixteen at the earliest that a boy married.

Varṇa hierarchy plays an important part in the choice of mates. Pāraskara Gṛhyasūtra allows marriages in direct order. He says: 'Three (wives are allowed) to a Brāhmaṇa in accordance with the order of the Varṇa.' Thus, a Brāhmaṇa can marry a Kṣatriya and a Vaiśya maiden apart from a Brāhmaṇa maiden. 'Two (wives are allowed) to a Rājanya or Kṣatriya.' Thus, a Kṣatriya can have a Vaiśya wife apart from a Kṣatriya wife. A Vaiśya is allowed to have only a Vaiśya wife. But Pārskara quotes some teachers who allow one Śūdra wife also to persons of all Varṇas. The marriage ceremonies with a Śūdra maiden should be performed without Mantras.[65]

From the way in which the Pāraskara Gṛhyasūtra allows a Śūdra wife it appears that marrying a Śūdra maiden was not permitted by all the law-givers. Manu and Yājñavalkya follow the rules laid down in Pāraskara Gṛhyasūtra.[66]

Manu provides that a man of thirty shall marry a maiden of twelve, a man of twenty-four a girl of eight.[67] Gautama Dharmasūtra provides that the maiden should be of equal caste. She should not belong to another man. She should be younger than the bridegroom. She should be of different Pravara.[68] Gobhila Gṛhyasūtra provides that the maiden should not belong to the same Gotra. She should not be a Sapinda.[69] Gautama Dharmasūtra says that the maiden should not be related within six degrees on the father's side or on the side of the begetter. She should not be related within four degrees on the mother's side.[70] Gobhila prescribes that the maiden should be a 'Nagnika' or one who is too young to wear clothes.[71] Gautama Dharmasūtra clearly lays down that a maiden should be given in marriage before she attains puberty. The father who neglects this, incurs sin. Gautama quotes some teachers who provide that a maiden should be given in marriage before she starts wearing clothes.[72]

Manu and Yājñavalkya follow the provisions of Gobhila Gṛhyasūtra and Gautama Dharmasūtra. Following Gautama Dharmasūtra Manu and Yājñavalkya also provide that a maiden should be given in marriage before she attains puberty. The father or guardian who neglects this incurs sin.[73]

In case a father does not gives away his daughter in marriage before puberty, Gautama allows the maiden to have three monthly periods to pass, and afterwards unite herself, of her own will to a blameles man, giving up the ornaments received from her father.[74] Manu and Yājñavalkya follow the dicta of Gautama Dharmasūtra.[75] Nārada Bṛahaspti and Parāśara follow the norms laid down by Manu and Yājñavalkya.

Thus marrying a maiden before she attain as puberty was

provided by a work as old as Gautama Dharmasūtra. The aphorisms of Gautama were consolidated around 600 B.C. During the Buddhist era the traditional norms were somewhat relaxed. But Manu, Yājñavalkya, Bṛhaspati, Nārada and Parāśara made an attempt to resurrect them.

The ancient Aryans aspired for many sons. In the Ṛgveda a poet prays to Indra for ten sons.[76] Sons were needed in battlefield in the ancient times. Later on when the Aryans colonized the vast lands of Indian sub-continent they needed many sons for carrying on the multifarious tasks connected with agriculture. Perhaps it was due to the requirement of large manpower that marriage before puberty was ordained for girls, so that they might bear the maximum number of sons. The Baudhāyana Dharmasūtra provides that as long as a girl who has attained puberty is not given in marriage the father or guardian incurs the sin of destroying an embryo every month.[77]

Manu and Yājñavalkya reasserted the dicta of the Dharmasūtras. The Parāśara Smṛti is the most conservative among all the texts in this respect. It provides that a Brāhmaṇa who marries a maiden who has attained puberty 'should remain unspoken, unadmitted in a row of dinner and called the husband of a Vṛṣalī'.[78]

The qualifications of a bridegroom have also been laid down by the sacred texts. Āśvalāyana Gṛhyasūtra provides that 'he (father) should first examine the family' and adds 'that a maiden should be given to a intellegent man.'[79]

Yājñavalkya also says that the family of bridegroom should be good, free from diseases that are hereditarily transmitted, young, intelligent and his virility must be carefully tested.[80] Nārada has discussed in detail the physical qualities and deficiencies of a bridgroom. Following Yājñavalkya, Nārada provides that the bridegroom must be tested for ascertaining his virility and discusses in detail impotence in man.[81]

Many Gṛhyasūtras provide that for selecting a bride a person should make lumps of different types of earth and let the girl touch one of these. On this basis the girl should be selected or rejected. According to Āśvalāyana Gṛhyasūtra one should make eight lumps of earth from a field that yields two crops in a year, from a cowshed, from a Vedi, from a pool which does not dry up, from a gambling place, from a place where four roads meet, from a barren spot, and from a funeral ground. Then the person should recite over the lumps the following formula. 'Ṛta has been born first, in the beginning; on the Ṛta truth is founded. For what (destiny) this girl is born, that may she attain here. What is true may that be seen'. Then he should say to the girl, 'Take one of these'. If she chooses the lump of earth from the field, her offspring will be rich in food; if from the cow-shed, rich in cattle; if the earth from an alter, rich in holy lustre; if from a pool, rich in everything; if from a gambling-place, addicted to gambling; if from a place where four roads meet, wandering to different directions; if from a barren spot, poor; if from a funeral ground, she will bring death to her husband.[82] In case she touches first four she will bring prosperity but if she touches the last four, obviously she should not be chosen. Such provisions are also found in Gobhila Gṛhyasūtra, Āpastamba Gṛhyasūtra and others. These rules indicate the belief that it is the wife who brings prosperity or destruction in the family.

Forms of Marriage

Āsvalyana speaks of eight types of marriage. These are: Brāhma, Daiva, Prajāpatya, Ārṣa, Gāndharva, Āsura, Paiśāca and Rākṣasa. Mānava Gṛhyasūtra provides only two forms of marriage: Brāhma and Śaukla. In the Brahma from the father gives away the maiden after decking her with ornaments, after pouring out a libation of water. A son born by the wife after wedding her according to this form brings purification to twelve descendants and to twelve ancesters on both the husband's and wife's side.

In the Daiva form, according to Āśvalāyana Gṛhyasūtra, the father shall give his daughter to the an officiating priest, who is performing a Śrauta sacrifice for him. A son born of this marriage brings purification to eight descendants and to eight ancestors on both sides.

In the Prajāpatya form of marriage, there is a stipulation that husband and wife fulfil the Dharma together. A son born of this union will bring purification to eight descendants and to eight ancestors on both sides.

In the Ārṣa form the bridegroom gives a bull and a cow to the girl's father. A son born of this union brings purification to seven descendants and to seven ancestors on both sides.

When the lover marrys the damsel, after a mutual agreement this is called a Gāndharva marriage.

In the Āsura form the bridegroom marries the maiden after gladdening her father by money.

When a person carries away the maiden while her relatives sleep or pay no attention, it is the Paiśāca form of marriage.

When a person carries away a girl after killing her relatives and cleaving their head while she weeps, it is the Rākṣasa form of marriage.

These are the forms of marriage according to Āśvalāyana Gṛhyasūtra.[83]

These forms of marriage are very ancient. The Āśvalāyana Gṛhyasūtra was consolidated into aphorisms around 600 B.C.

Though Āśvalāyana Gṛhyasūtra describes these eight forms, Mānava Gṛhyasūtra mentions only two forms, namely, Brahma and Śaulka. It appears that even in that remote past practically only two froms of marriage were prevalent as is the practice even now.

All the law-givers provide that the first four forms are the righteous or Dharmya forms. In these forms father or some other guardian performs the Kanyādāna or the gift of the Virgin. The guardianship of father is transferred to the bridegroom through this ceremony.

Manu prescribes that the first six forms are allowed to the Brāhmaṇas and last four to Kṣatriyas and the Gāndharva; Āsura and Paiśaca to Vaiśyas and Śūdras.[84] Thus Manu prescribes even Āsura and Gāndharva forms for the Brāhmaṇas. It appears that these forms were prevalent among Brāhmaṇas, therefore Manu had to honour the custom. For Kṣatriyas Manu provides that they may marry according to Āsura, Gāndharva, Rākṣasa and Paiśaca forms; and for Vaiśyas and Śūdras, Āsura, Gāndharva and Paiśaca.

But in the next verse Manu says that sages state that the first four forms are approved in the case of Brāhmaṇa, the Rākṣasa form is fit for a Kṣatriya and the Āsura form for Vaiśya and Śūdra. Again Manu adds that the Paiśāca and the Āsura forms must never be employed. For Kṣatriyas the Gāndharva and Rākṣasa forms whether separate or mixed are permitted by the sacred tradition.[85]

The Hindu marriage rites have an ancient Indo-Iranian origin. Essentially these involve an oath taken by the bride and bridegroom in the presence of water and fire. In ancient Iran also oath was taken in front of water and blazing fire.[86]

Varapreṣaṇa is the ceremony of sending persons to negotiate for the hand of the girl. As can be seen from the Ṛgveda and Gṛhyasūtras, the bridegroom's people used to send a messenger to the the father of girl. But perhaps due to strong patriarchal values this practice faded away in course of time. Now it is the girl's father who sends the offer to the bridegroom's father.

According to the Śankhayana Gṛhyasūtra when a youth wants to acquire a wife, he should recite the Ṛgvedic hymn, 'Thornless' (Ṛgveda X. LXXXV.23) over the wooers whom he sends to the girl's father. Vāgdāna is the giving of word for marriage. As the bridegroom's companions arrive they announce their presence. Then the visitors turn their faces to west settled, they touch a vessel full of water into which flowers, puffed grain, fruits, barley and gold have been put, and racite. 'Undisturbed art thou, the undisturbable vigour of the gods, not cursed, protecting against a curse, unexposed to a curse. May I staightaway attain truth. Put me into prosperity'.[87]

Then the Acārya of the girl's family, standing up, places the vessel on her head with the verse, 'So may Prajāpati bring children forth to us' (Ṛgveda, X. LXXXV. 43) and say, 'Offspring I put into thee, cattle I put into thee, splendour and holy lustre I put into thee'.[88]

This custom is not performed now.

Mandapa-karana is making of a temporaly thatch. Pāraskara Gṛhyasūtra prescribes that marriage, tonsure, initiation, cutting of the beard and parting of the hair are to be performed outside the house in a Mandapa.[89]

Vadhugṛhagamana is going to the bride's house. According to Śāmkhāyana Gṛhyasūtra the bridegroom, who has bathed and for whom auspicious ceremonies have been performed, is escorted by happy young women who are are not widows to the girl's house. The bridegroom would behave obedient with the women except when forbidden food or a transgression is involved.[90]

In later times, perhaps due to strong patriarchy, it became customary only for males and small girls to go to the bride's father's house. However in recent times ladies also have began to be a part of the bridegroom's marriage party.

Madhuparka[91] is the offering of honey-mixture to the bridegroom. Honey is added to curds. If no honey is available clarified butter is added. A seat, the water for washing the feet, the Arghya water (that is perfumed water into which flowers have been immersed), the water for sipping, the honey-mixture, a cow are to be annouced to the bridegroom three times. The bridegroom sits down on the seat made of northward pointed grass with the verse, 'I am the highest one among my people, as the sun among the lights. Here I tread on him whosoever infests me'. Or he should sit down after he has trodden on it. He should make his host wash his feet. The right foot he should stretch out first to a Brāhmaṇa. The left to a Śūdra. When his feet have been washed, he receives the Arghya water in the hollow of his joined hands and then sips the water with the formula, 'Thou art Madhuparka' when it is brought to him with the formula, 'I look at thee with the eye of Mitra'. He accepts it with his joined hands with the formula, 'By the inpulse of the god Savitr, with the arms of the two Asvins, with the hands of Pūṣan, I accept thee'. He than takes it into his left-hand, looks at it with the three verses of Ṛgveda, 'The winds blow honey to the rightous man' (Ṛgveda, I. 90. 6-8). He takes it into his left hand, stirs it about thrice from left to right with forth finger and thumb wipes his fingers towards to the east with the formula, 'May the Vasus eat thee with the Gāyatrī metre'; with the formula 'May the Rudras eat thee with the Triṣṭubha metre,' he wipes fingers towards south; with the formula 'May the Ādityas eat thee with the Jagatī metre,' towards the west; with the formula, 'May Viśve Devas eat thee with Anuṣṭubh metre' towards the north; with the formula, 'To the Bhūtas (being) eat thee', he three times takes some of the Madhuparka from the middle of it. He should partake thereof the first time with the formula, 'The milk of Viraj art thou', for the second time with 'The milk of Virāj may I obtain', the third time with 'may in me the milk of Padya Virāj dwell'. He should not eat the whole Madhuparka, He should not satiate himself. he should give the remainder to a Brāhmaṇa towards the north. If that cannot be done, should throw it into water. Or he may eat the whole Madhuparka. Then he should take Ācamana with the water intended for it with the formula, 'thou art the covering of Ambrosia'. He sips water a second time with the formula, 'Truth. Glory. Fortune. May fortune rest on me. When he has sipped water, they announce to him the cow, having mutteured, 'Destroyed is my sin, my sin is destroyed'. If he chooses to have her killed, he says, 'Om, do it.' If he chooses to let her loose, he mutters, 'The mother of the Rudras, the daughter of ṭhe Vasus' (Ṛgveda, VIII. 101. 15). He says 'Om let her loose. Let the Madhuparka not be without flesh.'[92]

Paridhāpana is making the bride put on new clothes. After taking the permission from the women, the bridegroom gives her garments with the verse, 'Raibhi was' (Ṛgveda, X. 85. 6.).[93]

Samanjana is anointing the bride. The bridegroom takes up the salvebox with the verse, 'Mind was the cushion.' The bride should be anointed with the verse, 'May the Viśve Devas anoint.'[94]

Pratisarabandha is tying an amulet string on the bride's hand. The bridegroom gives her into her right hand the quill of a porcupine and a string of three twisted threads with the words, 'As, this has protected Sacī the beloved one and Aditi the mother of noble sons and Apālā who was free from widowhood, may he thus here protect thee, N.N.' He gives into the left hand a mirror with the verse,'In every figure he had been the model' (Ṛgveda, VI. 47. 18.). Her relations tie to her hand a red and black woollen or linen cord with three gems with the verse, 'Dark-blue and red' (Ṛgveda, X. 85. 28). The bridegroom ties to her hand Madhūka flowers with the verse, 'Full of honey the herbs'.[95]

Then the bridegroom and bride come out from the inner part of the house to the Maṇḍapa.

Parasparasamikṣaṇa is looking at each other. First of all a piece of cloth is held between the bridegroom and the bride. At the proper astrological moment it is removed and they see each other.[96] The priest makes them look at each other while the bridegroom repeats the mantras (of Ṛgveda, X. 85. 44. 41 and 37).

'With no evil eye, not bringing death to thy husband, bring luck to the cattle, be full of joy and vigour.

'Give birth to heroes, be godly and friendly. Bring us luck, to men and animals.'

'Soma obtained her first, next the Gāndharva was her lord.

Agni was thy third husband: now the fourth is thy human'.

'Soma to the Gāndharva, and to Agni the Gāndharva gave.

And Agni hath bestowed on me, riches and sons and this my spouse'.

'O Pūṣan, send her on as most auspicious, her who shall be the share of my pleasures'.

Her who shall twine her loving arms around me, and welcome all my love and mine embraces.'[97]

Some of these ceremonies are not performed in the marriage ceremonies in north India among Hindus now.

Kanyādāna is the gift of the maiden. The bridegroom having accepted her who is given away by her father, takes her and goes away from that place with the verse, 'When thou wanderest far away with thy heart to the regions of the world like the wind, may the gold-winged Vaikarṇa grant that thy heart may dwell with me. N.N.'.[98]

In the Mānava Gṛhyasūtra we find a detailed description of this rite. The father or brother should, producing auspicious sound, say thrice, 'I am giving'. In case the bridegroom is giving the marriage-fee for the bride, he should give the fee money in his joined hands and offer it to the father of the bride. The father should say, 'I am giving you for wealth'. The bridegroom should say, 'I am taking you for sons'. Here the Gotras and names of Great Grandfather of the bride and bridegroom are uttered and it is said that 'Who has given, to whom given? Kāma or desire has given to Kāma or desire. Kāma or desire is the giver, Kama or desire is the taker. May you enter in the sea of desire, I am taking you for desire.[99]

Agnisthāpanā and Homa are establishing the fire and offering of Ājya obtations into the fire. According to Āśvalāyana Gṛhyasūtra the bridegroom should offer four Ājya oblations with the three of verses, 'Agni thou purifiest life' and with the one verse, 'Prajāpati, no other one than thou (Ṛgveda, X. 121. 10.)' or oblations may be offered with the Vyāhṛtis. At the marriage the fourth oblation should be offered with the verse, 'Thou art Aryaman towards the girls'(Ṛgveda, V. 3.2.).[100]

Pāṇigrahaṇa is the taking of the hand of bride by the bridegroom. At the west of the fire there should be placed a mill-stone, to the north east of the fire a water-pot. The husband should sacrifice, while the wife takes hold of him standing, with his face turned to the west, while the wife is sitting and turns her face to the east, he should say with the formula, 'I seize thy hand for the sake of happy fortune'. He should seize her thumb if he desires that only male children may be born to him. Her other fingers, if he desire that only female children may be born to him. The hand on the hairside together with the thumb, if desirous of both male and female children.[101] The translation of the whole Mantra of Ṛgveda is the following:

> 'I take thy hand in mine for happy fortune that thou mayst reach old age with me thy husband.
>
> God, Aryaman, Bhaga, Savitar, Purandhi have given thee to be my household's mistress.'[102]

Lājāhoma is the offering of puffed rice into the fire. The Āśvalāyana Gṛhyasūtra provides that the bride should make three offerings of puffed rice while the bridegroom should recite the Mantras. The fourth offering should be made silently by the bride.[103]

Agniparināyana is the leading of the bridegroom and the bride round the fire and water jar. Probably this ceremony is the original marriage ceremony. This is a very ancient rite. It seems to have been prevelant among Aryans long before they entered the Indian sub-continent. In the Avesta also we find such a rite for taking oath in front of blazing fire and a water filled jar is provided.[104]

Aśmārohaṇa is making the bride tread on a mill-stone. The whole procedure is the following, according to Āśvalāyana Gṛhyasūtra. The bridegroom leads the bride round the fire and water jar in such a way that their right sides are turned towards the fire and water jar and mutters: 'this am I, that art thou, that art thou, this am I; the heaven I, the earth thou; the Sāman I, the Ṛk thou. Come let us here marry. Let us beget offsprings. Loving, bright, with genial mind may we live a hundred autumns'. Each time after he leads her round, he makes her tread on the stone with the words, 'Tread on this stone; like a stone be firm. Overcome the enemies, tread the foes down'. Having first poured Ājya over her hand, her brother or a person acting in her brother's place pours puffed rice twice over the bride's joined hands, and three times for the descendants of Jamadāgni. Every time she goes round the fire and water jar, she should make oblations of puffed rice, without opening her joined hands; as if she did so with the spoon called 'sruk' while the bridegroom recites the verses.

'To god Aryaman the girls have made sacrifice, to Agni, may he, god Aryaman, loosen her from this and not from that place, Svāhā.

'To god Varuṇa the girls have made sacrifice, to Agni may he, god Varuṇa, etc.

'To god Pūṣan the girls have made sacrifice, to Agni, may he, god Pūṣan etc.'

The brother pours over Ājya over what has been left of the sacrificial food. Without that leading round the fire and water jar she sacrifices with puffed rice with the neb of a basket towards herself silently a fourth time.

Then the bridegroom loosens her two locks of hair if they are made, if two tufts of wool are bound round hair on the two sides with the Rk., 'I release thee from the noose of Varuṇa' (Ṛgveda, X. 85. 24). The left one with the following Rk.[105]

This rite of Keśamocana is not performed now but the other three rites still constitute the main ceremony of Hindu marriage.

Saptapadī is taking seven steps together. The bridegroom then causes her to step forward in a north-eastern direction seven steps with the words, 'For sap with one step, for juice with two steps, for thriving of wealth with three steps, for comfort with four steps, for offspring with five steps, for the seasons with six steps. Be friend with seven steps. So be thou devoted to me. Let us aquire many sons who may reach old age.[106]

Mūrdhābhiṣeka is the sprinkling of water (from the water jar). The Acārya joins together their heads and sprinkles them with water from the water-jar.[107]

Suryodikṣaṇa is making the bride look towards the sun. The bridegroom makes her look at the sun with the mantra 'Taccakṣr'[108] (Ṛk VII. 66. 16).

Hṛdayasparśa is touching the bride's heart with a Mantra. The bridegroom touches her heart reaching over her right shoulder with the words, 'Into my will I take thy heart, thy mind shall follow my mind in my word, thou shalt rejoice with all thy heart; may Prajāpati join thee to me.[109]

Preksakanumantraṇa is addressing the sepectaors. The bridegroom recites over the bride:

> 'Auspicious ornaments does this woman wear.
> Come up to her and behold her.
> Wish her prosperity, and then
> return unto your homes again.'[110]
> (Ṛgveda,XL. XXXV. 33)

Dakṣiṇadāna is the offering of fee to the priest. To the Ācarya a fee is to be given. A Brāhmaṇa should give a cow. A king or noble should give a village. A horse should be given by a Vaiśya.[111]

According to Āśvalāyana the bride should dwell that night in the house of an old Brāhmaṇa woman whose husband is alive and whose children are alive.

Dhruvarundhatī-darśana is looking at polar star and Arundhatī at the night. When the bride sees the polar star, the star Arundhatī and the seven Ṛsis, let her break the silence and say, 'May my husband live and I get offspring.[112]

According to Āśvalāyana Gṛhyasūtra the newly married couple have to make a journey to their new home. The bridegroom should cause her to mount to the chariot with the verse,

'May Pūṣan lead thee from her holding thy hand'(Ṛgveda, X. 85. 26). If on the way the couple has to cross a river by ship the bridegroom should cause her to ascend a ship with the hemistich, 'Here flows Aśmanvatī, hold fast each other'(Ṛgveda, X. 53. 8). And he should make her descend from the ship with the following hemistich, 'There let us leave the powers that brought no profit'. If the bride weeps, the bridegroom should pronounce the verse, 'They mourn the līving, cry aloud, at sacrifice' (Ṛgveda, X. 40. 10). They should constantly carry the nuptial fire in front. At a lovely place with trees, and cross-ways let him mutter the verse, 'May no way layers meet us' (Ṛgveda, X.85. 32). On their way at every dwelling place the bridegroom should look at the looker on with the verse, 'Good luck brings this woman'(Ṛgveda, X. 85. 33).

Gṛhaprasveśa is entering the bridegroom's house. When they reach the house of the bridegroom the bridegroom should make her enter the house with the verse:

> 'Happy be thou and prosper with thy children here:
> Be vigilant to rule thy household in this home.
> Closely unite thy body with this man, thy lord:
> So shall ye full of years, address your company' (Ṛgveda, X.LXXXV. 27).

Gṛhapraveśanīya Homa is the sacrifice on entering the bridegroom's house. After placing the nuptial fire, the bridegroom should spread the bull's hide with the neck to the east, with the hair outside. The bride sits on the hide and takes hold of the bridegroom. The bridegroom makes oblations with the four verses:

> 'May Prajāpati bring children forth to us (Ṛgveda, X. 85. 43 seq.)

With the verse,

> 'May all the gods,
> So may the waters join our hearts'(Ṛgveda,X. 85. 47).

He should eat some of the curds and gives to her, or he besmears their two hearts with the rest of the Ājya of which he has sacrificed.

Triratrāvrata is keeping certain observances for three nights. From that time they should eat no saline food, they should be chaste, wear no ornaments, sleep on the ground three nights or twelve nights, or one year. According to some teachers a Ṛṣi would be born a their son. When he has fulfilled this observance, he should give the bride's shift to the Brāhmaṇa who knows the Sūrya hymn (Ṛgveda, X. 85) and food to Brāhmaṇas. Then he should cause them to pronounce auspicious words.

Though Sindura Dana is not prescribed in the Gṛhyasūtras and is not observed in some parts of India, filling the parting of the bride's hair with Sindura by the bridegroom is an important marriage rite in Uttar Pradesh, Madhya Pradesh, Bihar and Bengal. All the married women apply Sindura in the parting of their hair as long as their husbands are live, for the long life of their husband.

We find no mention of this custom in the Sūtras or Smṛtis. Probably it is a non-Aryan custom.

Mañgalasūtra Bandhana is tying a string of black-beads with golden pendant round the neck of the bride. The mention of this custom is found in the Laghu-Āśvalāyana Smṛiti.[113] It is prevalent in Mahārāṣhtra and south India even now.

Antyeṣṭi

In the antiquated past when Aryans had not entered the Indian sub-continent they buried their dead like other Indo-European people. This practice continued for some time even after they entered India. This finds explicit mention in some of hymns of the Ṛgveda. The poets says:

> 'Heave thyself, Earth, nor press thee downwards heavily: afford him easy access, gently tending him.
>
> Cover him as mother wrapes her skirt about her child, O Earth.

Now let the heaving earth be free from motion: yea, let a thousand clods remain above him.

Be they to him a home distilling fatness, here let them ever be his place of refuge.

I put the earth on thee, while over thee I place this piece of earth. May I be free from injury.

Here let the Fathers keep this pillar firm for thee, and there let Yama make thee an abiding place.'[114]

Some time later, they adopted the custom of burning their dead. The early Indo-Iranians explicitly disapproved this custom. In the Avesta, it is said that during migrations from the original land of Aryans in thirteenth settlement, Angra Mainyu or the Satan created the custom of burning of cropses.[115]

When the death approaches it is a common practice in India to remove the dying man from the bed and lay him on the earth along with the bedding. The Kauśika- Sūtra provides that when the man is losing all his strength, the persons attending the dying man should spread grass on the ground and place him on it with the hymn 'Syonasmai bhava' or O earth may you be good to this man.[116] The Baudhāyana Pitrmedha Sūtra prescribes that sand should be spread on the earth and grass should be strewn on the sand with the sharp ends ends towards south and the dying man should be placed on it. His son or someone else should repeat the Anuvāka 'Ayusah pranam santanu.'[117]

The custom of laying the dying man on earth appears to be an ancient one. It was prevalent even before Aryans had entered the Indian subcontinent. In Europe there still survives the custom of laying the dying man on the earth or on straw.[118]

When Aryans settled down in India they began to burn their dead. In the Ṛgveda we find certain hymns in which the custom of burning the body on the funeral pyre is vividly described:

'Burn him not up, nor quite consume him, Agni:

Let not his body or his skin be scattered.
O Jātavedas, when thou hast matured him
Then send him on his way unto the fathers'
When thou hast made him ready, Jātavedas,
Then do thou give him over to the Fathers.
When he attains unto the life that waits him,
He shall become the Deities' controller.
The sun receive thine eye, the wind thy spirit;
Go, as thy merit is to earth or heaven.
Go, if it be thy lot unto the water;
Go make thine home in plants with all thy members.
Thy portion is the goat; with heat consume him;
Let thy firece flame, thy glowing splendour burn him.
With thine auspicious forms, O Jātavedas,
Bear this man to the region of the pious.
Again, O Agni, to the Fathers send him who,
Offered in thee, goes with our oblations.
Wearing new life let him increase his offspring:
Let him rejoin, a body Jātavedas.
What wound soever the black bird hath inflicted,
The emmet, or the serpent or the jackal,
May who devoureth all things heal it,
And Soma who hath passed into the Brāhmaṇas.'[119]

According to Āśvalāyana Gṛhya-Sūtra, if a person who has set up the sacred Srauta fire becomes ill, he should leave his home and go away to the eastern or northern or north-eastern direction. In the next Sūtras it is asserted that 'the sacred fires are fond on the village'. Therefore the sacred fires longing for it desirous of returning to the village they might restore him to health. In case he becomes healthy he should offer a Soma sacrifice, or he may offer no sacrifice and begin to live in the village again. If he dies, one should have a piece of ground dug up to the south- east or to the south-west, which is inclined towards the south or towards the south-east according to some teachers inclined towards south-west. The piece of ground dug up should be of the length of a man with upraised arms, of the breadth of one Vyāma or fathom and of the depth of one Vitasti or span. The funeral ground should be free from all sides. There should be plenty of herbs. If there are plants with thorns and with milky juice, they should be dug out. 'From which the waters flow off to all sides', this should be a characterstic required for the funeral-ground where the body is to be burned. They should cut off from the dead body the hair, the beard, the hair of the body and the nails. They should make provision for plenty of sacrificial grass and clarified butter. The clarified butter should be poured into curds. This is the Pṛṣadājya or spinkled clarified butter used in the rites for Fathers. The relatives of deceased should carry his sacred fires and his sacrificial vessels in that direction where the ground is dug up for cermation. After this, aged persons forming an odd number, men and women not going together, carry the dead body. Some teachers say that the dead body should be carried in a seat drawn by cows. Some prescribe that a she-animal covering the dead body with its limbs should be taken to the funeral ground. It may be a cow or a she-goat of one colour or a black one. A rope should be tied to its left forefoot and lead it behind the dead body. Then the relatives of the dead persons follow - wearing their sacrificial cords round their body. Their hair-locks should be untied. The older persons should go first, younger ones afterwards. When they have arrived at the place of cremation the performer of the rites walks three times round the spot with his left side turned towards it, and with a Śami branch sprinkles water on it, with the verse, 'Go away, withdraw and depart from here'.[120] The son or the performer of the rites places the

Āhavanīya fire to the south-east on an elevated corner of that place. He places to the north west the Dakṣiṇā fire. After that a person who knows the procedure piles up between the fires a pile of fuel. After sacrificial grass and a black antelope's skin with the hair outside has been spread out there they place the dead body thereon carrying it by way of the north side of the Gārhapatya fire and turning its head towards the Āhavanīya fire. They make the wife of the deceasd lie down on the pile to the north of the dead body, and also place his bow to the north if the deceased was a Kṣatriya. The wife's brother-in-law (husband's brother) or a representative of the husband or a pupil (of the deceased) or an old servant should make her riss from the pile with the verse, 'Arise, O wife to the world of life'.[121] If a Śūdra makes her rise from the pile, the performer of the rites should mutter that verse. He takes away the bow with the verse, 'Taking the bow out of the hand of the deceased.'[122] After that he should bend the bow and break it to pieces and throw it on the pile. He should then put the following sacrificial implements on the dead body. The spoon called Juhū should be put into right hand. Into the left hand he should put the other spoon called Upabhṛt. On his right side the wooden sacrificial sword called Sphya, on his left side the Agnihotrahavanī or the ladle with which the Agnihotra oblations are scrificed should be put. On his chest the big sacrificial ladle called Dhruva should be put. On his head the dishes. On his teeth the pressing stone should be put. On two sides of his nose the two smaller sacrificial ladles called Sruva should be put. These should be broken into two pieces. On his two ears the two Prāśitraharanas or the vessels into which the portion of the sacrificial food belonging to the Brahman should be put. If there is only one Prāśitraharana he should break it in two pieces. On his belly he should put the vessel called Patri and the cup into which the cut off portions of the sacrificial food are put. On his secret parts the staff called Śamyā is put. On his thighs two kindling sticks should be put. On his legs the morter and the pestle should be put. On his feet the two winnowing basket should be put. If there is only one basket, it should be torn into pieces. Those implements which have a hollow should be filled with sprinkled butter. The son of the deceased person should take the under and upper mill-stone and the implements made of copper, iron and earthenware for himself.

Taking out the omentum of the she animal he should cover the head and the mouth of the dead person with the verse, 'Put on the armour (which will protect thee) against Agni, by (that which comes from) the cows.[123] Taking out the kidneys (of the animal) he should lay them into the hands of the dead body with the verse, 'Escape the two hounds, the sons of Sarmā,'[124] the right kidney into the right hand and the left into the left. The heart of the Animal he should put on the heart of the deceased. Some teachers prescribe that two lumps (of flour or rice) should be put if there are no kidneys. Having distributed the whole animal, limb by limb (placing its different limbs on the corresponding limbs of the deceased), and having covered it with its hide, he recites the verse when the Pranita water is carried forward, 'Agni, do not overturn this cup'.[125] Bending his left knee he should sacrifice Ājya oblations into the Daksina fire with the formulas, 'To Agni Svāhā, To Kama Svāhā, To the world Svāhā, To Anumati Svāhā'. He should offer a fifth oblation on the chest of the deceased with the formala, 'Form this one verily thou has been born. May he now be born out of thee N.N.1. To the heavenly world Svāhā'.[126] He gives the order, 'Light the fires together'. If the Ahavanīya fire reaches the body first, he should understand, 'It has reached him in the heaven world. He will live there in prosperity, and so will this one that is his son, in this world'. If the Gārhapatya fire reaches first, he should know. 'It has reached him in the air-world. He will live there in prosperity and so will his son in this world.' If Dakṣinā fire reaches (the body) first he should know, 'It has reached him in the world of men. He will live there in prosperity, and so will this one, that is his son, in this world'. If the three fires reach the body at the same moment they say that this signifies the highest luck. While the body is burning, he recites over it the same texts, 'Go on, go on the ancient paths'.[127]

Being burnt by a person who knows this, he goes to the heavenly world together with the smoke of the funeral pile thus it is understood in the Śruti. To the north-east of the Āhavanīya fire he should have a knee-deep pit dug and should have an Avakā, i.e. the water-plant called Sipala put down into it. From that pit he (the deceased) goes out and together with the smoke he goes up the the heavenly world---thus it is understood in the Śruti. After he has recited the verse, 'These living ones have separated from the dead',[128] they turn round from right to left and go away without looking back. When they have come to the place where standing water is, having once plunged into it and emerged from it, they pour out one handful of water, pronounce the Gotra name and the proper name (of the deceased), go out of the water, put on other garments wring out the old garments once lay them away with their skirts to the north, and sit down until the stars appear. Or they may enter their houses when still a part of the sun-disc is seen, the younger ones first the older ones last. When they have come to the houses, they touch a stone, the fire, cow's dung, fried barley sesamum seeds and water. Let them not cook food during that night. Let them subsist on bought or readymade food. Let them eat no saline food for three nights. Let them for twelve nights avoid the distribution of gifts and the study of Vedic texts if one of the chief Gurus has died, ten days after the death of Sapindas and of a Guru who is no Sapinda and of unmarried female relations.

The Āpastmmba Dharma Sūtra provides shaving of hair for all Sapiṇḍas that are younger than the deceased.[129]

The gathering of the bones is performed after the tenth Tithi from the death, on a Tithi with an odd number, of the dark fortnight, under a single Nakṣatra. The performer of the ceremony walks three times round the spot with his left side turned towards it and sprinkles on it with a Śamī branch milk mixed with water, with the verse, 'O cool one, O thou that art full of coolness.'[130] With the thumb and the fourth finger they should put each single bone into the urn without making a noise, the feet first and the head last. Having well gathered them and purified them with a winnowing basket, they should put the urn into a pit at a place where the waters from the different sides do not flow together, except rain water, with the verse, 'Go to thy mother Earth there.'[131] With the following verse he should throw earth into the pit. After he has done so, he should repeat the following verse, having covered the urn with a lid with the verse, 'I fasten to thee,'[132] They then should go sway without looking back, should bathe in water and perform a Śrāddha for the deceased.[133]

Notes

1. Manu Smṛti, II. 27
2. Manu Smṛti, II. 66.
3. Manu Smṛti, II. 27.
4. Viśvarūpa on Yājñavalkya I. 13.
5. Gautama Dharmasūtra, VIII.14-20.
6. Manu Smṛti, II. 16.
7. Bṛhadaraṇyaka Upaniṣad, VI. 4.13.
8. Bṛhadaraṇyaka Jpaniṣad, VI. 4. 19-20.
9. Āśvalāyana Gṛhyasūtra, I. 13. 1.
10. Śankhayana Gṛhyasūtra, I. 18.
11. Pāraskara Gṛhyasūtra, I.II.
12. Āśvalāyana Gṛhyasūtra, I. 13. 2.7.
13. Āpastamba Gṛhyasūtra, 6. 14. 9-12.
14. Atharvaveda, VII.17. 2-3.
15. Ṛgveda, II. 32. 4-5.
16. Akhilasūkta after Ṛgveda, X. 184.
17. Ṛgveda, X. 121. 10.
18. Āśvalāyana Gṛhyasūtra, I. 14.
19. Taittirīya Saṁhitā, II. 2.52-3.

20. Śatapatha Brāhmaṇa, XI. 8.3.6.
21. Bṛhadārnyaka Upaniṣad, VI. 4. 24-28.
22. Śāmkhāyana Gṛhyasūtra, I. 24, Asavalayana Gṛhyasūtra, I. 15. Pāraskara Gṛhyas sūtra, I. 16; Āpastamba Gṛhyasūtra, 6.15.
23. Maṇu Smṛti, II. 29.
24. Mantra-Brāhmaṇa, I. 5. 14.15.
25. Gobhila Gṛhyasūtra, II. 8.8-18.
26. Pāraskara Gṛhyasūtra, I. 17.4.
27. Manu Smṛti, II. 30-32.
28. Ṛgveda, I. CXXII. 14.
29. Baudhayana Gṛhya Śesasūtra, I. 12.
30. Samskāraprakāśa, p. 258.
31. Pāraskara Gṛhya sūtra, I. 17. 5-6. The verse is from Vajasaneya Saṁhitā, XXXVI. 24.
32. Manu Smṛti, II. 34.
33. Śamakhāyana Grhysūtra, I. 27. 1-3; Āśvalāyana Gṛhyasūtra, I. 16.1-3.
34. Śāmkhāyana Gṛhyasūtra, I. 27.
35. Manu Smṛti,II.34.
36. Āśvalāyana Gṛhyasūtra, I. 17.
37. Manu Smṛti,II.35.
38. Arthaśāstra of Kautilya. I. 5.
39. Aparārkapp. 30-31, Smṛti Candrika, I. p. 26.
40. Atharveveda, XI. 7.
41. Śatapatha Brāhmaṇa,XI. 5.4.
42. Gopatha Brāhmaṇa,II. 5-7.
43. This has been discussed in some details inthe chapter of Asramas.
44. Śāmkhāyana Gṛhyasūtra, II. I. 26- 28.
45. Āpastamba Gṛhyasūtra, IV. 10.9.
46. Śāmkhāyana Gṛhyasūtra, II. 1.30.
47. Śāmkhāyana Gṛhyasūtra, II. 2-9.
48. Manu Smṛti, II. 101.

49. Āpastamba Dharmasūtra I. 2.5.19; I. 3. 10.17. Manu Smṛti,II. 71.
50. Āśvalāyana Gṛhyasūtra, I. 19. 5- 7.; Baudhayana Gṛhyasūtra, III.13. 5-6; Āpastamba Gṛhyasūtra, I. 1.2.2; Manu Smṛti, II. 39; Yājñavalkya Smṛti, I. 37-38.
51. Āpastamba Dharmasūtra, I. 1.1.1. 24-27.
52. Manu Smṛti, XI. 191.
53. Manu Smṛti, XI. 211.
54. Āpastamba Dharmasūtra, I. 1.1.28. I. 1.2.18.
55. Śāmkhāyana Gṛhyasūtra, I. 28. 20.
56. Āśvalāyana Gṛhyasūtra, I. 18.1-9.
57. Manu Smṛti,II. 65.
58. Āśvalāyana Gṛhyasūtra, III. 9.4.
59. Āśvalāyana Gṛhyasūtra, III. 8-9.
60. Manu Smṛti,II.IV. 13. FF. Yājñavalkya Smṛti, I. 129-166.
61. Śatapatha Brāhmaṇa, V. 2.1.10.
62. Āpastamba Dharmasūtra, II. 5. 11. 12.
63. Mahābhārata, Adiparva, 74. 40.
64. Manu Smṛti, IX. 28.
65. Pāraskara Gṛhyasūtra, I. 4.8.11.
66. Manu Smṛti, III. 13. Yājñavalkya Smṛti, I. 56.
67. Manu Smṛti, IX. 94.
68. Gautama Dhrmasūtra, IV. 1-2.
69. Gobhila Gṛhyasūtra, III. 4.4-5.
70. Gautama Dharmasūtra, IV. 3-5.
71. Gobhila Gṛhyasūtra, III. 4.6.
72. Gautama Dharmasūtra, XVIII. 21-23.
73. Manu Smṛti,III. 4-5. Yājñavalkya Smṛti, I. 52-53.
74. Gautama Dharmasūtra XVIII. 1.20.
75. Manu Smṛti,IX. 88; and 4; Yājñavalkya Smṛti, 1.64.
76. Ṛgveda, X. LXXXV. 45.
77. Baudhāyana Dharmasūtra, IV. 1. 14.
78. Parāśara Smṛti, VII. 7-9.

79. Āśvalāyana Gṛhyasūtra, I. 5.2.
80. Yājñavalkya Smṛti, I. 54-55.
81. Nārada Smṛti, XII. 8- 18.
82. Āśvalāyana Gṛhyasūtra, I. 5.5.
83. Āśvalāyana Gṛhyasūtra, I. 6.1-8.
84. Manu Smṛti,III. 23.
85. Manu Smṛti,III. 24-26.
86. Zend-Avesta, I. Vendidad, IV. 46.
87. Śāmkhāyana Gṛhyasūtra, I. 6.1.

    It appears that this ceremony was usually performed by the bridegroom himself.
88. Śāmkhāyana Gṛhyasūtra, I. 6. 2-6.
89. Pāraskara Gṛhyasūtra, I. 4.2.
90. Śāmkhāyana Gṛhyasūtra, I. 12. 1- 2.
91. The Madhuparka is offered to honoured guests such as to priest officiating at sacrifices, to a Snātaka, to the king, the ruler of the country, to one's Acarya, father-in-law, paternal and maternal uncle, to bridegroom it is offered because he is a Snataka and most honoured.
92. Āśvalāyana Gṛhyasūtra, I. 24. 1- 33.
93. Śāmkhāyana Gṛhyasūtra, I. 12.3.
94. Śāmkhāyana Gṛhyasūtra, I. 12.5.
95. Śāmkhāyana Gṛhyasūtra, I 12. 6-9.
96. Āśvalāyana Gṛhyasūtra, pariśiṣṭa, I. 23.
97. Pāraskara Gṛhyasūtra, I. 4. 16.
98. Pāraskara Gṛhyasūtra, I. 4. 15.
99. Mānava Gṛhyasūtra, I. 8. 6-9.
100. Āśvalāyana Gṛhyasūtra, I. 4. 3-8.
101. Āśvalāyana Gṛhyasūtra, I. 7. 3-5.
102. Ṛgveda. X. LXXXV. 36.
103. Āśvalāyana Gṛhyasūtra,, I. 7. 7- 18.
104. Zend-Avesta, I. Vendidad IV. 46.
105. Āśvalāyana Gṛhya Sūtra, I.7. 19.

106. Āśvalāyana Gṛhya Sūtra, I.7.20.
107. Pāraskara Gṛhyasūtra, I.8.7.
108. Pāraskara Gṛhyasūtra, I.8.8.
109. Pāraskara Gṛhyasūtra, I.8.9.
110. Pāraskara Gṛhyasūtra, I.8.14.17.
111. Āśvalāyana Gṛhya Sūtra, I.7. 21- 22.
112. Āśvalāyana Gṛhya Sūtra, I.8. 1- 14.
113. Laghu Āśvalāyana Smṛti, 15. 33.
114. Ṛgveda, X 11-13.
115. The Zend-Avesta I. Vendidad. I. 17.
116. Kauśika Sūtra LXXX. 3.
117. Baudhayana Pitrmedha Sūtra, III. 1. 18.
118. Prof. Edgerten, 'The hour of death', *Aunals of the Bhandarkar Oriental Research Institute,* Vol. VII 219-249.
119. Ṛgveda, x, xvi. 1-6.
120. Ṛgveda, x. 14. 9.
121. Ṛgveda, X. 18.8.
122. Ṛgveda, X. 18.9.
123. Ṛgveda, X. 16.7.
124. Ṛgveda, X. 14.10.
125. Ṛgveda, X. 16.8.
126. Vajsaneya Samhita, XXXV. 22.
127. Ṛgveda, X.14.7.
128. Ṛgveda, X.18.3.
129. Āpastamba Dharmasūtra, I. 3. 10. 6.
130. Ṛgveda, X. 16.14.
131. Ṛgveda, X. 18.10.
132. Ṛgveda, X. 18.13.
133. Āśvalāyana Gṛhyasūtra, IV. 1-5.

VII

The Āśramas

We do not find the term Āśrama in Vedas or the Brāhmaṇa Granthas. However in the Taittirīya Brāhmaṇa human life is described as having four parts.[1] Āpastamba speaks of four Āśramas. But their names and sequence are not the same as became prevalent later. These are Gārhasthya or the stage of householder; Ācāryakula or staying in teacher's house; Mauna or stage of being a Muni and Vānaprasthya or stage of living in woods.[2] The Gautama Dharmasūtra speaks of four Āśramas in the same sequence which came to be traditionally established. Brahmacārī or student, Gṛhastha or householder, Bhikṣu or ascetic and Vaikhānasa or hermit in the woods.[3] The Baudhāyana Dharma Sūtra also enumerates four Āśramas. These refer to Brahmacārī or student; Gṛhastha or householder; Vānaprastha and Parivrājaka[4]. After discussing the four Āśramas Baudhāyana says that there is only one order because in other orders people do not beget offsprings. He makes a rather surprising observation that 'there was forsooth, an Asura, Kapila by name, the son of Prahlāda. Striving with gods, he made these divisions. A wise man should not take heed of them'.[5] Gautama also says that since the order of householder is explicity prescribed (in the Vedas) therefore the venerable teacher (prescribes) only one order.[6]

It appears that the system of Āśramas has a non-Aryan origin. In the Ṛgveda we find a hymn in which the priest exhorts the newly married couple to live in the house happily with sons and grandsons.[7] Thus, in the Ṛgveda, we do not find mention of Vānaprastha or Sannyāsa. Manu speaks of four Āśramas. These are Brahmacarya, Gṛhastha, Vānaprastha and Sannyāsa. Human life is conceived to be of one hundred years. It is divided into four equal parts for four stages of life.

Brahmacarya Āśrama

In the Atharvaveda we find the mention of Upanayana or initiation for the first time, nearly with all its main features. From the initiation starts the Brahmacarya Āśrama. The ceremony of initiation seems to be very ancient. It may have already been practised by the Aryans when they had not entered the Indian sub-continent. We find the ceremony of initiation among the Parsis also. In the Ṛgveda, the word Brahmacārī occurs for Bṛhaspati when he wanders without his wife.[8] Thus, it indicates that during studentship the student had to live the life of celibacy. In the Atharvaveda, the Sun is described as a Brahmacārī. It describes that he wears a girdle, offers fuel sticks on the fire, wears the skin of black antelope, has a long beard; and it is said that he takes birth again by initiation.[9] In the Taittirīya Samhitā of black Yajurveda we find the story of Nābhānediṣṭha, the son of Manu, who was student and was deprived of the property by his father.[10] We find no mention of begging and the teaching of Sāvitrī in the Samhitās.

In the Brāhmaṇa Granthas also we get a description of the stage of Brahmacarya. In the Taittirīya Brāhmaṇa we find the story of Bhāradvāja who remained a Brahmacārī for three parts of his life. But Indra commented that despite the long period spent in the Brahmacarya stage, what he had mastered out of the Vedas was as insignificant as three handfuls out of three mountains. The Vedas are endless.[11] In this story, though the four Āśramas are not mentioned, human life is described as having four parts.

The Śatapatha Brāhmaṇa describes the ceremony of Upanayana or initiation in a elaborate way. We find the various duties prescribed for a Brahmacārī or a student. These are teaching Sāvitrī Mantra, serving in teacher's house, begging for alms, putting fuel-sticks on the fire, not sleeping during day and not taking honey. A student is called Antevāsī or one who lives near a teacher in Śatapatha Brāhmaṇa.[12]

The proper age for entering the Brahmacarya Āśrama differs according to the Varṇa of the boy. According to Āśvalāyana Gṛhya Sūtra a Brāhmaṇa should be initiated in the eighth year after the conception. The maximum age limit for performing initiation of a Brāhmaṇa is sixteen years. He should wear an antelope skin or a reddish yellow garment. He should wear the girdle of Muñja grass and take the staff of Palāśa wood.

A Kṣatriya boy should be initiated in the eleventh year after the conception. The maximum limit for performing initiation of a Kṣatriya boy is the twenty-second year. He should wear the skin of a spotted deer or a light red garment. His girdle should be made of bow-string. His staff should be made of Udumbara wood.

A Vaiśya boy should be initiated in the twelfth year. The maximum limit for performing initiation of a Vaiśya boy is twenty-four. He should wear a goat skin or a yellow garment. His girdle should be made of wool. His staff should be of Bilva wood.[13]

Manu follows the Sūtras. But in the very next verse he provides even lesser age for all the three higher Varṇas. He says that in case a Brāhmaṇa desires proficiency in sacred learning his initiation should be performed in the fifth year after conception, that of a Kṣatriya who wishes to become powerful in the sixth, and that Yajñopavīta of a Vaiśya who longs for success in his business in the eighth.[14]

Wearing Yajñopavīta is an essential feature of initiation since ancient times. The Parsis also wear a sacred cord like Yajnopavīta. In the Taittirīya Samhitā we find the mention of sacred cord.[15] The Taittirīya Brāhmaṇa and Śatapatha Brāhmaṇa also mention it.[16] The Gṛhyasūtras of Gobhila and Khadira prescribe that an initiated student should take as his Yajñopavīta a cord or a garment or simply a rope of Kuśa grass. When the cord is suspended over his left shoulder, so that it hangs down on his right side he becomes Yajñopavitin. When the cord is suspended over his right shoulder, so that it hangs down on his left side, he becomes Prācīnavitin. Being Prācīnavitin he offers sacrifices to the Manes.[17] The Āpastamba Dharma Sūtra provides that a householder must always wear a garment over his left shoulder and under his right arm; or he may use a cord instead of a garment.[18] Baudhāyana provides that the sacred cord should be made of Kuśa grass or cotton and should consist of thrice three strings.[19]

Manu prescribes different types of sacred cords for the persons of different Varṇas. The sacred cord of a Brāhmaṇa should be made of cotton, should be twisted to the right, and consist of three threads, that of a Kṣatriya of hempen threads and that of Vaiśya of woollen threads.[20]

Teaching of Sāvitrī is also an essential feature of initiation. The Śatapatha Brāhmaṇa mentions it.[21] All the teachers of Dharma Sūtras follow this.

The initiated student should wear two garments. The Pāraskara, Āśvalāyana and Baudhāyana Gṛhyasūtras prescribe that the upper garment of a Brāhmaṇa should be the skin of black deer for Kṣatriya the skin of Rūrū deer and for a Vaiśya the skin of a cow or a goat. Baudhāyana and Āśvalāyana prescribe only the skin of goat for a Vaiśya.[22] According to Pāraskara Gṛhyasūtra if a suitable skin can not be secured the cow skin should be employed by students of all Varṇas.[23]

The student should avoid certain things, some for short time, others during the whole period of studentship. The

Āśvalāyana Gṛhyasūtra prescribes that for three nights or twelve nights or a year after initition the student should not eat 'Kṣāra' and 'Lavaṇa' and should sleep on the ground.[24] Baudhāyana, Bhārdwāja, Pārskara and Khadira Gṛhyasūtras also provide similarly.[25]

The period of studentship may last for forty-eight years, or twenty-four years or twelve years or until the student has learnt the Vedas according to Hiraṇyakeśin Gṛhyasūtra.[26] Manu provides that a student should study thirty years or eighteen years or nine years or until he has perfectly learnt the Vedas.[27]

According to the Śānkhāyana Gṛhyasūtra, the daily putting on of fuel, going for alms, sleeping on the ground and obedience to the teacher are the standing duties of a student.[28] Other Sūtras make a similar provision. Manu follows them. He provides that a student should offer fuel in sacred fire, beg for food, sleep on the ground, offer libations of water to the gods, sages and manes.[29]

The student should say Saṁdhyā prayer in the morning and evening according to the Āśvalāyana Gṛhyasūtra.[30] Manu prescribes that a student should perform prayer standing during morning and sitting in the evening. He should keep all his organs and mind, under control.[31] Later Smṛti writers follow Manu.

Gṛhastha Āśrama

Gautama calls householdership as the source of all Āśramas or orders because only in this order offsprings are produced, in others people do not procreate.[32] Baudhāyana makes a similar provision and quotes passages from Vedas for support.[33] In the Ṛgveda we find: 'May we, O Agni attain immortality through progeny.'[34] In the Taittirīya Samhitā it is said : 'A Brāhmaṇa when born owes three debts, he owes Brahmacarya to the sages, sacrifice to the gods and progeny to his ancesters.'[35]

Manu follows the Dharmasūtras. He provides: 'As all living creatures subsist by receiving support from air, similarly people of all orders subsist by receiving support from the householder.' Manu declares the order of householder the most exalted. He says: 'Because men of the three orders are daily supported by the householder with gifts of sacred knowledge and food therefore the order of householder is the most excellent order.'[36] Gautama provides that the householder should worship gods, manes, men, beings and Ṛsis. It is obligatory on him to recite a portion of the Vedas daily and to offer libation of water to the manes. Other rites than these he may perform according to his ability. The sacred fire must be kindled on his marriage or on the division of the family estate. The domestic rituals are to be performed in that fire.[37]

Āpastamba provides that food of a householder for Vaiśvadeva should be prepared by the persons of the first three Varṇas. But in a following verse he provides that even a Śūdra may prepare food under the superintendence of men of the first three Varṇas. The nails and hair of Śūdra cooks should be cut daily or on eighth day or on the days of the full and new-moon. In case the Śūdra cook prepares without supervision the food should be kept on fire and should be spinkled with water.[38]

Manu also provides that with the sacred fire kindled at the wedding a householder should perform domestic ceremonies and five great sacrifices and should cook his food. He also gives an explanation for the daily performance of the five great sacrifices. He says that the householder has five slaughter houses: the hearth, the grinding stone, the broom the pestle and mortar, the water-vessel---by using these he is bound by the fetters of sin. In order to successfully expiciate the sin committed by means of all these five slaughter houses the great sages have prescribed for householders the daily performance of the five great sacrifices.[39] It appears that Manu was influenced by Buddhists and Jain religions, because in the earlier texts we do not find such explanations for atoning the guilt for killing creatures even unknowingly.

Gautama provides that the householder should make gifts

to the persons of the Brāhmaṇa Varṇa begging for their teachers or in order to defray the expenses of their wedding or for medicine for the sick, to those who are without means of subsistence, to those who are going to offer a sacrifice, to those engaged in study, to travellers and to those who have performed the Viśvajit sacrifice.[40] But he should not give anything for unlawful purposes even though he may have made such a promise.[41] Āpastamba also provides similarly.[42]

A householder is expected to feed his dependents before he takes his meal. Gautama and Āpastamba provide that the householder should feed his guests, the infants, the sick people, the pregnant women, the females under his protection, the very aged men and those of low condition.[43] But when especial guests like teacher, parents, friends visit his house, he should ask for orders before the preparation of the dinner.[44] According to Gautama and Āpastamba, when an officiating priests, his teacher, his father-in-law, paternal or maternal uncles visit him Madhuparka or honey-mixture must be offered to them. If they have been once hououred in this manner, the ceremony need be repeated only after a year.[45] Manu adds a king, Snātaka and son-in-law to the list.[46] It appears that honouring son-in-law is a later development.

Vānaprastha

Vanaprastha is the third stage of life. Manu says that when a householder sees his skin wrinkled, and his hair white and the sons of his sons, then he may resort to the forest. He should abandon all food raised by cultivation and all his belongings. His wife may either accompany him or she may live with his sons. He should take with him the sacred fire and the implements required for domestic sacrifices. He should live in the forest duly controlling his senses.[47]

Gautama provides that while living in the forest the Vānaprasthī should subsist on roots and fruits and should practice austerities.[48] He should eat wild growing vegetables only and he should worship gods, manes, men, beings and Risis, according to Gautama Dhrmasūtra. Manu follows him.[49] Gautama Dharmasūtra also provides that a Vānaprasthī may even use the flesh of animals killed by carnivorous beasts.[50]

Gautama prescribes that he should wear a skin or a tattered garment. He should take bath in the evening or in the morning. He should always wear his hair in braids, the hair on his body, his beard and his nails being unclipped.[51] Manu follows Gautama. At another place Manu provides that he should take bath thrice daily-in the morning, at noon and in the evening. Yājnavalkaya also makes a similar provision.[52]

The Vānaprasthī should not eat anything grown on ploughed land, though it may have been thrown away by somebody, nor roots and fruits grown in a village though he may be tormented by hunger.[53] The Vānaprasthī may store sufficient food for a months or for a year.[54] According to Āpastamba Dharmasūtra, he should throw away his old grain in the month of Āśvin. Manu and Yājnavlkya Smṛtis follow this.[55]

Manu says that a Vānaprasthī may live according to the rules of the Cāndrāyaṇa Vrata or lumar penance, daily diminishing the quantity of his food in the bright half of the month and increasing it in dark half or he may eat on the last days of each fortnight, once a day only, and that too boiled barley-gruel.[56] The Āpastamba Dharmasūtra provides that the Vānaprasthī may live on water and then on air. Manu follows this. According to Manu he should continue this practice until his body sinks to death.[57] It a kind of sucide, the reason for making such provision could be the asceticism propagated by the Buddhists and the Jains. In order to combat the influence on these heterodox sects the Brāhmaṇa elites took over many of their ideas pertaining to non-violence and ascetism which made them venerable among the people, thus taking out the wind from there sails.

Sannyāsa

Sannyāsa is the fourth stage of human life. According to Āpastamba Dharmasūtra, in this stage the Sannyāsī should live without a fire, without a house, without pleasures, without protection. Remaining silent and uttering speech only on the occasion of the daily recitation of the Vedas, begging so much food only in the village as will sustain his life, he should wander about neither caring for this world nor for the heaven.[58]

Gautama says that an ascetic shall not possess any store. He must be chaste. He must not change his residence during the rainy season. He should enter a village only in order to beg. He should beg late after people have finished their meal, without returning twice, abandoning all desires for sweet food. He should wear a cloth to cover his nakedness. Some declare that he should wear an old rag after having washed it.[59] Āpastamba and Baudhāyana make a similar provision.[60] Āpastamba further adds that abandoning truth and falsehood, pleasure and pain, the Vedas, this world and the next, he should seek the Ātaman. But Āpastamba asserts that this opinion is opposed to the Śāstras. Because if salvation were obtained by the knowledge of the Ātaman alone then he ought not feel any pain even in this world.[61]

Baudhāyana disapproves the last two orders. He says that only studentship and the order of householder are to be followed by people. One who praises other orders 'becomes dust and perishes.[62]

Manu says that a twice-born person should enter the order of Sannyāsa only after studying Vedas having begotten sons and having offered sacrifices. He should offer Prājāpatya sacrifice, give all his property as the sacrificial fee and then he should become a Sannyāsī.[63]

Manu follows the Dharma Sutras and lays down the proper conduct of a Sannyasī. He prescribes that a Sannyasī should neither possess a fire nor a dwelling, he may go to a village for his food, he should be indifferent to everything, firm of purpose, meditating and concentrating his mind on Brahman: 'A potsherd instead of an alms-bowl, the roots of trees for a dwelling, coarse worn-out garments, life in solitude and indifference towards everything are the marks of one who has attained liberation.'[64]

It seems that the Manu Smṛti was also influenced by the Jain doctrine. It is provided in the Manu Smṛti that a Sannyāsī should drink water after straining it with a cloth.[65] His hair, nails and beard being unclipped, carrying an alms-bowl, a staff, and a water-pot, let him continually wander about controlling himself and not injuring any creatures.[66]

Following Gautama Dharmasūtra, Manu prescribes that a Sannyāsī should always go to beg when no smoke ascends from the kitchen , when the pestle lies motionless, when the embers have been extinguished, when the people have finished their meal, when the remanants in the dishes have been removed.[67] Manu says that a Sannyāsī should not desire to die, let him not desire to live; let him wait for his appointed time, as a servants for the payment of his wages.[68]

A Sannyāsī is expected to remain always alone. Dakṣa Smṛti prescribes that a Sannyāsī should remain lone because if they are two, they would form a pair; if they are three, they are like a village; and if more than three live together, they become like a town. A Sannyāsī should not form a pair or village or a town; by doing so he swerves from his Dharma, because then a Sannyāsī would talk about the ruler, about the alms obtained and due to closeness, sentiments of affection, jealousy would arise among them. Bad ascetics undertake many activities interpreting texts for gaining money or honour and gathering pupils around them. There are four actions for a Sannyāsī: meditation; purity, begging and remaining alone.[69] Smṛtimuktāphala quotes Vyāsa who forbids Sannyāsa on the ground of its having become a Kali-Varjya or forbiddened in the Kali age.[70] These last two orders appear to be of non-Aryan origin. The first inkling of the Vānasprastha Āśrama is found in the Chāndogya Upaniṣad as Yājnavalkya wants to distributes his property among his wives. It is well known that the Upaniṣads represent a revolt against the Brahmanical supremacy and orthodoxy.

Notes

1. Taittirīya Brāhmaṇa, III. 10.11.
2. Āpastamba Dharmasūtra, II. 9.21.1.
3. Gautama Dharmasūtra, III. 2.
4. Baudhāyana Dharmasūtra, II. 6. 11. 12.
5. Baudhāyana Dharmasūtra, II. 6. 11. 26-27.
6. Gautama Dharmasūtra, III. 36.
7. Ṛgveda, X. LXXXV. 42.
8. Ṛgveda, X. 109. 5.
9. Atharvaveda, XI. 46.
10. Taittirīya Saṁhita, III. 9.5.
11. Taittirīya Brāhmaṇa, III. 10. 11.
12. Śatapatha Brāhmaṇa, XI. 5.4.1-17, XI. 3.3.3-6.
13. Āśvalāyana Gṛhyasūtra, I. 19. 1- 13.
14. Manu Smṛti, II.37.
15. Taittirīya Brāhmaṇa, II. 5.11.1.
16. Taittirīya Brāhmaṇa, I. 6. 8; Śatapatha Brāhmaṇa, II. 4. 2.1.
17. Gobhila Gṛhyasūtra, I. 2. 1-4; Khadira Gṛhyasūtra, I. 4-6.
18. Āpastamba Dharmasūtra, II. 2. 4.21- 22.
19. Baudhāyana Dharmasūtra, I. 5. 8. 5.
20. Manu Smṛti, II.44.
21. Śatapatha Brāhmaṇa, XI.5.4.1-17.
22. Pāraskara Gṛhyasūtra, II. 5. 16. Āśvalāyana Gṛhyasūtra, I. 17.10. Baudhāyana Gṛhyasūtra, II. 5. 16.
23. Pāraskara Gṛhyasūtra, II. 5.
24. Āśvalāyana Gṛhyasūtra, I. 22. 17.
25. Baudhāyana Gṛhyasūtra, Ii. 5.55, Bhārdvaja Gṛhyasūtra, I. 10; Parakara Gṛhyasūtra, II. 5. Khadira Gṛhyasūtra, II. 4. 33.
26. Hiranyakeśin Gṛhyasūtra, I. 28. 14.
27. Manu Smṛti, III. 1.
28. Śānkhāyana Gṛhyasūtra, II. 6. 8.

29. Manu Smṛti, II. 108, 176.
30. Āśvlāyana Gṛhyasūtra, III. 7. 3-6.
31. Manu Smṛti, II. 100-101.
32. Gautama Dharmasūtra, III. 3.
33. Baudhāyana Dharmasūtra, II. 6. 11. 27, 33.
34. Ṛgveda, V. IV. 10.
35. Taittirīya Samhitā, VI. 3. 10. 5.
36. Manu Smṛti, III. 77-78.
37. Gautama Dharmasūtra, V. 3-8.
38. Āpastamba Dharmasūtra, II. 2.3.1-9.
39. Manu Smṛti, III. 67-69.
40. Gautama Dharmasūtra, V. 21.
41. Gautama Dharmasūtra, V. 23.
42. Āpastamba Dharmasūtra. II. 5. 10. 1-3.
43. Gautama Dharmasūtra, V. 25; Āpastamba Dharmasūtra, II. 2. 4. 11-12.
44. Gautama Dharmasūtra, V. 26.
45. Gautama Dharmasūtra, V. 27. Āpastamba Dharmasūtra, II. 4. 8. 6-7.
46. Manu Smṛti, III. 119.
47. Manu Smṛti, VI. 2-4.
48. Gautama Dharmasūtra, III. 26.
49. Gautama Dharmasūtra, III. 28-29, Manu Smṛti, VI. 5.
50. Gautama Dharmasūtra, III. 31.
51. Gautama Dharmasūtra, III. 34; Manu Smṛti, VI.6.
52. Manu Smṛti, VI. 22. 24. Yājñ avalkya Smṛti, III. 48.
53. Manu Smṛti, VI. 16.
54. Manu Smṛti, VI. 18.
55. Āpastamba Dharmasūtra, I. 9. 22. 24. Manu Smṛti, VI. 15, Yajnavalkya Smṛti, III. 47.
56. Manu Smṛti, VI. 20.
57. Āpastamba Dharmasūtra, II. 8. 23. 2. Manu Smṛti, VI. 31.

58. Āpastamba Dharmasūtra, II. 9.21.10.
59. Gautama Dharmasūtra, III.11-19.
60. Āpastamba Dharmasūtra, II. 9.11-12; Baudhāyana Dharmasūtra, II. 6. 11. 19, 22.
61. Āpastamba Dharmasūtra, II. 9. 21. 13-16.
62. Badhayana Dharmasūtra, II. 6. 11. 33-34.
63. Manu Smṛti, VI. 36-38.
64. Manu Smṛti, VI. 43-44.
65. Manu Smṛti, VI. 46.
66. Manu Smṛti, VI. 52.
67. Manu Smṛti, VI. 56.
68. Manu Smṛti, VI. 45.
69. Dakṣa Smṛti, VII. 34-38.
70. Smṛtimuktāphala, Varnāśrama. p. 76.

VIII

The Position of Woman: Socio-Cultural Compulsives of Attitude Towards Woman

The status a society assigns to woman largely depends upon the basic structure of that society itself. While considering the emergence of the traditional social structure in India, we have seen how diverse struggling racial groups became parts of an integrated hierarchial society in which the invading immigrants formed the elite stratum. We have also seen how the values of the elite stratum were imposed on the integrated culture that emerged as a result of this interaction, and how the immigrants suffering from a deep-seated feeling of insecurity performed various rites and rituals to ward off the fear of extermination. The womenfolk belonging to a stock which was racially and culturally different were regarded inimical and given a low position. Due to extraneous origin of womenfolk a feeling of suspicion against them was deeply ingrained in the society.

In India from the earliest times many races entered and settled. The Aryans entered the Indian sub-continent in the second millenium B.C. They fought with the earlier settlers and ultimately settled down in India. Like all invading hordes the Aryans were short of women. They had to take women from the earlier settlers who were their enemies. Though they married these women, they could not completely shed their suspicion and disdain for them. This matrix seems to be considerably responsible for the shape that traditional attitudes towards woman took. The circumstances were such that it was natural for the victorious Aryans to be suspicious of their wives who were enslaved forcefully by them. Thus, the low assessment of woman became embedded in the very roots of traditional Indian thought and social structure.

Among the earlier settlers the position of woman was not very low. Among the early Ṛgvedic Aryans too the status of woman was not so low as it became later. We find about twenty Ṛśikās or woman poets in the Ṛgveda itself. It is true that some of them appear to be mythical personages but many of them must be real persons. In any case accepting women as composers of sacred lore is indicative of a high status accorded to woman by that society. Thus, during the early Ṛgvedic era, the women enjoyed a position which was not very much lower than that of man. But after the Aryans settled in India, and took women from the subjugated people as their wives, the picture altogether changed.

It appears that among pre-Aryan settlers woman occupied a position which was somewhat equal to that of man. Woman fought in the battlefield together with menfolk. In the Ṛgveda, Indra refers to Dāsa Śambara with contempt, because his army consisted of women soldiers: 'The Dāsa Śambara has made woman his instrument; What can his *Abalā* or vigorless army do to mine?'[1] The word *'Abalā'* became a synonym for woman, and this use of the word is current even now.

Even in the Ṛgveda we find certain disparaging remarks about woman. The poet asserts that 'Indra has ordained that women have non-controllable minds, therefore they must see downwards not upwards.'[2] Urvaśī consoles Pururavas with the words that the friendship of woman does not last; they have the hearts of hyenas.[3]

During the period of their expansion, the Aryans abducted

women on a large scale from the subjugated enemy as war booty, and turned them into wives. It is remarkable that the word *'Vadhu'* is used both for bride and female slave in Ṛgveda.[4] The following general principle enuncinted in Atharvaveda supports this hypothesis : 'When a Brāhmaṇa grasps the hand of woman, though she be married, she becomes his wife.'[5]

The racial admixture of the Ṛgvedic Aryans was vehemently disaproved by the Iranian Aryans, the close cousins of the Ṛgvedic Aryans. The Avesta alludes to this admixture when it calls it the birth of abnormal issues to women.[6] In the Pahlavi texts we find the myth that Yim (Yama in Sanskrit) took a demoness as wife and gave Yimuk, his sister, to a demon as wife; and from them have originated the tailed ape and bear.[7]

Many hymns of the Ṛgveda expressly mention the existence of polygamy. Aryans aspired for many wives. Their gods and kings or tribal leaders aided them in the fulfilment of this wish. Many hymns praise the two Aśvins for providing good consorts. For example, 'they made Cyavana the husband of many maidens.'[8] Similarly king Trasdasyu gave fifty brides to Sorabhi at the bank of Suvāstu river.[9] Vaśiṣṭha also got many brides seated on two chariots from king Sudāsa.[10] However, the unenviable plight of a man with many wives also finds vivid portrayal. A husband of many wives is compared to a man who had fallen in a well; for he is obstructed and made miserable from many sides.[11]

The feeling of rivalry among co-wives is well reflected in Vedic hymns. These hymns are very near to folksongs in their content and tenor. Feminine jealousy finds forceful expression. We find mention of certain herbs which are supposed to have the magical power of keeping away the other co-wife from the husband's favour. Indrānī, the archetypical woman, gives vent to her feelings thus :

> 'I dig out this most potent drug,
> Through which a co-wife is obstructed and the husband is won.

O, the beloved of gods strong, beautiful, and one whose leaves are up,

May you keep away my co-wife so that the husband may belong only to me.

O the best one may I be the best,

May I be the best among the best.

While my co-wife be the lowest among the low,

I do not speak her name, I do not like that person;

I send the co-wife even farther than far away.

O herb I am strong and so art thou;

May both of us, being strong, crush my co-wife.'[12]

In the Atharvaveda a wife who has taken over all the possessions of the co-wife wishes that the co-wife may not come back from her parents' house:

'I am taking all the property of that wretch (co-wife),

All the riches, as if I am making a garland of of flowers from the tree;

Just as a big mountain with its large base stands there forever,

May she too for ages get stuck in her parents' house.'

Her envious sentiments find no limit. She seeks the help even of the god of death in her mission :

'O Yama, my that woman be capable of becoming your wife,

Till then may she remain fortunate with her mother, with her father, with her brother.'[13]

Certain hymns of Ṛgveda portray the woman as proud, dominant, and full of vigour:

'The sun arose (as though) my luck arose,

Knowing that I the victorious one, control my husband.

I am ardent and I speak beautifully,

My husband follows me.

My sons are killers of enemy, my daughter is brilliant.

I am the best winner, my husband has the best hymns for me.'[14]

The later Vedic literature inherited the norms of Ṛgveda. The Taittirīya Saṁhitā justified polygamy in a very simple way on the basis of ritual: 'He ties two ropes to the sacrificial post, therefore a man marries two wives; he does not tie one rope on two sacrificial posts, therefore a wife does not marry two husbands'.[15] Similarly, the Aitareya Brāhmaṇa says: 'Therefore a person marries many wives but a wife cannot have many husbands.'[16] The Śatapatha Brāhmaṇa mentions four categories of wives for a king. These are: Mahiṣī or consecreated queen, Vāvātā or the fovourite queen, Parivṛktā or the discarded queen, and Palāgalī or the low caste queen.[17]

The position of woman shows a perceptible decline with the passage of time. The Taittirīya Saṁhitā says: 'Woman is without senses, not capable of inheriting, and lower even to sinful man.'[18] She is not recognized as a legal person. The feeling of suspicion towards the fidelity of the wife also finds expression. Maitrāyaṇī Saṁhitā says that : 'Woman is falsehood because though bought by her husband she lives with others'. The same Saṁhitā provides that the Sabhā (assembly) should not be attended by women.[19]

In the Śatapatha Brāhmaṇa during the performance of the Varunapraghāsa[20] offerings the sacrificer's wife has to confess her extraconjugal relationships before the Pratiprasthatṛ priest. The priest leads the scrificer's wife aside. 'He asks her, 'with whom holdest thou intercourse?' Now when a woman who belongs to one (man) carries on intercourse with another, she undoubtedly commits (a sin) against Varuṇa. He therefore asks her thus, lest she should sacrifice with a secret pang in her mind; for when confessed the sin becomes less since it becomes truth, this is why he thus asks her. And whatever (connection) she confess not, that indeed will turn out injurious to her relatives'.[21] The underlying principle is that confession before the priest destroys or reduces the sin.[22]

Chastising womenfolk seems to be a normal practice. In Śatapatha Brāhmaṇa it is asserted that even the gods used to do this occasionally; therefore men should also do likewise. The Śatapatha Brāhmaṇa states : '*Ghee*' or clarified butter is a thunderbolt, and by that thunderbolt, the *ghee,* the gods smote their wives and unmanned them; and thus smitten and unmanned they neither owned any self nor did they own (have right to) any inheritance. And in like manner does he now, by that thunderbolt, the *ghee,* smites the wives and unmans them; and thus smitten and unmanned, they neither own any self nor do they own any inheritance.'[23]

But the picture changes in the Upaniṣads. The Upaniṣads represent a revolt again Vedic orthodoxy. We find a number of women scholars in the Upaniṣads. These scholars participated in metaphysical discussions. In the Bṛhadāraṇyka Upaniṣad we find that Gārgī asks so many questions of a profound and esoteric nature that Yājñavalkya loses his patience and says: 'O Gārgī, Do not ask too much lest thy head should fall off. Thou asketh too much about a deity about which we are not to ask too much.'[24] But Gārgī challenges Yājñavalkya : 'As the son of a warrior from Kāśis or Videhas might string his looseded bow, take two pointed foe-piercing arrows in his hand and rise to engage in battle, I have risen to fight thee with two questions.' Yājñavalkya explains the character of the ultimate reality to her satisfaction.[25] Not only women philosophers like Gārgī, but some housewives also showed their keen interest in the newly emerged metaphysical thought. Instead of taking property, Maitreyī, the wife of Yājñavalkya, preferred to know the way to immortality from her departing husband.[26]

Due to strong patriarchal society the birth of a daughter is considered a misfortune in the Vedas and later literature. But in Upaniṣads we find a ritual for having the birth of a learned daughter, in addition to the rituals for the birth of sons.[27]

The picture, however, changes in the Gṛhya Sūtras. The Gṛhya Sūtras appear to be a systematic effort of the priestly elites to revive the pre-Upaniṣadic Vedic tradition. In the Upaniṣadic era the women seem to enjoy a position similar to that of the men. But the Gṛhya Sūtras revived the norms of the later Vedic literature. In the marital and post-marital rituals prescribed in Gṛhya Sūtras, the feeling of suspicion towards the wife finds an even stronger expression. The wife is supposed to bring some evil elements with her, which can harm her husband, his forthcoming progeny, cattle, house and fame. Apprehending these dangers, the husband performs ritual and prayers to direct these elements towards his wife's earlier lover or spouse. On the fourth day after the marriage ceremony, before the consummation of marriage, a fire sacrifice is made in which after offering each oblation the husband pours the remainder of the oblation into the water pot, and out of that pot he sprinkles it on her head with the words: 'The evil substance which dwells in thee that brings death to thy husband, death to thy children, death to cattle, destruction to the house, destruction of fame that I change into one that brings death to thy paramour. Thus live with me to old age.'[28]

The desire to secure male child finds strong expression in the Gṛhya Sūtras. We find many pre-natal rituals for securing a male child. Puṁsvana is the chief sacrament for having male offsprings. It is be performed when the stars are of the male gender. During the sacrament of Sīmantonnyna, all the implements that are to be used should be (that is, have the names) of the male gender.

During the Ṛgvedic era, Aryans used to take the women of the non-Aryan subjugated people. But Aryan women were never given in marriage to non-Aryans. However, during the Upaniṣadic era some kings gave their daughters in marriage to persons belonging to lower Varṇas, in gratitude for the higher knowledge received from the latter. Again through the Sūtra literature hypergamy was revived. Sūtras recommend hypergamous marriages along with the marriages in one's own Varṇa. Thus, a Brāhmaṇa can marry three wives of three lower Varṇas along with one of the Brāhmaṇa Varṇa.

We can witness the gradually lowering position of woman through the successive texts. In the Vedas men used to acquire wives without any guilt just by grasping their hands, though they be already married. They did not mind the existence of their former husbands. In the Brāhmaṇas, during ritual the wives had to confess their extramarital relations, if any. In the Gṛhya Sūtras it is presumed that every woman had a lover who wanted to harm the husband and his property. To forestall this threat the husband had to seek the help of various gods. In the Smṛtis, despite the fact that marriage of girls is recommended at a very tender age, we find a great deal of suspicion about the character of women.

The essential attitude towards a daughter which still prevails in Indian society seems to have taken shape long ago. The birth of a daughter was considered undesirable in the later Vedic times just as it is regarded even now. In many later Vedic texts we find derogatory remarks regarding the daughter. The Taittirīya Saṁhitā says: 'The daughter is left aside after she takes birth while the son is gladly accepted.'[29] The Aitareya Brāhmaṇa calls a daughter 'an insult', while the son is described as the 'light of the highest heaven'.[30] In the Sūtras we find a number of prenatal rituals to ensure the birth of a male child. In Smṛtis 'the mother of female children is equated to a barren woman'. It is prescribed that the husband of such a woman may have another marriage.[31]

The generally low estimate of woman in the patriarchal social structure may have induced the law-givers to prescribe an early marriage for girls also for combating the influence of matriarchy prevalent among the earlier settlers. The Gautama Dharma Sūtras prescribes that girls should be given in marriage before they attain puberty.[32] However, in the Sūtras, the difference of age between the bride and bridegroom does not seem to be much, because a boy of seventeen who has completed his studies is described as an eligible suiter. But in Smṛtis the difference between the respective ages of bride and bridegroom became excessively pronounced. Manu prescribes that a man of thirty should marry a maiden of twelve, or a man of twenty-four a girl of eight.[33] This difference of age ensured the full dependence of woman on man, and male superiority over her.

The Vedic literature explains the conjugal relationship through the analogy of Dyau and Pṛthvī or heaven and earth. This myth of divine parents of the universe probably originated in the remote past among the Indo-Aryans, long before they entered the Indian sub-continent. Heaven and earth are complements of a single whole. Father heaven makes the earth pregnant through rains,and 'beings of manifold forms grow'.[34] This imputed perenthood of heaven and earth is transferred to the human couple. A *mantra* of Atharva Veda recited by the bridegroom at the time of the wedding says : 'I am Dyau, you are Prthvī.'[35] This *mantra* has been adopted by many Gṛhya Sūtras. The implicit idea seems to be that though the earth is the mother of all beings yet beings manifest the divine father. Like the parents of the universe the husband and wife too form a single whole. In the Śatapatha Brāhmaṇa it is said: 'The wife is indeed the half of one's self. Therefore, as long as a man does not secure a wife, as long as he does not beget a son until then he is not complete or whole. But when he secures a wife and begets progeny, he becomes complete.'[36] The son is the manifestation of the father. In the Ṛgveda, a father prays, 'O Fire may I enjoy immortality through the children'.[37] The Nirukta also says: 'The son is my own self. May he live a hundred autumns.'[38] This idea has found even more vivid expression in the Kauṣītaki Upaniṣad : 'One's own self takes birth as the son.'[39] Auddalika, as referred to by Vātsyāyana in the Kama Sūtra, asserts: 'The women can not enjoy the act of creation for she does not contain the seeds. Her joy is only the reflection of the man's joy.'[40]

In the Sūtra period the Brahmanical tradition was revived. It was again challenged by Buddhism. Buddha struck at the very foundations of the Brahmanical social structure---the Varna hierarchy. The discourses of Buddha were in the common man's language which Śūdras and women could also understand. Buddha even allowed women to get admitted to his order. But he agreed to this very reluctantly. This shows that he too did not consider woman to be an equal of man. He declared that because of allowing admission to women in his order it would last for only half the time of what it would have lasted otherwise. However, several women entered the order and made contributions to knowledge. Many of them were unmarried while some were married. Following this tradition, King Aśoka sent his daughter Saṅghamitrā to Ceylon. All these women chose the life of celibacy in pursuit of the truth.

Buddha preseribed strict discipline for nuns. They had always to live under the protection of monks. They were enjoined to avoid company of men of bad character. Only the righteous monks were allowed to give sermons. They were expected to remain always in groups of two or three. Every woman who wanted admission to the order had to be examined jointly by monks and nuns; while men could be admitted by monks themselves. And all the nuns were considered junior to all the monks however accomplished or elderly they might be.[41] Even so, according to Buddhism a woman can achieved the state of Niravāṇa or salvation.[42]

But Brāhmaṇical elites could not reconcile to this situation. For them this was an aberration. The old Vedic norms were breakings up due to threats which came from many sides. The most vigorous challenge was from Buddhism. Another threat was posed by non-Aryan popular heterodox religious sects. Still another came in the shape of foreign invaders—the Greeks, the Parthians, the Śaka and the Kuṣāṇas who were settling in India. These invaders were very close in their physical features to the recognized attributes of the Brāhmaṇa Varṇa. They fitted in very well with the criteria of fair complexion and blonde hair which were indentified as characteristics of a Brāhmaṇa by Patañjali.[43]

Systems of philosophy and legal codes seem to have developed in such a way as to support the social norms concerning women. Certain systems of metaphysics personified the material cause of the world, Prakṛti or Māyā, as the wife of the Puruṣa or ultimate reality. This provides a metaphysical justification for the role which woman actually enjoy in the traditional social order. Similarly, the theory of Karma explains her low position as a consequence of sins incurred in previous births. The law givers also maintained conformity to those norms. Woman was not considered a full legal person. Religion too played its part. Plentiful heavenly rewards were promised to boost the morale of the woman who abided by these norms despite injustices and hardships.

The myth of divine parents of the universe is found in the Manu Smṛti also. It equates the woman to the field or *Kṣetra* and man to the seed; and after some discussion as to which of the two is more important it is concluded that seed is more important because the 'offsprings of all created beings are marked by the characteristics of the seed'. To further emphasize the idea the Smṛti says that though earth is called the primeval womb of all created beings, the properties reflected in the created beings are not of earth but of the seed.[44]

The role of woman in procreation is minimized to such an extent that the seed of man is considered efficatious enough to produce a child even without the aid of woman. In the Mahābhārata we find that the great teacher, Droṇa, was born because of semen falling into a *drona* or a vessel of wood. Certain metaphysical systems which grew up in ancient Indian society provide an elaborate cosmic justification for the dependent and low status of woman.

In the Sāṅkhya and Advaita philosophical systems, the relationship of woman and man is imputed to the supreme being and Prakrti or Māyā. Through this analogy many attributes of nature were transferred to woman.

Thus, a similarly between the macrocosm and the microcosm was established. The role of the ultimate reality was conceived as that of a powerful patriarch who manifests himself through Māyā or Nature in the form of creation. Though Prakṛti or Māyā has been recognized as the mother of the universe, the fatherhood of the Lord overshadows her because it is the Lord who has been manifested. Similarly, it is the patriarch who creates his family; woman is only his instrument or medium.

The theory of Karma too played an important part in justifying the social system and in inducing woman to reconcile herself to her lot as the natural consequence of her own deeds in past lives.

The legal ideas provide further support to patriarchy. The Śatapatha Brāhmaṇa and other texts call woman 'Adāya' or one who does not inherit. The law-givers following it provided no share in property to woman. The process of depriving woman of the ownership of property through use of physical force is reflected well in the passage of Śatapatha Brāhamaṇa cited above. It says that the women were smitten so hard that they become unable even to think of inheriting property. This strongly suggests that among the earlier settlers who belonged to a matriarchal order, woman owned property; and later on she was deprived of its ownership because of the strong patriarchal structure of the Aryans. The Dharma Sūtras carried on the ancient Vedic tradition and did not recognize woman as a legal person. She can neither inherit nor can give evidence or be a surety. However, the Gautma Dharma Sūtra provides a share to a sonless widow.[45] The later Dharma Sūtras denied that too. The Manu Smṛti, being the earliest work of the revivlist era, adhered to the ancient tradition. The later law-givers, Yājnavalkya and Bṛhaspati, took a liberal attitude and recognized a widow and daughter of a sonless person as full heirs.[46] But this too was denied by the commentators. None of the law-givers allowed woman to enter into any transaction or give evidence.

Manu had to provide a solid foundation to a patriarchal society which was in crisis. To have a smooth and harmoniously functioning mechanism based on old norms, it was essential for Manu to lay down codes which imply perpetual subjugation of woman and Śūdra. Manu prohibited the customs of Niyoga, or the appointment of the younger brother-in-law to raise a son on the widowed sister-in-law for his elder brother, the taking of bride price, and marriage of a twice-born man to a Śudra woman. By the time of Manu the first two customs had lost their currency and the changed norms of society did not permit him to revive them. This austere Smṛti writer called Niyoga 'a beastly act.'[47] Similarly about the practice of bride-price Manu remarks, 'it is selling one's child' and is therefore sinful.[48] The marriage with a Śūdra female was also vehemently condemned by Manu[49] because he wanted to preserve the caste hierarchy. Rejecting the first two customs certainly had the impact of lowering the position woman. The sonless widow who was not allowed levirate had to live on the mercy of her relatives. Prohibition of bride-price also made the daughter totally undesired.

Though the dicta of Manu assigning a low status to woman may appear inequitous today, one has to remember that the norms about the status and role of woman were not very different in other partiarchal societies such as those of ancient Greece and traditional China; just like the ancient Chinese law of three obediences for woman, Manu has laid down that a woman has to obey the father in her childhood, the husband in her youth, and the sons in her old age—a woman never remains independent. This may at first sight look inconsistent with another oft quoted dictum of Manu which says that gods dwell where women are 'worshipped' (or honoured). However, the two dicta are not necessarily contradictory. Worshipping is one thing and giving freedom is quite another. For example, the Hindus do worship the cow; but they do not leave it free.

The statements made in Smṛtis and in the epics show a high degree of consistency. The fundamental values of Indian society are well enunciated in them. Long inculcations about the glory of chastity, and obedience and devotion to the husband, marred the natural affectionate conjugal relations. It was expected that the wife should submerge her personality into that of her husband. The position of the wife was reduced to a pupil or a mute follower rather than a companion or a friend. Manu compares a woman to a student. He says, 'The nupital ceremony is similar to the initiation, serving the husband is equal to living in the teacher's house and the household duties are equal to the worship of the sacred fire'.[50] He further prescribes that like a teacher or father the husband can chastise his wife with lashes of a rope or cane on her back.[51]

All the works of the revivalist era adhered to the norms established by Manu. The ideal established for the wife is to serve her husband with mind, speech and body, though he be poor, sickly or foolish.[52] A number of supernatural rewards have been promised to the woman who steadfastly adheres to these norms, while the deviators have only suffering in store for them. Manu says that a woman who through her thought speech and actions remains dutiful to her husband gets the highest heaven with her husband, besides worldly renown; whereas the violator of the norms of duty becomes a she-jackal and remains afflicted with diseases.[53] Parāśara says that the wife who insults a poor, sickly or foolish husband, takes birth as a bitch, and after that again and again she becomes a she-pig.[54]

The Mahābharata contains several stories of devoted wives who acquire divine power by serving their husbands. Through her tremendous supernatural power Sāvitrī retrieved her husband from the clutches of Yama, the god of death. A young hunter, who being stricken by lust tried to approach Damayanti, fell dead by her curse. Śāṇḍilī attained celestial regions by virtue of obedience and devotion to her husband. Gāndhārī had powers to burn up the universe and stop the movements of sun and moon. All these stories provided the psychological motivation for bearing the disproportionate load of a large number of odd jobs that were deliberately prescribed to preoccupy a wife.

Manu, Yājnavalkya and Bṛhaspati provide that woman should be kept busy in cleaning utensils, performing rituals, cooking and doing other domestic chores, besides keeping account of income and expenditure, so that she may remain pure.[55]

The Smṛtis and epics vie with each other in recounting the bad qualities of women. Many wholesale abusive statements have been issued. Mahābharata outnumbers other texts in such declarations: 'Nobody is as wicked as woman; they are the edge of knife, poision, snake and fire at the same time'.[56] The same text asserts that 'women are non-controllable, they live under their husband's control only because nobody approaches them and they are afraid of servants'.[57] The Vālmīkī Rāmāyaṇa says : 'By nature women are indifferent to religion, fickle, fierce and a cause of conflict.'[58]

It has been said in the Mahābharata that it is impossible to enumerate all the bad qualities of woman even for one who is endowed with a thousand tongues and a hundred years of life, even if he devotes himself to nothing else but to this task alone.[59] Manu Smṛti is no milder in its disdain for woman: 'Through their passion for men, through their natural cruelty, they become disloyal towards their husbands, however carefully they may be guarded.'[60] Later the status of woman declined further. Śankara, the great philosopher proclaimed : 'Woman is the gate for hell.' The commentaries too, meticulously adhered to the norms for subjugating woman. It is ordained that the wife should take food in the same plate in which the husband has taken his meals. Obviously, the wife was expected to eat the left-overs of her husband. But the lawgiver was careful enough to forbid the husband from leaving in his plate delicacies like curds, honey, *ghee*, and milk.[61]

Thus, the patriarchal elite stratum of ancient India through its conscious efforts, and perhaps unconsciously too through the instinct of self-preservation inherent in culture itself, evolved a strong normative pattern for the subjugation of woman, so that she was prevented from becoming a threat to the solidarity of the patriarchal joint family. These norms were justified and buttressed by law, religion and metaphysics.[62] The system thus evolved not only met successfully the inner and outer challenges but influenced all the people who came in contact with it.

Notes

1. Ṛgveda, V. 30., 9.
2. Ṛgveda, VIII. 33.17-19.
3. Ṛgveda, X. 95. 15.
4. Ṛgveda, VIII. 19. 36-37.
5. Atharvaveda, V. 17. 8-9.
6. Zend-Avesta, I. Vendidad. I.17.
7. Pahlavi Texts, I Bundahis. XXIII. 1.
8. Ṛgveda, X. 116. 10.
9. Ṛgveda, VIII. 19. 36-37.
10. Ṛgveda, VII. 18-22.
11. Ṛgveda, I. 105. 8.
12. Ṛgveda, X. 145
13. Atharvaveda, I. 14.
14. Ṛgveda, X. 159. It is interesting that just like contemporary Indian folk-songs this hymn mentions a number of sons but only one daughter.
15. Tattirīya Saṁhitā, VI. 6. 1.3.
16. Aitareya Brāhmaṇa, XII. II.
17. Śatapatha Brāhmaṇa, XIII. 4. 1. 9.
18. Taittirīya Saṁhitā, VI. 5. 8. 2.
19. Maitrāyanī Saṁhitā, I. 10. 11; IV. 7. 4.
20. These offerings are given to Varuṇa in order to deliver ones progeny from Varuṇa's noose.

21. Śatapatha Brāhmaṇa, II. 5. 2. 20.
22. The provision of confession seems to be borrowed from Assyrians as in the Vedas we do not find the concept of confession.
23. Śatapatha Brāhmaṇ, IV. 4. 2. 13.
24. Bṛhadaranyaka Upaniṣad, III. 6. 1.
25. Bṛhadaranyaka Upaniṣad,III. 2-12.
26. Bṛhadaranyaka Upaniṣad, II. 4. 1-4.
27. Bṛhadaranyaka Upaniṣad, VI. 4. 17.
28. Śānkhāyana Gṛhyasūtra, I. 3.
29. Taittirīya Saṁhitā, V. 10. 3.
30. Aitareya Brāhmaṇa, XXXII. 1.
31. Nārada Smṛti, XII. 94.
32. Gautama Dharmasūtra, XVII. 20. 30.
33. Manu Smṛti, IX. 94.
34. Ṛgveda, VI. 70.
35. Atharvaveda, XIV. 11. 71.
36. Śatapatha Brāhmaṇa, V. 2.1.10.
37. Ṛgveda, V. 8. 10.
38. Nirukta, III. 4.
39. Kauśītaki Upaniṣad, II. 11.
40. Vātsyāyana, Kamasūtra (Madhavacarya ed.), Bombay, Venkateshwara Steam press, 1934), vol. 11. 1.10.
41. *Vinaya.* Chullvagga, X. 1.4.
42. *Therigatha,* 61.
43. Mahābhasya of Patañjali, II. 2. 6.
44. Manu Smṛti, IX. 32-37.
45. Gautama Dharma Sūtra, XXVIII. 21.
46. Yājnavalkya Smṛti, II. 135; Brhaspati Smṛti, XXVI, 87, 90.
47. Manu Smṛti, IX. 64-68.
48. Manu Smṛti, III. 51-52.
49. Manu Smṛti, III. 17-18.
50. Manu Smṛti, II. 67.

51. Manu Smṛti, VIII. 299-300.
52. Manu Smṛti, V. 154; Yājnavalkya Smṛti, I. 77; Parasara Smṛti, IV. 17-18; Rāmāyaṇa Ayodhya Kanda. XXIV. 26-27. Mahābharata Anuśāsanaparva. 146-155; Narada Smṛti, XVIII. 22.
53. Manu Smṛti, V. 164-166.
54. Parāśara Smṛti, IV. 17-18.
55. Manu Smṛti, IV. 11; Yājnavalkya Smṛti, I. 83, Brahaspati, Smṛti, XV. 6.
56. Mahābhrata, Anuśāsnaparva, 12. 29.
57. Mahābharata Anuśāsanaparva, XXXVIII. 16.
58. Rāmāyaṇa, Āraṇyakānda, XXXXV. 29-30.
59. Mahābharata, XII. 75. 9.
60. Manu Smṛti, XI. 14.
61. Pārāśara Madhavīya, I. I. 422.
62. For a more detailed discussion of how the metaphysical systems provided justification to the lower status of woman, and thus strengthened the patriarch order, see the following chapter.

IX

Correspondence between Woman and Nature in Indian Thought : An Essay in Sociology of Knowledge

A metaphor persistently occurs in Indian thought. Woman is compared in innumerable ways to Prakṛti (Nature), Māyā (Illusion), and earth. This correspondence has moulded not only thinking but also the social institutions. It has influenced the whole of Indian tradition. It pervades so many aspects of life and thought that it seems to be one of the basic modes of perception and understanding with regard both to woman and to Nature. An exploration of the forms this comparison has assumed in traditional Indian thoguht should bring out certain basic attitudes toward woman in India. It may also provide a background for an ampler understanding of the conception of material cause in Indian tradition. The metaphor runs right from the Vedas through the Sūtras, Smṛtis, Purāṇas, and literary works of various kinds. In fact, it is found in mythological, literary and philosophical writings of all varieties. Because the evidence is so ample, it is difficult to decide where to begin.

Nevertheless, an attempt in this direction is sure to deepen our understanding of the traditional Indian view regarding woman and her (supposed) essential attributes. Such an analysis can be reasonably expected to shed interesting light on certain basic assumptions of Indian social order. The status and role ascribed to woman determines to a great extent the nature of the family, and the family has undoubtedly been the cornerstone of the whole social structure in India.

In different contexts woman is conceived to be comparable to Prakṛti, Māyā, and earth. The fact that woman is considered comparable to each of these concepts is not necessarily a disadvantage from the viewpoint of analysis. The concepts are akin, and comparison with each of these illuminates some aspect of the traditional image of woman. Certain fundamental ideas regarding the proper role of woman and her constitution are implicit in the comparison. The role of woman in the formation of the family, procreation, sexual union, etc., has been conceived by Indian thinkers from this angle. This comparison is based on the comprehensive principle of analogical correspondence found in Indian as well as other traditional systems of thought. The principle implies a correspondence between the general and the specific—the macrocosm and the microcosm. In accordance with this notion, the relationship of woman and man is considered to correspond to that of the Supreme Being and Māyā, or Puruṣa and Prakṛti.

Though in the prolification of Indian thought nature has been conceived variously, the general conception of Nature as inert but necessary for creation, seems to persist despite finer diffierences. For instance, in the Saṁkhya philosophy we find this kind of relationship between Puruṣa and Prakṛti. Though Prakṛti is the material cause of the physical universe, it lacks consciouseness. But it behaves as if it were conscious through the reflection of Puruṣa, which is conscious. Thus change (Vikāra) occurs in the Avyakta-Mūlaprakṛti, that is, Prakṛti in its original nonmanifested form. It becomes manifest (Vyakta). Only a reflection of Puruṣa sets Nature in motion and leads it to the creation of the universe.

In the Ṛgveda, the supreme God manifests himself through

Māyā in the form of universe : 'God manifests himself in many forms through Māyā.'[1] The Supreme God, the creator, employs Māyā as an instrument or support which manifests him in the form of universe. Māyā is the mother of the whole world. She brings the universe from her womb. The conception of Māyā is related to that of the Mother Goddess, who is worshipped throughout India in twelve forms. The Mother Goddess is referred to as Śakti (the personified energy of God). As the Śvetāśvatara Upaniṣad says: 'God's Śakti is hidden by its properties (guṇas).'[2] God, the creator, creates with his Śakti as the instrument. She has been recognized as God's power. Becoming the medium for the manifestation of God is her fulfillment.

The role of Nature in creation has been brought out through an interesting metaphor in the Gītā. This metaphor imputes the role of father to God and the function of mother to nature in the creation of the universe. Lord Kṛṣṇa says: 'Nature is my Yoni (womb), and I am the seed-giving father.'[3] Here we find fatherhood enthroned as the primary quality of the supreme God. All creation is but the progeny of the Lord. The role of God is that of the powerful patriarch. Though Nature has been recognized as one of the parents, her role is certainly the inferior one. Although it is Nature that apparently brings forth the universe, no independent status has been assigned to it. The fatherhood of God overshadows the motherhood of Nature. In fact, she herself belongs to him. She has been regarded as his attribute and has been referred to as his Māyā, Śakti, and womb. While God is the ultimate truth, the only utility of Nature is that it bears the seed of God and brings forth the universe. Its function is only to manifest God in the form of the universe. God is represented as the creator of the universe, and Prakṛti as his support, through which he acts. Prakṛti is the ultimate source of the physical universe. In the Brahma Sūtra, we find the aphorism: 'Yoni (the womb) is the source of universe according to revelation.'[4] In his famous commentary, Śaṁkara, discussing this sūtra, inter alia, says that the word 'Yoni' is used by common people in the sense of 'Nature' and 'birth.' He further points out that the Yoni (womb) of the woman also is the organ which is the instrument of conception (Garbha).

The place woman occupied in the higher Hindu society of ancient India seems to be related to this conception. Motherhood has been the pivotal role for woman. The woman is the mother. The son is considered a manifestation of the father. As the Nirukta, Kauṣītaki Upaniṣad, and Yājñavalkya Smṛti put it, the father himself takes birth in the form of his son. In the Nirukta, the father says: 'The son is my own self. May he live a hundred autumns.'[5] A similar idea is found in the Kauṣītaki Upaniṣad: 'One's own self takes birth as the son.'[6] The Yājñavalkya Smṛti, while forbidding a twice-born (Dvija) from marrying a Śūdra maiden, points out that 'one takes birth himself (as the son).'[7] Commenting on this verse, Vijñāneśvara in his Mitākṣarā cites the Śruti (revelation): 'The wife (Jayā) alone is Jayā in whom the husband takes birth again.'[8] In short, the woman is considered the medium through which man manifests himself.

Man and woman both are the root of the family. Just as ultimate consciousness and nature create the universe, in the same way man and woman create the world of the family. Indian society is patriarchal. Man is the powerful father, the real creator of the family. Woman is his medium. In Vedic literature, the contact of woman and man has been explained through the analogy of Pṛthvī (earth) and Dyau (heaven). A Mantra (verse) recited by the bridegroom at the time of the wedding says: 'I am Dyau, You are Pṛthvī.'[9] Earth and heaven are complements of a single whole. Clouds of heaven make the earth pregnant through rain. The earth gives birth to various vegetation. The value of the earth depends upon its fertility. Similarly, the worth of woman lies in her ability to become the mother of sons. Nārada ordains that: 'The husband should not bestow love on a wife who is barren or the mother of girls. If he does so, he is a sinner.'[10] But even the motherhood of woman depends upon the man. Man is considered the real creator. He is the master of his wife (Svāmin). Woman is dependent on her husband in every way. According to Auddālika, as referred to by Vātsyāyana in the Kāma Sūtra: 'She cannot even enjoy the act of creation like man, because she does not contain seeds; it is the man who gives her the real thing. Whatever joy she gets is only the reflection of man's joy.'[11] In the commentary on the above Sūtra the statement of the Sanskrit grammarian Patañjali, that in the act of creation 'woman becomes active through the fatigue of man,'[12] is often quoted.

The supremacy of man over woman in the patriarchal order was reinforced also by certain beliefs regarding their respective roles in procreation. It appears that with the strengthening of patriarchy in ancient India, the importance of the part played by woman in procreation was minimized, while the role of man was emphasized to the extreme. In the Mahābhārata, we come across several stories which imply that the semen of man is alone efficacious in producing a child. Thus, the great teacher Droṇa was born because of semen falling into a vessel made of wood (Droṇa in Sanskrit). This story, and several others of this kind, show that the part of woman in procreation was thought to be only that of a container for the semen of man. A similar conclusion is reached in the discussions in the Dharma Śāstras of the relative importance of the parts played by man and woman. In the Manu Smṛti, woman is equated to the field (Kṣetra) and man to the seed; and after some discussion the conclusion is drawn that, while the field is necessary, the nature of the tree and the fruit depends upon the nature of the seed, that is, the masculine principle. This comparison of woman to the field is found throughout Indian literature. Even in folk literature, which thrives through oral tradition, the word 'medinī' stands both for the earth and the female genitals. The double entendre riddles and some folk songs push forward the metaphor by comparing pubic hair with grass.

However, even though the place assigned to woman is inferior to that of man, she is nevertheless considered indispensable. In this she is important just like Nature. Just as there can be no creation without Nature, there can be no procreation without woman. Śaṁkara says: 'The Lord with his Śakti can create; without Śakti He cannot even move.'[13] In this sense, woman and man are complementary; and Prakṛti and Puruṣa are complementary. There are numerous references to this idea in Indian literature through the ages. The two complementary entities are often referred to as parts of the same whole. In the Śatapatha Brāhmaṇa it is said that the wife is the portion of the husband through which the husband gets a son and becomes complete: 'The wife is indeed the half of one's self. Therefore, as long as man does not secure a wife, as long as he does not beget a son, until then he is not complete or whole. But when he secures a wife and begets progeny, he becomes complete.'[14] Many centuries later, the famous Muslim poet Malik Muhammad Jāyasī (sixteenth century) expresses a similar idea: 'One tree has two leaves, the father heaven and the mother earth.'[15] Even to this day the most common objects of worship in Hindu temples are the images of the male and female genitals in union. This image symbolizes the god Śiva (the ultimate goodness) and his Śakti (power).

Woman is necessary for establishing the fatherhood of man and continuing his family line. These functions have significance also from the ritual and spiritual viewpoint. Marriage is a sacrament in Hindu tradition and continuance of the family line is one of its primary aims. The following verse has to be recited by the bridegroom during the marriage ceremony: 'I take your hand for good progeny.'[16] The bridegroom has to recite during wedding the following verse: 'From whom all the beings have emerged, from whom has emerged the whole world; I shall sing the song of the great glory of woman.'[17] The son is the continuation of father. A father says in the Ṛgveda: 'Oh Fire! may I enjoy immortality through my children.'[18] In the Vedic age, at the completion of education, the teacher exhorted his pupil: 'Do not break the line of progeny.'[19] The son (Putra) means one who saves the father from being cast into a hell named 'Put.'

A man cannot fulfill his obligations (social, ritual, and spiritual) without his wife. In the Ādiparva of the Mahābhārata the wife is called the root of the Puruṣārthas (basic values of life). The Puruṣārthas are the four supreme values of life: Dharma, or duty; Artha or wealth; Kāma or pleasure of the senses; and Mokṣa or salvation. According to Pāṇini, the great grammarian, the word 'Patnī' is etymologically proved by an aphorism which mens that 'the contact which is established through marriage sacrifice, gives the woman wifehood.'[20] No sacrifice, therefore, can be performed without a wife. Tīrtha (visit to holy places), Japa (recitation of holy words), Homa (fire sacrifices), Dāna (gifts), and Vrata (fasts), can be performed only together with the wife. A hymn which has to be recited during the marriage ceremony says: 'We will perform religious duties together.'[21] In the Rāmāyana, King Janaka, while giving his daughter Sītā in marriage to Rāma, says to him: 'Here is Sītā, my daughter and your coperformer of religious duties.'[22]

Woman is the companion of man in enjoying the pleasures of wealth and the senses. But these, according to traditional thought, she cannot enjoy herself. She always needs a guide or a master. Like Nature she has no power of manifestation. The fulfillment of Nature is the manifestation of the ultimate consciousness. Similarly, woman's fulfillment is in the wifehood and motherhood or manifestation of her husband. The wife is only the medium through which the husband himself takes birth in the form of the son and thus attains immortality. As pointed out above, this idea is clearly put forth in the Vedic and the Dharma Śāstra literature. Moreover, woman is persistently compared to the field or the earth. The seed comes from the father or heaven and through its growth the seed-giver is manifested. Even in the sexual act the woman's pleasure is solely dependent on man's. According to ancient authorities, whatever pleasure she derives is only the reflection of man's joy. Assuming the dependence of woman in all fundamental matters, it is natural to argue that she should never remain independent. This is what the traditional Hindu does. Thus Manu ordains:

> 'The father protects her in maidenhood,
> The husband protects her in youth,
> Sons protect her in old age,
> Woman can never be independent.'[23]

This famous dictum enunciates well the patriarchal principle underlying traditional Hindu social thought. The woman is always dependent.[24] She can never own movable or immovable property. Her self (Sva) cannot exist separately from the self of her father, husband or son. The Gautama Dharma Sūtra states: 'Lack of independence is the nature (or duty) of woman.' The Vasistha Dharma Sūtra says: 'Woman lacks independence, and man is her master.' In Hindu society, the idea of the dependence of woman and her conception as the medium or instrument has been carried to its logical conclusion. It is considered good for a woman to die before her husband; for she is considered only as an instrument for the husband. If the husband dies first, a devoted wife is expected to end her life. This is the basis of the well-known system of Satī referred to in the Viṣṇu Dharma Sūtra[25] and prevalent about a century ago, under which the widow wearing ornaments and rich clothes immolated herself on the dead husband's funeral pyre.

In the Vedānta it is said that to make sorrow vanish from its root, to attain the ultimate reality, one should leave the 'cause of contact between Prakṛti and Puruṣa'.[26] The word used here for 'contact' is 'Saṁyoga.' This word is used also to refer to sexual union. Nature is a help to a certain extent in the process of attainment of Mokṣa (salvation) because the seeker has to start from his body, which itself is a part of illusion (Māyā). In the Saṁkhya system we find a similar idea. Puruṣa is uncontaminated, conscious, different from the three properties of Nature, and eternal. Prakṛti is also eternal. The image of Puruṣa falls on Prakṛti, because of which Prakṛti in its first manifestation intellect behaves as if it were conscious. On the other hand, the image of the intellect flashes back on Puruṣa. Thus the uncontaminated Puruṣa appears to be the creator and the enjoyer. This conceptual and imputed contact of Puruṣa and Parkṛti is bondage. Salvation is the removal of this bondage. From intellect to gross elements, all creation is the path of salvation. This is the Svabhāva (intrinsic tendency) of Prakṛti. 'Just as the milk from the teats of the cow goes itself to the mouth of the calf to nourish it, so also Prakṛti is active by its own intrinsic tendency towards the saliation of the Puruṣa.'[27] On the acquisition of this ability of discrimination the Puruṣa recognizes his real self. The influence of intellect vanishes and the Prakṛti becomes detached, and the Puruṣa gains the ultimate state (Kaivalya). After this, even though the Puruṣa has attained salvation, he continues to look upon the Prakṛti as an indifferent spectator.[28] He remains free from its bondage.

Similarly, woman is helpful in creation; so she should not be neglected up to a certain stage. But after completing the Gṛhasthāśrama,[29] man should treat his wife like his mother or sister, and in the next Āśrama (stage of life), Sannyāsa (stage of complete renunciation) he should give her up altogether.

We find thus, that in Indian traditional thought woman and Nature have many basic attributes in common. Nature (Prakṛti) is the material cause of the world, and it is the medium through which the Puruṣa is manifested. Similarly, woman is the medium or instrument which makes possible the manifestation of man. It is through her that man procreates. Yet she is essentially comparable to the earth: necessary for procreation but dependent on the seed which has to come from outside. The creation of the world is due to union (Saṁyoga) between Prakṛti and Puruṣa; human procreation is due to the Saṁyoga between woman and man. For salvation, the Saṁyoga between the former as well as the latter has to be transcended. The conceptions of woman and Nature, thus, correspond in a number of ways; and the metaphysical notion of this analogical correspondence has deep implications for the actual position of woman in traditional society.

Notes

1. Ṛgveda, VI. xlvii. 18.
2. Śvetāśvatara Upaniṣad, 1.3.
3. Gītā, XIV. 3-4.
4. Brahma Sūtra, Śāmkarabhāṣya, I.iv. 27.
5. Nirukta, III. 4.
6. Kauṣītaki Upaniṣad, II. 11.
7. Yājñavalkya Smṛti, I. 56.
8. See Mitākṣarā on Yājñavalkya Smṛti, I. 56.
9. Mānava Gṛhya Sūtra, I.x. 15.
10. Nārada Smṛti, XII. 94.
11. Vātsyāyana, Kāmasūtra, Madhavacarya, ed. (Bombay: Laxmi Venkatśwar Steam Press, 1934), Vol. I. (Adhikarana II, chap. I, verse 10), p. 231.
12. Ibid., p.13.
13. Śamkara, Ānandalaharī (Wave of Bliss), Arthur Avalon, ed. (Madras: Ganesh & Co., 1948), p. 1.
14. Śatapatha Brāhmaṇa, V. ii. i. 10.
15. Malik Muhammad Jāyasī, 'Akhravata,' in Jāyasī Granthāvalī, Mataprasad Gupta, ed. (Allahabad: Hindustani Academy, 1952), p. 654.
16. Ṛgveda, X. lxviii. 36.
17. Pāraskara Gṛhya Sūtra, I. ix. 2.
18. Ṛgveda, V. viii. 10.
19. Taittirīya Upaniṣad, I. xi. 1.
20. Pāṇini, IV. i. 33.
21. Āśvalāyana Gṛhya Sūtra, I. vi. 1.
22. Rāmāyaṇa, I. lxiii. 26.
23. Manu Smṛti, IX. 3.
24. Incidentally, this dictum of Mnu is strikingly similar in import to the law of three obediences for woman in the Chinese Code of Li chi.

25. Viṣṇu Dharma Sūtra, XXV. 14.
26. Commentary on Brahma Sūtra (Śaṁkarabhāṣya), II. ii. 10.
27. Saṁkhya Kārikā, 57.
28. Ibid., 65.
29. The second of the four stages in man's life, in which he should perform the duties of householder.

X

Religion of India : The Reassertion of Subjugated Cultures

It seems that whenever there is a struggle between cultures, the culture of the victorious people becomes the culture of the people as whole in the beginning, but later on the culture of the subjugated people asserts itself and many of its essential elements have to be integrated in the elite culture. We can see this process at work in the making of the Indian civilization. In the beginning the culture of the newly triumphant Aryan hordes naturally became the dominent culture of the Indian sub- continent. But later on the culture of the subjugated non-Aryans asserted itself, and during the second Brahmanical revival it found full-blooded expression in the Māhabhārata, the Ramāyaṇa and the Purāṇas. As we shall see in this chapter eventhough the Aryans were conscious of the non-Aryans influence and resisted it, their attempts could not prevent copious inflow of non-Aryans culture.

The Aryans hated the phallus worshippers and considered the dark complexioned non-Aryans to be Amanuṣya or non-human. But later on the Vedic god Rudra was unified with the phallus god and was given the Aryan name Mahādeva or the great god. This is only one example. Many gods and Mother goddesses were included in later mythology which constitutes the basic sub-stratum of Hinduism. In this chapter we propose to examine the process which led to the emergence of Hindu mythology, the bulk of which came from non-Aryans subjugated cultures. The priestly elites could not save the purity either of the Aryan race or original Aryan religion but they succeeded in securing for themselves the supreme position in the social structure. Another interesting feature of this process is that those very people whose culture and religion the priestly elites took over, were denied a respectable place in the social order that was sustained by the doctrines borrowed from them and even the right to enter the temples where gods who originally belonged to their own cultures were worshipped.

Many of the basic metaphysical doctrines like the theory of Karma (transmigration of soul) and that of the illusory nature of this world seem to be of non-Aryans origin. They are not found in the Ṛgveda which is believed to be the original word of God by all orthodox Hindus. Similarly, most of the gods of the elite religious tradition of Hinduism seem to have non-Aryans origins. We shall try to outline how the vast and many-faceted edifice that is Hinduism took shape as a result of the interplay of numerous contending and cohesive forces in its long and turbulent history.

The Ṛgvedic Religion and Gods

We find the earliest glimpses of the ancient religion of the Aryans in the prayers of the Ṛgveda. The Ṛgvedic Aryans were very much devoted to their gods. They were robust, active and fond of good life. Their gods also were conceived to be like them. They worshipped gods for gaining riches. They believed in heaven. The Aryans considered themselves superior and were proud of their race, religion and language. They called non-Aryans non-humans, or Amanuṣya.[1] They maintained a distance from the non-Aryans. The poet Vasiṣṭha says : 'The worshippers of phallus should not come near Ṛta'.[2] Ṛta was conceived to be the universal law.

It is remarkable that the doctrine of transmigration of soul, 'Punarajanma' which is one of the cardinal principles of later Hinduism finds no mention in the Ṛgveda.[3] The Aryans of the Ṛgveda performed fire sacrifices and prepared Soma to apease the gods. In return gods were believed to fight with them and bestow various favours. All the gods were anthropomorphic. It is explicitly asserted that all of them are virile and none among them is a child.

Through their sacrifices the Ṛgvedic Aryans offered to the gods the food that they themselves ate. It consisted of different preparations made from barley. It included ground, roasted barley or Karambha, roasted barley and barley cake[4], apart from *ghee* or clarified butter. They also offered horses, bulls, oxen, barren cows and rams in the fire sacrifices.[5] Agni or the fire-god carries the food offered to all the gods.

The heaven of the Aryans was believed to be placed at 'lofty heights above'.[6] In heaven 'the ancient fathers live together with gods, those ancestors who have satiated the gods'.[7] The heaven is described as 'deathless and undecaying world', 'where everlasting lusture shines. Where food and full delight are found. Where there is happiness, joys and felicities combine, and longings are fulfilled'.[8] We find an indirect description of hell also in the Ṛgveda. To this hell 'sinners', 'unfaithful' and people of 'evil conduct'[9] go. Aryan gods are personified forces of nature. Prominent among them are the following.

Indra

The god Indra is the hero and leader of the Ṛgvedic Aryans. He has a golden beard and golden hair.[10] He wears a crown of gold and weilds thunderbolt as his weapon.[11] The horses of Indra 'have tails like peacocks' plumes'.[12] Indra is called 'immortal'.[13] He fights with the enemies of Aryans in battles and plunders the wealth of non-Aryans for Aryans.[14] He drinks Soma with Aryans.[15] Aryans prepare the meat of bulls for Indra and invite him to eat.[16] Indra is also called the destroyer of cities—'Purandara'. This is significant. Early Aryans were pastoral people. Their hordes attacked and devastated the urban settlements of the Paṇis (who perhaps were civilized Mediterreneans) and plundered them. It is natural therefore that their leader Indra is given the title of 'Destroyer of Cities'. Indra bestows victory, booty, power and glory. More than one fourth of the hymns of Ṛgveda are devoted to Indra.

Agni or Fire

Agni is second only to Indra in prominence. He is called immortal, bearer of offering to gods, and envoy of men.[17] Ṛgvedic Aryans also used fire against their enemies.[18] He has 'flashing teeth and golden beard'.[19] His hair are 'flame'.[20] He has got two red horses.[21] He is called lord of house, the great priest. He grants offsprings and prosperity.

Varuṇa

Varuṇa is the ancient god of Aryans. The old Slav god Perūna appears to be connected with Varuṇa. Many scholars think that Ahuramazda of Iranians was originally Varuṇa. Varuṇa is the upholder of the cosmic order, Ṛta, which regulates all activities of the universe. It regulates day and night, the flow of rivers, and all human behaviour.[22] He is connected with water.[23] Varuṇa binds down sinners with his noose or Pāśa. In the Ṛgveda we come across prayers addressed to Varuṇa to loosen his fetters.[24]

Soma

Soma is a very important god. It is a plant. The juice of its shoots was the favourite bevarage of Aryans. All the Aryans and their gods, especially Indra and Agni, are fond of Soma. Poets give credit to Soma for the exploits of Indra and Agni. Soma gives great exhilarating power.[25]

Heaven and Earth

Heaven and earth are called Pitarau or parents. They are ancient gods of early Indo-European times. Through the rains of Heaven the earth produces different kinds of vegetation and creatures.[26] Dyaus seems to be akin to the Greek god Zeus. He is also akin to the Roman god Jupiter (Dyaus-Pitara or Father Heaven).

Viṣṇu

Viṣṇu is a minor god in the Ṛgveda. He is conceived as the Sun. He is personified as a moving luminary who traverses the three worlds. Though the priests employ these hymns for god Viṣṇu of the later Hinduism, the character of Viṣṇu of Ṛgveda is obviously different from this later god. Viṣṇu is described as a god who has taken three strides which represent the three divisions of universe enlightened by the Sun.[27] Of course the Purāṇas, which contain later classical mythology, have adapted this myth from the Ṛgveda in their own way.

Rudra

Rudra is invoked much less than Viṣṇu in the Ṛgveda. He is conceived as fierce and destructive. Poets offer prayers to him so that he may not kill men, cows or horses.[28] He is described as 'strong, great, tawny and fair-complexioned'.[29] He is the one who has a 'thousand medicines'.[30] He is quite different from the later phallus-god Śiva with whom he was unified later. While the Ṛgvedic Rudra is feared by men for the damage that he may cause, Śiva is essentially bonevolent and is believed to be satisfied easily, 'Āśutoṣa'.

Through the synthesizing process of Indian tradition which integrated cultural elements from diverse sources, the Ṛgvedic Rudra was related to the classical and popular god Śiva. But the two are essentially different. Śiva of the popular and classical tradition is typically represented and worshipped as phallus, but the Ṛgvedic Aryans had great disdain for the worshippers of phallus. Yet there is a tendency among Hindu scholars to mix up the two. This is true even of such a great scholar as

P.V.Kane. However, the references from Ṛgveda which he has cited are all only to Rudra, and none of them is to Śiva as such.[31] The Ṛgveda belongs to the era when the primary concern of the Aryans was that of overpowering and subjugating the non-Aryans. But the later Saṁhitās and the Brāhmaṇa Granthas were composed when the Aryans had established their supremacy and settled down. The higher stratum of this society consisted of the Aryans and they were divided into three higher Varnas. The non-Aryans formed the serving class---the Śūdras.

Later Saṁhitās and Brāhmaṇa Granthas

The later Saṁhitās and Brāhmaṇa Granthas contain detailed rules of procedure of grand sacrifices. This is especially true of the Yajurveda and Sāmaveda Saṁhitās and the Brāhmaṇa Granthas. For performing such elaborate sacrifices the priests divided themselves into four large groups, each headed by a head priest. These expensive sacrifices presuppose the presence of powerful kings and wealthy householders.

The four head-priests perform specialized functions in such sacrifices. The first of these is called Hotā. He invokes the gods by uttering hymns of the Ṛgveda. The second is Udgātā who sings the melodies of the Sāmaveda. The third is Avadharyu who performs various sacrificial acts while muttering the Yajuṣ. The fourths one is called Brahmā. He keeps a watch over all sacrifical activities. The Brahmā priest should be well versed in all the three Vedas, so that even a minor error of speech or procedure is corrected. The householder or sacrificer had to give liberal fees to the priests.

By the times of the later Saṁhitās and the Brāhmaṇa Granthas simple rituals had been transformed into complex and expensive sacrifices. The contents of the Brāhmaṇa Granthas are of two kinds—precepts and rationalizations. We come across many myths which prescribe and rationalize certain sacrificial rituals. The Śatapatha Brāhmaṇa prescribes five great observances or sacrifices of Panca Mahayajnas which the Sūtras and the Smṛtis followed. These are mentioned in the following order: the sacrifices to beings or the Bhutayajna, which consist of offering oblations to beings everyday; the Manusyayajna, or the sacrifices to men which is offering men a cupful of water daily; Pitṛyajna or offering Svadhā or a cupful of water to fathers; Devayajna or making offerings of the log daily with the word 'Svahā' in the fire for the gods; and Brahmayajna or the study of Vedas daily.[32] The Śatapatha Brāhmaṇa introduced the five great sacrifices for the first time in a rudimentary fashion. These were for the three higher Varnas or classes. The later works systematized and elaborated them further.

Upaniṣads

Elaborate sacrifices did not suit all sections of the society. The Ksatriya kings who had to pay for them found them too costly. There was a kind of revolt, and it found expression in the Upaniṣads. The Upaniṣads were in a simple language, and they introduced the concept of 'Brhama'. Brahma is the ultimate reality, devoid of adjuncts. When one realizes Him, he becomes one with the ultimate reality. In the Upaniṣads we find even Śūdras and women participating in philosophical discussions. The Upaniṣads challenged the ritualistic way of life. There are instances in the Upaniṣads where Brāhmaṇa teachers went to learn the knowledge of the Self from Kṣatriya kings. A king approached even a cartman for gaining the knowledge of the Ultimate reality.

We find a story in the Chāndogya Upaniṣad in which a procession of white dogs are portrayed as priests who recite, 'Om let us eat; Om let us drink; Om, may the divine Varuṇa, Prajapati, Sāvitri brings us food; Lord of food bring hither food, bring it, Om'. Through such stories the Upaniṣads expose the parasitism of priests with scathing sarcasm.[33]

The Upaniṣads are far more liberal than the earlier Vedic literature. We do not find racial prejudice in the Upaniṣads. In the Ṛgveda persons of dark complexion are declared non-humans or Amanuṣya. Due to strong patriarchal values the birth of a daughter was considered a misfortune. But in the Bṛhadāraṇyaka Upaniṣad we find rituals for securing the birth of a dark complexioned son along with those for a blond son. There is a ritual even for securing the birth of a daughter.[34] In marked contrast to the common traditionalistic viewpoint, the Upaniṣads do not look backwards for a golden past. It is expected from the younger generation to be better than the older. In the Brhadāranayaka Upaniṣad the father blesses his newborn son to make more progress than his father and grandfather.[35]

The idea of rebirth is found for the first time in the Upaniṣads. It seems to have a non-Aryans origin. In the Ṛgveda and the Avesta the dead go to live with their forefathers in heaven. The introduction of the idea of transmigration of soul is thus a radical departure. It is another matter that it was made the foundation-stone of the system of Varṇa hierarchy and was effectively employed for legitimizing the inequality based on birth. In systems of metaphysics like Sāmkhya, Yoga and Vedānta it crystallized into the theory of Karma which provided a strong basis for rationalizing the ascription of social status by birth over the millenia.[36]

The Upaniṣads mark the revolt of people against the priestly elites. In the course of this revolt many non-Aryan ideas got entry into the elite tradition. The idea of transmigration of soul and rebirth was among them. Paradoxically, later on this idea proved to be a most effective instrument in the hands of the priestly elites for rationalizing, justifying and enṣuring almost universal acceptance for the system of Varṇa hierarchy, which originally was a system based on racial discrimination enforced through physical might.

This doctrine propounds that everyone takes high or low birth according to his own deeds in previous births. Therefore a Brāhmaṇa earns his higher status due to his good deeds of previous births and a Śūdra gets the low position due to his own bad deeds in previous lives. A firm and pervading belief in this doctrine seems to have induced a general apathy towards all human suffering. The common attitude tends to be that every sufferer is bound to be sinner, and therefore one should not interfere in the divine dispensation of justice lest he may himself get inflicted by the sins of the sufferer. Even the exploited sections accepted and internalized this doctrine.

The doctrine of the Upaniṣads asserted that sacrifices lead only to superficial gains such as earning heaven by performing various sacrifices, but one cannot get to the ultimate reality through sacrifices. Only after attaining real knowledge one becomes free from all the worldly sufferings.[37]

The Bramanical priestly elites lost their grip over the society during the Upaniṣadic era. The Varṇa hierarchy and the patriarchal order were both weakened.

The First Brahmanical Revival : Subtitution of Ritual for Race

In order to revitalize and preserve the tradition that gave these institutions the supreme position in society, the priestly elites consolidated the ancient Vedic lore in the form of aphorisms—the Kalpa Sūtras. Kalpa Sūtras consist of Gṛhya Sūtras, Śrauta Sūtras and Dharma Sūtras.

Since the racial purity of the elites had already been greatly compromised, racial features could no more provide the basis for their supremacy. It seems that scruples of ritual purity were put forward as a substitute for the earlier criterion of racial purity. And for the first time a number of Sanskāras or sacraments were introduced in the Gṛhya Sūtras. These sacraments are to be performed by all male members of the three higher Varṇas. The sacrements begin before the conception and last even after death. In this dispensation, priestly elites were the chief gainers and the Śūdras as well as women became the primary losers.

Since the priestly elites wanted to preserve, revive nd derive authority from ancient past, we find the mention of Ṛgvedic gods in the Gṛhya Sūtras. We find in them the mention of ancient god Yama who was originally the leader of Aryan migration but had become the god of death even in the Ṛgveda; though in one hymn of the Ṛgveda too he is referred to as the leader of migration and the first mortal.[38]

Besides the sacraments connected with *rites de passage* a number of other rituals too are prescribed in the Gṛhya Sūtras. The presence of a priest in the rituals is optional. In some rituals animal sacrifice is also prescribed. They include those of marriage; offerings to the manes; and the reception of guests. Many household rituals have a high degree of magical content.

The Śrauta Sūtras contain elaborate procedures for performing various sacrifices. They follow the later Saṁhitās and the Brāhmaṇas. These sacrifices are performed by a team of priests for the householders.

Dharma Sūtras are primarily the law-books of Aryans. These also contain the earlier norms of the Aryans pertaining to conduct, custom, and religion. In the Dharma Sūtras we find the ancient Aryan insistence of keeping the non-Aryans (Śūdras) away from their scriptures. The Gautama Dharma Sūtras provide that if a Śūdra intentionally listens to the recitation of the Vedas, his ears shall be filled with molten lead or lac. If he recites Vedic texts, his tongue shall be cut off; if he remembered them his body shall be split into two parts.[39]

The Gautama Dharmasūtra speaks of four Āśramas. These are Brahmacari or student, Gṛhastha or householder, Bhikśu or ascetic and Vaikhanasa or hermit in the wood.[40] But Āpastmba provides Āśramas in a different order.[41] These are Grhasthya or the order of householder; Ācāryakula or the order of student; the Mauna or the order of ascetics and Vānaprasthya or the order of hermit in the woods. Baudhāyana enumerates four Āśramas[42] and then makes the startling remark that these Āśramas were introduced by an Asura Kapila, the son of Prahlāda and that a wise man should not take heed of them.[43]

In the Baudhāyana Dharmasūtras we find a strange practice. It is that of carrying of water in a pot which is to be used for toilet as well as for washing and in ritual.[44] This was an ancient

Aryan practice. But in Smṛtis and Purāṇas this custom is declared Kalivarjya or 'forbidden because of the Kali age.' Many ancient Aryan practices which became unpopular among the people were forbidden and declared Kalivarjya.

The Mānava Gṛhyasūtra says that the four Vināyakas are evil spirits. These are : Śālakantaka, Kuṣmanḍarajaputra, Usmita and Devayajana. People when seized by them have bad dreams of inausicious sight such as shaved persons, persons with matted hair or wearing yellowish garments, camels, hogs asses and Cāṇḍālas. Seized by them, princes though capable donot get their kingdoms, maiden though endowed with all accomplishments cannot secure husbands, married women have no children, even virtuous wives lose their children in infancy, husbandmen lose their crops, and so on. For removing the evil influences of Vināyakas' seizure, Mānva Gṛhyasūtra prescribes propitiatory rites. Unlike Aryans gods, they were offered oil, fish and liquer.[45] Probably the Vināyakas are gods of non-Aryan origin and therefore they were considered destructive by the Aryans and were to be propitiated differently.

We find a gradual change in prescribed mode of worship. In the Deva Yajña as prescribed by the Śatapatha Brāhmaṇa only a fuel stick was to be offered to the fire for being transmitted as offering to the gods. But in the Āśvalāyana and Śankhāyana Gṛhyasūtras offering of cooked food were to be placed on earth for various gods in different directions. This change in the mode of sacrifice was probably due to the non-Aryan influence. The Aryans used to make offerings in the fire. The Śākhāyana Gṛhya Sūtra includes even the name of non-Aryans godsess, Bhadrakāli, among the Aryan gods whom offerings are to be made.

The Āpastamba Dharmasūtra provides that a householder should collect the left-over food and wash it with water and put at a clean place to the north and offer them to Rudra.[46] It is asserted that in this way the house will become properous. This manner of offering food to gods also appears to be of a non-Aryan origin.

The Impact of Buddhism

The social norms established by the Sūtras were again threatened by Buddhism. The teachings of Buddha were in Pālī, the language of the people. These were meant for all the sections of the population. Therefore Buddhism gained influence among the people. Buddha propounded equality of all castes. Once a young Brāhmaṇa Āssalāyana, challenged him. He said:

'Brahāmaṇas maintain that only they are the highest class and the others are lower. They are white, the others black; only they are pure and not others. Only they are the true sons of Brahmā, born from his mouth, born of Brahmā, heirs of Brahmā. Now what does worthy Gautama say to that.'

'Do the Brāhmaṇas really maintain this, Āssalāyana, when they are born of women just like anyone also, of Brāhmaṇa women who have their periods and who conceive, give birth and nurse their children, just like any other women?'[47]

Ultimately the Buddha convinced him that the people of all castes are equal.

The Buddha also challenged the efficacy of sacrifices. He said that performing a sacrifice is as futile as throwing a stone into deep water and then imploring it to spring up on the shore, but of course the stone remains at the bottom.[48]

The Buddha says that decent in not important but conduct is important.[49] Through right conduct even the persons of low castes could accomplish a higher position and ultimately get salvation for which he used the terms Nirvāṇa or 'blowing out of the lamp.' He compares life with a lamp.

The Buddhist doctrine, though it was deeply influenced by the Upaniṣadic philosophy, rejects the concepts of Brahma and soul. But he did emphasize the importance of life without passion. He compares life with a lamp. Just as a new lamp may be lighted by another lamp, similarly rebirth is possible without soul. Good and bad actions determine the fate and fortune in the next birth. Though Buddha rejected the Varṇa hierarchy he was not able to reject the theory of Karma, which has played such an important part in rationalizing and justifying the Varṇa inequality.

He says : 'Be thy own lamp. Do not seek external support. Hold fast to the truth as lamp. Every individual if he performs good actions in many births will ultimately achieve the final stage of Naibbāna or Nirvāṇa or the blowing out of the lamp.'[50]

Origin and Nature of the Second Brahmanicial Revival

Buddhism became widely accepted in India and abroad. It deprived the priestly elites of their priviledged status. This led to ressertation of their status by the Brahamanical elites around the second century A.D. Due to weakening of the Varna system and also the widespread racial admixture that had inevitably taken place, the norms of racial purity even of the priestly elites had been compromised. The foreign hordes, which continued to enter India from time to time had a complexion which was fairer than even the established priestly elites. Norms of the people of non-Aryan origin also began to assert themselves. Many Ancient Aryan customs had lost their hold on people and became repugnant. By that time it must have become quite clear to the priestly elites that ancient religion of the Aryans could not be revived in its original form. To combat these challenges the priestly elites composed various Smṛiti texts. These texts bear the names of ancient Vedic seers. The Manu Smriti is the first among these. Manu followed the dicta of Dharma Sūtras. Yājñavalkya, Bṛahspati, Nārada, and Kātyāyana followed the Manu Smṛti.

Manu tried hard to revive the ancient religion of Aryans. But it could not be revived in its pure form. The priestly elites were declared the repositories of the Vedic religion. Manu says that 'The Brahmaṇa from the very birth is an eternal incarnation of the scared law.'[51] To establish the priestly elites, Manu revived the ancient Ṛgvedic myth of the origin of the four Varnas and called them 'lords of this whole creation.'[52] Manu prescribes six duties for the Brāhmaṇa. One of the duties of the Brāhmaṇa is sacrificing for others.'[53] The non-Aryan religious practices which were prevalent among Brāhmaṇas were disapproved by Manu. Manu prescribes that those Brāhmaṇas who worship idols in temples as priests and those who offer sacrifices to the Gaṇas or the four Vināyakas must be avoided at sacrifices offered to the gods and manes.'[54] But it appears that non-Aryan gods had already become popular among the Aryans. For example, following Śānkhāyana Gṛhya Sūtra, Manu had to provide that a householder should offer a Bali or offering to Bhadrakālī near the foot of the bedstead.[55] Vaikhanasa-Smārta Sūtra and Uśanas provide that a Parāśava or the son of Brāhamaṇa with a Śūdra woman may worship the goddess Bhardrakālī or may learn the Śaiva Āgama.[56] It appears that despite the provision by Manu that a Brāhmaṇa householder should make an offering to Bhadrakālī many elites did not favour this even at a later time. An exception was made in case of a Parāśava son of Brahāmaṇa man and a Śūdrā woman. He could perform that offering without fear of pollution (for he was not as pure as a pure Brāhmaṇa).

Though the Mahābhārata enumerates Buddha among incarnations of Viṣṇu. It does not make complimentary remarks about him. It says that "during the Kali age I (god Viṣṇu) am taking birth as Buddha, the son of Śuddhodana; dressed in yellow garments I would confuse people. The Śūdra would wear yellow garments. Priests would neither study nor sacrifice. Śruti and Smṛti would be forgotten".[57] The Ramāyana also condemns the Buddha. It calls him an atheist and a thief.[58]

The Vṛddha Hārīta Smṛti clearly states that an Aryan householder should not enter the shrines of Śaiva, Bauddha, Skanda and Śākta cults.[59] Medhātithi on Manu Smṛti was so conscious of the non-Aryan and non-Vedic origins of these sects that he declares that the Pāncarātras or Vaiṣṇavas, Niragranthas or Jaina and Pāśupatas or Śaivas are outside the pale of Vedic orthodoxy.[60] The Kūrma Purāṇa asserts that "various

Śāstras opposed to the Vedas and Smṛtis which are popular among people such as Kāpāla, Bhairava, Yamala, Vāma and Arhata are for deluding the world and are based on ignorance".[61] The Brahmāṇḍa Purāṇa quoted in the Mitākṣarā commentary on the Yājñavalkya Smṛti, and the Smṛti Candrikā quotes the Śattrimsanmata to provide that if a man touches a Bauddha, Pāśupata, Jaina, Lokāyatika, atheist, a Dvijati or twice-born living by condemned actions or a Śūdra, he should bathe with his clothes on.[62] The four Vināyakas who are considered demons in the Mānava Gṛhya Sūtras appear in the Yājñavalkya Smṛti as one single god.[63] There is evidence that at one time even the outcaste people such as the Cāṇḍālas and the Pukkasas used to worship in the temples of Viṣṇu along with Brāhamaṇas. And even the Cāṇḍālas could establish the temples of Bhairava. It is provided the Nityācārapaddhti that if a Brāhmaṇa touches outcastes such as Cāṇḍālas and Pukkasas who came to worship god Viṣṇu in the temple, the Brahmaṇa need not take bath.[64] The Nirṇayasindhu quotes a passage of Devi Purāṇa which provides that Antyajas or outcastes could establish a temple of Bhairava or Śiva.[65] But later on even the Śūdras, not to speak of the outcastes, were forbidden from visiting temples.

As time passed even the basic Aryan ritual, Agnihotra or fire-sacrifice was declared Kalivarjya or forbidden in Kali age by Vyāsa.[66] Thus the non-Vedic religious practices were almost completely adopted by the priestly elites and Hinduism which is substantially different from the religion of the Vedas came into being. Despite the disapproval of some Brahmanical elites, the Pāñcarātra or Vaiṣṇava cult and Paśupata or the Śaiva cult were accepted in the elite Brahmanical tradition. Vināyaka or Gaṇeśa became the chief god who was the first to be invoked, before all other ceremonies commenced. This is considered imperative for ceremonies to be completed without hinderance. It seems that one of the reasons for such adaptation was the temptation of monetary gain for the Brahamana priests.

Since the Aryan religious practices had no longer remained

popular among the masses the Brahmanical priests felt compelled to give up the Vedic sacrifices and ultimately adopted the popular non-Aryan idol worship. And so many popular folk beliefs, customs, myths and historical incidents have been interwoven in the complex fabric of Hinduism that it is hard to isolate or identify them. Undoubtedly, the two great epics, the Mahābhārata and the Rāmāyana, and numerous Purāṇas profoundly influenced and unified the people of the whole of the Indian subcontinent by integrating elements from diverse sources. Priests made concerted effort for many centuries to make a consistent mythology and popularise it. Thus, a broad and strong base was provided to Hinduism. During the period between the second century B. C. and the third century A. D. Hinduism seems to have acquired the shape that was to last for much more than a millennium and a half.

In the Purāṇas, the cultures of the subjugated people can be seen to have overpowered the culture of the victorious Aryans. The most evident example is the legend of the struggle of the Vedic hero-god Indra and cowherd-god Kṛṣṇa. Kṛṣṇa challenged the power and position of Indra. To teach him a lesson, Indra brought rains continuously for seven nights while Kṛṣṇa held up a mountain on one finger and gave shelter to the people. Ultimately Kṛṣṇa won the battle and prevented people from offering sacrifice to Indra.

The Vedic god Rudra was unified with the non-Aryan phallus god and was given the name of Paśupati, and called Śiva or one who bestows welfare. The mother goddesses were unified and made his spouse. But inspite of this mythical arrangement, various mother-goddesses are still worshipped independently. The mother goddess is call Śakti or power. The worshippers of Śakti are called Śākta. Śakti is said to be the power of Śiva. It is said that without her Śiva becomes Śava or a dead body. Kumāra who figures as a demon in the Pāraskara Gṛhya Sūtras and according to these Gṛhya Sūtras caused epilepsy among Aryan infants,[67] was Brahamanized as called Subrahamanya or Skanda the god of youthful powers and bravery. He was recognized as the first born son of Śiva. Similarly, the four Vināyakas who were described as demons in the Mānava Gṛhya Sūtras,[68] were unified into one god and given the Aryan name of Gaṇeśa, who became the second son of Śiva. Similarly, Rāma and Kṛṣṇa were unified with the Ṛgvedic sun-god Viṣṇu, through the notion that they were incarnations of the god Viṣṇu. His spouse is the Vedic goddess Śrī who was later on called Laksmī, the goddess of wealth. The worship of these deities consists of bathing the idol, offering him food, water, flowers, leaves, incense; and music and dancing. The integration of the Vedic gods with the goddesses of non-Aryan origin, helped the unification of the people of different races and cultures of the Indian sub-continent. Thus, the worship of phallus and idols of non-Aryan gods and goddesses which were intensely repugnant to the Aryans became an important part of the elite tradition of later Hinduism. In fact, Hinduism as it has been actually practiced over the centuries gives scarce importance to Vedic Yajñas and gods of the Ṛgveda. Brahma Purāṇa and Mastya Purāṇa make an interesting observation that in Kṛta or earliest age there was a single Varṇa but at the end of the Kali age almost all people will be Śūdras.[69]

The main sects of Hinduism which developed later on are Vaiṣṇavas or the worshippers of Viṣṇu, Śaivas or worshippers of Śiva, and Śāktas or worshippers of Śakti. These are devotional sects. Viṣṇu, Śiva and Śakti are the deities of these sects. These deities are supposed to be omnipresent, omniscient and omnipotent. When the devotee surrenders himself unreaservedly to his deity, he goes to the heaven of that deity. This surrender might be through the worship of the idol of his deity or by singing devotional songs or chanting the name of his chosen deity. The worship of an idol of the deity consists of bathing the idol, offering him food, water, flowers, leaves, incense, music and dancing. By the whole hearted worship of the deity the sins of the devotees are condoned by the deity and the devotee goes to the heaven of that particular deity.

Behind the unification of various gods and goddesses of different origins, and making a consistent mythology, one attraction for the priestly elites must have been economic. And this process still continues. Whichever new deity emerges and becomes popular, the Brahmanical priests take over its priesthood from the low caste person who is its initial priest.

Notes

1. Ṛgveda, X. XXII. 8.1
2. Ṛgveda, VII. XXI. 5.
3. Ṛgveda, VII. XXX. 1.
4. Ṛgveda, III. LII. 7.
5. Ṛgveda, X. XCI. 14.
6. Ṛgveda, X. XIV. 1.
7. Ṛgveda, I. 125.5
8. Ṛgveda, IX. CXIII. 7-11.
9. Ṛgveda, IV. V. 5.
10. Ṛgveda,X. XCXI. 8.
11. Ṛgveda, III. XXXII. 3
12. Ṛgveda, III. XLV. 1.
13. Ṛgveda, IV. XVI. 14.
14. Ṛgveda, IV. XVII. 9.
15. Ṛgveda, III. XXXII. II.
16. Ṛgveda, X. XXVIII. 3.
17. Ṛgveda, VI. XV. 8.
18. Ṛgveda, VI. XVI. 32.
19. Ṛgveda,V. VII. 7.
20. Ṛgveda, III. XIV. 1.
21. Ṛgveda, VII. XVI. 2.
22. Ṛgveda, I. XXIV. 10; CV. 12
23. Ṛgveda, VII. XXXIV. 10-11.

24. Ṛgveda, V. LXXXV. 8.
25. Ṛgveda, VI. XVII. 1-6.
26. Ṛgveda, VI. XXX. 1-5.
27. Ṛgveda, I. CLIV. 1-4.
28. Ṛgveda, I. CXIV. 7-8.
29. Ṛgveda, II. XXXIII. 8.
30. Ṛgveda, VII. XLVI. 3.
31. P. V. Kane, History of Dharma Sastra, Bhandarkar Research Institute, Poona 1962, Vol. V., part II, p. 1622.
32. Śatapatha Brāhamaṇa, XI. 5-6. 1-3.
33. Chāndogya Uhaniṣad, I. 12. 1-5.
34. Bṛhadāranyaka Upaniṣad, VI. 4. 14-17.
35. Bṛhadāranyaka Upaniṣad, VI. 4. 28.
36. For a more elaborate discussion of this thesis, see Shrirama Indradeva; The doctrine of Karma towards a Sociological Perspective, Diogenes !40, 1987.
37. Mundaka Upaniṣad, I.2. 7-13.
38. See Shrirama Indradeva "Cultural interaction, between Ancient Civilizations ; A Study of Indo-Iranian Relations" *Diogenes* no. 111 (July-Sept. 1980)
39. Gautama Dharmasūtra, XII. 4-6.
40. Gautama Dharmasūtra, III.2.
41. Āpastamba Dharmasūtra, II. 9.21.1.
42. Baudhāyana Dharmasūtra, II.6.11.12.
43. Baudhāyana Dharmasūtra, II.6.11.28.
44. Baudhāyana Dharmasūtra, I.4.7.1-8.
45. Mānava Gṛhyasūtra, II. 14.1-21.
46. Āpastamba Dharmasūtra, II.2.4.23.
47. Majjhima Nikāya, 2.147.ff.
48. Saṁyutta Nikāya, XLII.6.
49. Vinaya Mahāvagga, 4.9.
50. Buddhist Suttas, II.33.
51. Manu Smṛti, I.98.

52. Manu Smṛti, I.92.
53. Manu Smṛti, X. 75-76.
54. Manu Smṛti, III.152., 164.
55. Manu Smṛti, 89.
56. Vaikhānasa Smārta Sūtra, X.13, Uśanas Smṛti, 36.
57. Mahābhārata, 12. 48.2
58. Ramāyana Ayodhya Kanda. 109.34.
59. Vṛddha Hārita Smṛti, XI.143.
60. Medhātithi on Manu Smṛti, II.6.
61. Kūrma Purāṇa I.12.161-162.
62. Brahmānda Purāṇa quoted in Mitākṣarā on Yājñavalkya Smṛti III. 30, Śaṭ-trimsan-Mata quoted by Smṛti-Candrikā, I.p.118.
63. Mānava Gṛhyasūtra, II.14.1-2, Yājñavalkya Smṛti I.282-283.
64. Nityācāraapaddhati, p. 130.
65. Nirnayasindhu, III. Devapratistha.
66. Vyāsa quoted in Smrtimuktaphala, p. 176.
67. Pārskara Gṛhya Sūtra, I. 16.24-25.
68. Mānava Gṛhya Sūtra, II. 14.1-21.
69. Brahma Purana 220. 52; Matsya purana, 144.78.

XI

Latent Function of the Doctrine of Karma

It is well known that in India, over the last two thousand five hundred years and more, there has been a pervasive belief in the doctrine of Karma. Various forms and variants in which this doctrine has found expression in the multifarious texts and metaphysical systems have drawn a good deal of attention. In this chapter, an attempt has been made to analyze the function of this doctrine in the sustenance of the traditional social system, and particularly, the scheme of social stratification. As we shall see, an unshakable faith in this doctrine by people belonging to all strata of society provided tremendous strength to the caste hierarchy based on birth, and ensured a secure place for the Brāhmaṇas and their progeny on the top of the social pyramid.

Since most of the traditional texts are the creations of the Brāhmaṇas, it is easy to conclude that the doctrine of Karma has been deliberately designed by them to secure the highest status and privileges for themselves. Such a conclusion may not be entirely correct. As a sociological concept, function "refers to observable objective consequences and not to subjective dispositions".[1] Any cultural or structural element which helps in the sustenance or adjustment of the system as a whole is said to be functional—whatever be the intentions or motivations of various actors in the situation. In fact the noted sociologist, Robert K. Merton, has put forth thus the concept of latent function—those functions which are neither intended not recognised by the members of that culture.[2] The function of the doctrine of Karma in justifying and strengthening the social hierarchy based on birth may well be a "latent" function.

Non-Aryan Origin of the Doctrine of Karma

Though the doctrine of Karma has been entrenched for long in the orthodox and heterodox religions and metaphysical systems, it seems to be of non-Aryan origin. In the Rgveda, the dead go to live in the world of forefathers (Pitara). There is no concept of transmigration of soul or rebirth in the Ṛgveda. It is in the Upaniṣads, which were composed much later, that we find an ample and vivid exposition of the doctrine of Karma. These ideas became an integral part of the foundation of the traditional Indian thought.

According to the doctrine of Karma every soul's fate is determined according to the deeds performed in the past lives. The characteristics of the body, birth in a particular species, caste, or family—everything is decided by the deeds performed in previous lives. According to the Hindu view of life, every soul is rewarded or suffers as an inevitable consequence of deeds and conduct in his past lives. The ultimate aim of human life is to get rid of the cycle of birth and rebirth. This is salvation or Mokṣa.

Though the idea of transmigration of soul is not found in the Ṛgveda, the Śatapatha Brāhmaṇa does say that by performing certain sacrifices by the correct procedure one can get rid of repeated deaths or Punaramrtyu.[3] In fact this idea occurs rather suddenly for the first time in the Śatapatha Brāhmaṇa. The Śatapatha Brāhmaṇa bears clear impress of Assyrian influence in many ways. For instance, the story of deluge described in this work seems to be the result of contact with Assyrians. The idea of repeated deaths, Punarmṛtyu, too seems to have come through diffusion, by culture contact with the Assyrians.

Similarly, the Assyrian idea that one can get rid of his or her sins by confessing them before a priest also finds expression in the Śatapatha Brāhmaṇa. During the Varuṇapraghāsa offerings the priest takes the sacrificer's wife aside and asks her to confess her extraconjugal relations. It is asserted that sins turn into truth after confession, but those sins that are not confessed remain injurious.

This contact became possible because the easternmost part of the vast Assyrian empire covered the Saptasindhu. This is confirmed also by the accounts of Arrian (Indica I. 1-3.) which state that the Indians between the river Sindhu and Kabul (Cophen) "were in ancient times subject to Assyrians, the Medes, and, finally to the Persians under Cyrus to whom they pay tribute he imposed upon them." It is also remarkable that no mention of Saptasindhu, which is the land described most of all in the Ṛgveda, is found in the Śatapatha Brāhmaṇa. This further suggests that the Saptasindhu had to be given up by the Aryans in the times when they composed the Śatapatha Brāhmaṇa.

Explicit discussion of transmigration of soul is not found in any work earlier than the Upaniṣads. The Upaniṣads mark the revolt of the princely elites against Brahamananical orthodoxy and supremacy. The Upaniṣads often assert that the Brahmanas are devoid of the real knowledge. What is more, in the Upaniṣads we find some low caste persons like Raikva, the cartman, so well versed in the knowledge about the ultimate reality that even the Kṣatriaya kings go to learn from them. The lower castes are categorized as Śūdras, the lowest of the four Varṇas, and are predominantly of non-Aryan origin—the Dāsas of Ṛgveda. It is not surprising, therefore, that many non-Aryan ideas such as transmigration of soul and asceticism have found expression in the Upaniṣads. The Upaniṣads propound that deeds performed in previous lives determine the next life.

The idea of transmigration of soul has been deeply rooted

in the Indian folk-mind since ancient times. The doctrine of Karma implies that the low status of the people of the Śūdra and untouchable castes is due to their own misdeeds committed in their previous births. It is because of these that they are born in the lowest castes. According to this doctrine, the only hope of improving their lot lies in performing properly the duties of their particular Varṇa and caste.[4] The Śūdras, for instance, can hope to benefit only through serving the higher Varṇas and thus becoming eligible for birth in higher Varṇas in their later lives.

Social Background of the Articulation of the Doctrine of Karma in Upaniṣads

It is interesting that the idea of transmigration of soul and re-birth was introduced in the Upaniṣads which themselves are an expression of revolt against Brāhmanical supremacy. The Upaniṣads seem to have borrowed this and many other meta-physical ideas and attitudes from the non-Aryan settlers. The doctrine of Karma as developed by the Brāhmaṇa elites has had such a pervasive and firm grip that even the most exploited sec-tions have faith in it since ancient times. It is a popular theme of Jātaka tales, many of which belong to the pre-Buddhist era ac-cording to T. W. Rhys Davids.[5] These ideas seem to have influenced the Buddhist doctrine so much that though Bud-dhism does not believe in the existence of soul, it nevertheless maintains that Karmas or deeds continue after death and deter-mine the next birth.

Belief in the transmigration of soul, which is an integral part of the doctrine of Karma, finds ample expression in all the later texts. It is found in the Sūtra literature; and in all the works of the era of Brāhmanical revival such as the Mahābhārata, Rāmāyana and Manu Smṛti. This doctrine is ac-cepted as a self-evident truth.

The doctrine of Karma is a common feature of all the schools of Indian philosophy. The only exception is the materialist school of Cārvāka. Not only the orthodox schools of thought, but also the heterodox religions such as Buddhism and Jainism subscribe to this fundamental doctrine. All these schools relate transmigration of soul to the nature of deeds. They also believe, in one way or the other, in salvation as freedom from transmigration.

The idea that a soul takes many births appears to have a non-Aryan origin. This belief is widely prevalent among many proto-Austroloid tribes, such as Santhala. Many of these tribes believe even now that after death the soul becomes a tree or an animal.

The Upaniṣads have meticulously worked out and propounded the doctrine of Karma. The Chāndogya Upaniṣads says: "Those whose conduct has been good will quickly attain a good birth, the birth of a Brāhmaṇa, or a Kṣatriya or a Vaiśya. But those whose conduct has been evil, will quickly attain an evil birth, the birth of a dog, or a hog or a Cāṇḍāla (an untouchable outcaste)."[6]

In the Bṛhadaranyaka Upaniṣad we find the theory of transmigration together with the description of the supreme bliss, the unification with non-qualifiable absolute—the Brahman :

> "And as a caterpiller, after having reached the end of a blade of grass, and after having made another approach (to another blade), draws itself together towards it, so does this self, after having thrown off this body and dispelled all ignorance, and after making another approach (to another body), draws himself together towards it.
>
> "And as a goldsmith, taking a piece of gold, turns it into another, newer and more beautiful shape so does this self, after having thrown off this body and dispelled all ignorance, makes unto himself another, newer and more beautiful shape, whether it be like the ancestors, or like the Gandharvas, or like the Devas, or like Prajāpati or like Brahman or like other beings.
>
> "That self is indeed Brəhman, consisting of knowledge, mind, life, sight, hearing, earth, wind, ether, light and no light, desire and no

desire, anger and no anger, right or wrong and all things. Now as a man is like this or like that, according to the way he acts and according to how he behaves, so will a man of good acts becomes good, a man of bad acts, bad. He becomes pure by pure deeds, bad by bad ones.

"And there they say that a person consists of desires. And as is his desire so is his will; and as is his will, so is his deed and whatever deed he does that he will reap.

"And here there is this verse : To whatever object a man's own mind is attached to that he goes strenuously together with his deed, and having obtained the end of whatever deed he does here on earth, he returns again from that world to this world of action.

"So much for the man who desires. But as to the man who does not desire, who not desiring, freed from desires, it satisfied in his desires, or desires the self only, his vital spirits do not depart elsewhere being Brahman, he goes to Brāhmaṇ."[7]

In this passage of the Bṛhadāranyaka Upaniṣad, it is explained that if a man improves his desires and deeds in the successive births he achieves the ultimate Goal, the Brahman. In the case that he desires some worldly object he inevitably attaches himself to that object and returns to this world. In this passage we also find a passing reference to the other world, probably heaven. Perhaps, the Upaniṣads could not completely get themselves rid of the Aryan concept of heaven; and the belief in the existence of heaven is probably sought to be reconciled with the doctrine of transmigration of soul. Before taking a new birth in this world the soul remains in heaven for some time.

The Śvetāśvatara Upaniṣad explains the nature of Brahman, the Ultimate Reality :

"He is the creator and knower, the destroyer of time, possessing qualities, knowing everything. lord of Pradhāna (material cause), of individual souls and the Gunas (Sattva, Rajas, Tamas) and of the cause of release from Saṁsāra (births and deaths), of sustaining it and of bondage."[8]

Incidentally, these basic concepts of the material cause, the three-fold qualities and the cause of release, have been employed in the metaphysical theory of the Sāmkhya system.

The Sūtras seem to have inherited the idea of transmigration of soul from the Upaniṣads. The Gautama Dharmasūtra propounds that:

> "Members (Brāhmaṇa etc) of the Varṇas and of Āśramas (Brāhmaṇacari etc.) who are devoted to performing the appropriate duties (of their Varṇa and Āśrama) enjoy the fruit (heaven) of their actions after death and then by virtue of the residue (of their actions) they attain a new birth (in this world) endowed with a good country, caste, family, long life, learning in Vedas, character, wealth, happiness and wisdom."[9]

This passage indicates that the concept of heaven also persisted along with the doctrine of transmigration of soul in the Sūtra period. Similarly, the Āpastamba Dharmasūtra says :

> "Men of all Varṇas, if they fullfil their prescribed duties, enjoy (in heaven) the highest, measureless happiness. Afterwards when (a man who has fulfilled his duties) returns to this world, he obtains, by virtue of a remainder of merit, birth in a distinguished family, beauty of form, beauty of complexion, strength, aptitude for learning, wisdom, wealth and the gift of fulfilling the laws of his (Varṇa and Āśrama). Therefore in both worlds he dwells in happiness, (rolling) like a wheel (from the one to the other)."[10]

Similarly, if the men of higher Varṇas commit sins they shall be born as outcastes. Āpastamba provides that a Brāhmaṇa, a Kṣatriya and a Vaiśya, who has stolen gold or killed a Brāhmaṇa, is born again if he was Brāhmaṇa as a Cāndāla, if he was a Kṣatriya as a Pualkasa, if he was a Vaiśya as a Vaina, after undergoing torments in hell for a limited time.[11] In this provision, too, it is implicit that these castes are the most sinful, and their low birth is due to their own sins. Thus on the one hand this belief functions as a means of social control by supporting the traditional norms, and on the other it provides an explanation and justification for the low status assigned to the untouchable castes. Both ways it ensures the supreme position of the Brāhmaṇas and promotes internalisation of norms and values conducive to the maintenance of their privilages.

Buddhism and the Doctrine of Karma

Even in very early times, the doctrine of Karma had become such an integral part of the life and thought of the people that the Buddhists too had to accept it though they denied the existence of soul. Buddhism inherited and in certain ways pushed farther the tradition of Upaniṣads. The doctrine of Karma was refined and systematized meticulously in Buddhism. In the Mahāvagga of Vinaya texts we find the mention of Pratityasamutpāda or the doctrine of dependent origination. It says that life originates due to ignorance. This doctrine is attributed to the Buddha : "Then the Blessed one during the first watch of the night fixed his mind upon the chain of causation, in direct and in reverse order :

> "From ignorance spring the Saṁskāras[12] or predispositions, from the Saṁskāras springs consciousness, from consciousness spring name and form, from name and form spring the six provinces (of the six senses, eye, ear, nose, tongue, body or touch and mind), from the six provinces springs contact, from contact springs sensation, from sensation springs craving, from cravings springs attachment, from attachment springs becoming, from becoming springs birth, from birth spring old age and death, grief, lamentation, suffering, dejection and despair. Such is the origin of this whole mass of suffering. Again, by the destruction of ignorance, which consists in the complete absence of lust, the Saṁskāras are destroyed; by the destruction of the Saṁskāras consciousness is destroyed; by the destruction of consciousness, name and form are destroyed; by the destruction of name and form the six provinces are destroyed; by the destruction of contact, sensation is destroyed; by the destruction of sensation, craving is destroyed; by the destruction of attachment, becoming is destroyed; by the destruction of becoming, birth, old age and death, grief, lamentation, suffering, dejection and despair are destroyed. Such is the cessation of this whole mass of suffering."[13]

In the Majjhima Nikāya this wheel of causation is divided into those elements which are due to the past life, those elements which are due to the present life and those of the future life. Among these Avidyā or ignorance and Saṁskāras or predispositions are declared to be due to past life. Vijñāna or consciousness, Nāmarūpa or name and form, Śaḍāyatana or the six sense organs, Sparśa or contact, Vedanā or emotion, Tṛṣṇā or craving, Upādāna or clinging or attachment, are due to present life. Bhāva or coming to be, Jāti or rebirth, Jarāmaraṇa or old age and death are of future life.[14]

Thus, according to Buddhism, the very human existence is due to ignorance. Saṁskāras or predispositions follow the ignorance. They determine the rebirth. in the Majjhima Nikaya it is said : "It happens, my disciples, that a monk, endowed with faith, endowed with righteousness, endowed with knowledge of the doctrine, with resignation, with wisdom, communes thus with himself : "Now then could I, when my body is dissolved in death obtain rebirth in a powerful princely family." He thinks this thought, dwells on this thought, cherishes this thought. These Saṁskāras and internal conditions which he has thus cherished within him and fostered lead to his rebirth in such an existence. This, disciples, is the avenue, this the path which leads to rebirth in such an existence."[15]

Next follows Vijñāna or consciousness from which name and form come into being :

> "If consciousness, Ānanda, did not enter into the womb would name and form arise in the womb?" "No, sir". And if consciousness, Ananda, after it has entered into the womb were again to leave its place would name and form be born into this life?" "No sir" "And if consciousness, Ananda, were again lost to the boy or to the girl while they were yet small, would name and form attain growth, increase and progress?" "No sir, it is through this consciousness that new birth is possible?" "If, Ananda, consciousness were not to find name, and material form as its resting place, would then birth, old age and death the origin and development

or sorrow, reveal themselves in succession?" "No sir, they should not."[16]

Buddhism was deeply influenced by Upaniṣads. And the ultimate goal of both is to get rid of rebirth. It is interesting that in the Śatapatha Brāhmaṇa also there is a reference to getting rid of Purarmṛtyu or recurring death. It is probable that belief in rebirth was prevalent among the vast body of the non-Aryan people, and it was from them that all the three, the Śatapatha Brāhmaṇa, the Upaniṣads and Buddhism derived it, and refined and systematized it in their own way.

Buddha says : "Therefore, O Bhikkus, whatever body has been, will be, and is now, belonging or not belonging to sentiment beings, gross or subtle, inferior or superior, distant or near, all that body is not mine, is not me, is not my self : this should be considered by right knowledge according to the truth." He further says :

> "Considering this, O Bhikkhus, a learned, noble hearer of the world becomes weary of body, weary of emotion, weary of perception, weary of the Samskāras or predispositions, weary of consciousness. Becoming weary of all that he divests himself of passion, by absence of passion he is made free, when he is free, he becomes aware that he is free; and he realises that re-birth is exhausted; that holiness is completed, that duty is fulfilled; and that there is no further return to this world."[17]

This is the state of Nirvaṇa or the blowing out or extinction. Though Buddhism is regarded as a hetrodox system, the orthodox schools of metaphysics, specially Vendānta, were greatly influenced by Buddhism.

The Brāhmanical Revival and the Latent Function of the Doctrine

It was during the period of Brāhmanical revival that the doctrine of Karma, together with other beliefs and rituals, was given the shape that persisted till contemporary times. The

Brāhmanical revival sought to revive the norms established during the Sūtra period, and the theory of Karma was further strengthened and elaborated by the systems of metaphysics.

In the Mahābhārata we find an interesting statement which explains the doctrine of Karma well :

> "Just as the calf finds his own mother out of a thousand cows, similarly action performed in a previous life follows the doer."[18]

Many stories of the Mahābhārata are inspired by a firm belief in the doctrine of Karma and transmigration. In a story, the son of an old women, Gautamī, died of snake-bite. A hunter caught the snake and said that he would kill the snake for biting the boy. But Gautami forbade him saying that the killing would not revive her son. Then Kala, or time himself, came an informed Gautamī that,

> "Just as the potter moulds from a lump of clay whatever he desires, so man secures, fruits of deeds done by himself; the boy's death was due to his deeds in previous life."[19]

The Manu Smṛti explains the creation of the universe on the basis of the Sāmkhya system of metaphysics. It explains that all deeds are performed by gods, men and animals because of the three Guṇas, qualities of the nature or the material cause of the universe. These qualities are Satoguṇa or light, Rajoguṇa or activity, and Tamoguṇa or darkness. Manu says that the three qualities of nature or the material cause of the universe are responsible for the creation of gods, man and animals. Among these, gods, sages and Brāhmaṇas etc., are created by light or the Satoguṇa, kings and Kṣatriyas are created by activity or Rajoguṇa; while Śūdras, elephants, horses, etc., are created by darkness or Tamoguṇa.[20] The Manu Smṛti further explains that

> "In consequence of attachment to (the objects of) the sense, and in consequence of the non-performance of their duties, the fools, the lowest of men, reach the vilest of births."[21]

Thus, it has been emphasized again and again that persons of the Śūdra Varṇa are themselves responsible for their low position in society.

As a metaphysical theory, the doctrine of Karma has been integrated in various sophisticated ways in the traditional philosophical systems. At the same time it has been a vital part of the living faith of the vast massess in India for more than two millenia. As a belief system, unquestioningly accepted by the people of all strata, it has been exceedingly functional for the sustenance of the social order.

It has been invaluable as a means of social control in general. Social control refers to the processes which are conducive to the maintenance of a social system. Every society has its own agencies and means of social control. These include institutions like the family and he state; social codes such as customs and law; and values and belief system. The vitality and survival of a social system depends on the conformity to its norms by the vast majority of its members; for it is on this that the stability of the established forms of social relationships, and ultimately that of the social structure as a whole, depends. Belief in the doctrine of Karma implies that the consequences of all one's deeds---good or bad---are bound to be endured by the doer in this or later lives. Any deviance from the prescribed norms, whether watched or unwatched, is bound to entail automatic punishment. A deep faith in this doctrine, therefore, deters people from violation of norms.

There is another aspect also of the function of the doctrine of Karma as a means of social control. For the smooth functioning of the social organisation it is essential that conflict or confusion between various statuses and roles is kept to a minimum. Belief in the doctrine of Karma tends to ensure this by inculcating the idea that everyone gets (or is born into) his vocation in accordance with his own predispositions (Saṁskāras) based on the deeds of his past lives. He should therefore assiduously attend to the duties appropriate to his own role, and never crave for the role of someone else. As the Gītā puts it: "It is glorious even to die doing one's own duty. The duty of someone else is perilous."[22] This is repeatedly quoted as a maxim in everyday parlance. Thus, in this pervasive Weltanschauung, every individual man or woman is expected to perform, to the best of his or her ability, the role assigned to him or her in the traditional social structure, without being attracted by any other role, and without any concern about whether others are performing their duties or not. This explains, for instance, how traditional Indian women continue to worship their husbands despite the frequently erring behaviour of the latter. One may be distressed at the oppression that this involves, but the fact remains that it is conducive to the sustenance of the social system.

It is perhaps in the justification and legitimization of the traditional pattern of social stratification that the function of the doctrine of Karma has been most effective and telling. The firm belief that one is born into a caste, low or high, strictly according to his own deeds in past lives, has reconciled to their lot people belonging even to the most oppressed and exploited castes, generation after generation. This doctrine thus has been a great support to the caste system. And when we consider the deep implications that the caste system has for all aspects of social life, the significance of the doctrine of Karma is brought out in its true proportions. The caste system is not just a device for reckoning status hierarchy. Traditionally, a person's caste is related also to occupation, marriage, eating and drinking, dress, mode of worship, and almost everything else. Though there is no one-to-one relationship between caste and occupation, for every caste certain occupations are forbidden, some others are permissible, and one or more are favoured. As for marriage, there are stringent and elaborate caste norms of endogamy, exogamy and hypergamy. In fact endogamy is the defining characteristic of a caste. Castes are endogamous groups—marriage outside one's caste is traditionally inadmissible, and even unthinkable. Exogamy too is governed by caste norms—one has to marry within one's own caste, but outside certain specified groups within it. And the regulation of hypergamy depends solely on the hierarchical sub-structures within various castes. The caste system has intricate norms concerning the sharing of food and water between persons belonging to different castes. In addition certain foods and beverages are forbidden or favoured for different castes. Castes puts severe restrictions on social intercourse—the touch or even the shadow or the sight or people of certain castes is considered to be polluting. There are a plethora of other caste norms which cover almost all aspects of life. When caste is so pervasive in traditional Indian society, it is hardly possible to overemphasize the importance of the social function of the doctrine of Karma, which has played a vital part in sustaining the caste system.

In the Upaniṣadic period this belief was refined and systematized and was given the sophisticated form of the metaphysical doctrine of Karma. In that period it was used by a section of the Aryan elites, namely, the Kṣatriyas (warriors and rulers), as a weapon in their revolt against the overbearing priestly elites, the Brāhmaṇas. Eventually the doctrine received wide acceptance, both by heterodox systems such as Buddhism and Jainism and in orthodox works like the Sūtras. It appears, however, that it was in the period of Brahmanical revival that the doctrine became an almost perfect instrument for the sustenance of the social order, ordained by the Brāhmanical elite. It has effectively performed this function chiefly because of the unquestioning acceptance that this doctrine has enjoyed among all sections of society. That faith in this doctrine is not confined to elite is borne out by the fact that it finds ample expression in the oral tradition of the unlettered folk as well. In fact even those religious movements which marked a revolt against Brāhmanical supremacy (such as the ones led by low caste saint poets like Kabīra and Raidāsa), and which gained wide popularity among the lower castes, nevertheless subscribed to the basic tenets of the doctrine of Karma.

Notes

1. Robert K. Merton, "Manifest and Latent Function", *Social Theory and Social Structure*, New York, The Free Press, 1968, p. 78.
2. Ibid, p. 114-136.
3. Śatapatha Brāhmaṇa, X.4.4. 9-10.
4. The term Varṇa refers to the fourfold ideal division of society mentioned in the classical texts of Hinduism, while the word caste (jāti in Sanskrit and Hindi) is generally used for the numerious endogamous groups which actually form the traditional social hierarchy. The Varṇas are only four in number while the castes are well over two thousand, and they are a social reality in the sense that they are recognised as such and determine the flow of social interaction. However there is often a dispute about a caste's belonging to a particular Varna. It would be difficult to place nearly all the castes in the four Varṇas.
5. Buddhist India, Delhi, Motilal Banarasidas, 1971, p. 197.
6. Chāndogya Upaniṣads, V. 10.7.
7. Bṛahadāranyaka Upaniṣad, IV, 4, 3-6.
8. Śvetāśvatara Upaniṣad, 6.16.
9. Gautama Dharmasūtra, XI. 29-30.
10. Āpastamba Dharmasūtra, II. 2. 2-3.
11. Āpastamba Dharmasūtra, II, 1, 2-6.
12. This word is used in the same sense among the Hindus even today.
13. Vinaya Texts, Mahāvagga, I, 1, 2-3.
14. Majjhima Nikāya, 140.
15. Majjhima Nikāya, 120.
16. Digha Nikāya, 15.
17. Vinaya texts, Mahāvagga, I, 6.44, and 46.

18. Mahābhārata, Anuśāsanaparva, 7.22.
19. Mahābhārata, Anuśāsanaparva, I, 74, 78-79.
20. Manusmṛti, XII, 40-50.
21. Manusmṛti, XII, 52.
22. Bhagvat Gītā, III, 35.

XII

The Rise of Elite Tradition and Genesis of Indian Civilization

The genesis of civilization has been an enigma for the historian and the social scientist. How does it happen that the homogenous stream of a tribal culture differentiates into the elite and folk traditions? The duality of cultural tradition in civilized societies is widely recognized and is designated by such paired terms as the classical and the lay, the aristrocratic and the common, and the great and the little traditions of culture. Apart from architechtonic formulations of the philosophers of history and the various metaphysical and mythological models that we have inherited, this question has to be approached from an empiric angle on the basis of cultural data about ancient civilizations available to us.

There can be no adequate comprehension of the existing sociocultural reality without a proper knowledge of the dynamics of its growth and the historical forces that shaped it. Such knowledge is all the more necessary for a country like India, which has maintained remarkable continuity in its cultural tradition through its thousands of years of existence.

The Indian civilization is an indigenous one in the sense that its elite stratum of culture has been formed by carrying forward (through refinement, sophistication and articulation) the indigenous elements of the lay culture. A better comprehension of the growth of the elite stratum of culture in ancient Indian civilization is sure to sharpen our understanding of the genesis of civilization as such. Form this angle the study of the Gṛhya Sūtras can be of immense value. These aphorisms composed before the sixth century B.C. seem to contain elements pertaining to the stage of the transformation of lay rituals and beliefs into the elite ones. Ordinarily, the Gṛhya Sūtras together with the Dharma Sūtras are unquestionably accepted as parts of the sacred elite (Śāstric) tradition of Indian culture. Their authority in matters dealt with by them would scarcely be challenged by any orthodox learned Hindu who is steeped in tradition. But a close look at the Gṛhya Sūtras would reveal that in their content as well as their tenor, they are closer to folklore rather than to classical works. A study of these features vividly brings out the folk roots of the articulated elite tradition.

The Gṛhya Sūtras as their name indicates contain aphorisms on household rituals. They belong broadly to the period when the Vedic Aryan tribes had decisively vanquished the Dāsas, the indigenous people, and were fanning out to colonize the vast lands that came under their sway. The militant spirit of the conquerors which characterised the Ṛgveda seems to have diminished by that time and it was assuming ritualistic form. The result of changing social conditions is amply reflected in these aphorisms. When these works were in the process of composition the turbulent tribal hordes were being transformed into simple villagers.

The Gṛhya Sūtras seems to provide the missing link in the evolution of the Indian civilization from the Vedic Aryan state to the stage of classical Hinduism found in works like the Smṛtis. The early Vedic civilization was marked by the vigorous militancy of the Aryans who enjoyed taking intoxicants and eating meat of cows, bulls and horses. The life of these invading immigrants was understandably rugged and devoid of much embellishment. As a contrast, the classical Hinduism, the tradition of which still survives in some form, is characterized by a surfeit of ritualism and intricate codes governing purity and pollution. The Gṛhya Sūtras help to reveal the processes which brought about this transformation. In these Sūtras we find on the one hand the glimpses of the simple life of the settler, and on the other certain ritualistic ideas which foreshadow the later sacramental complex of classical Hinduism.

A striking example of how the Gṛhya Sūtra era constitutes the period of transition from the early Vedic norms to the classical Hindu values is provided by the changing attitude towards cow slaughter and beef eating. Today beef eating is considered a most reprehensible sin by the Hindus, and this has been so for many centuries. But in the early Vedic period beef eating was enjoyed by the Aryans and when a respected guest arrived a cow was slaughtered in his honour. As a mark of respect the guest was given Madhuparka and requested to slaughter the cow himself. But, in the Gṛhya Sūtras, the householder does offer the cow with a butcher's knife to the guest; though he does implores the latter to let the animal live if he so wishes. It is provided, nevertheless, that the feast for the guest should not be without meat. This is only one example. Similar transitional positions are found on matters related to gods, rituals and social institutions in these Sūtras.

The interaction between the culture of Aryan settlers and the indigenous inhabitants whom they met and overpowered holds the key to the understanding of the origin of characteristically Indian institutions like caste, joint family based on subjugation of women, and the village community. While similar social institutions are not unknown in other civilizations, the peculiar circumstances of the clash between the Aryan and the indigenous cultures endowed the traditional Indian institutions with certain unique features which have engaged the attention of the social scientists. As the Gṛhya Sūtras belong to the period when the relationship between the Aryans and the non-Aryans was in the process of acquiring institutionalized forms, they can tell us a good deal about the elements and forces which went into the making of these institutional patterns.

It would be wrong to assume that the origin of the two cultural traditions in Indian civilization, namely, the classical and the folk, can be neatly traced to the Aryan and the non-Aryan sources respectively. Many of the gods and goddesses of classical Hinduism are clearly derived from the non-Aryan sources. The evidence of the Gṛhya Sūtras is illuminating on this point also.

The Gṛhya Sūtras inherited the Vedic gods with a few insignificant female goddesses dependent on their spouses. Some of the gods and demons which are considered harmful and ferocious, became popular Hindu deities in later literature. Among them are Rudra, the howler; the four Vināyakas, who make the person mentally distracted and with an adverse fate; Kumāra; Kubera and a she-demon whose description is quite close to the famous goddess Kālī. All these are considered in the Gṛhya Sūtras as bearers of different diseases. Rudra, who was later called Āśutoṣa or one who is pleased easily, was considered till the Gṛhya Sūtra period the bearer of storm and plague in cattle. He was propitiated to save the sacrificer from his wrath, and thus from cattle disaster. He was regarded so wrathful and ferocious that in the Śūlagava ritual the calf for him was sacrificed outside the village unwatched, and it was cremated at the same place. The Āsvalāyana Gṛhya Sūtra gives the reason. "They should not take to the village anything belonging to Śūlagava; for this god (Rudra) will do harm to creatures."[1] The four Vināyakas which were later integrated into one Vināyaka or Gaṇeśa, were also considered destructive—destroying even Yajñas. Unlike Aryan gods, they were offered oil, fish and liquor.[2] Probably these are the gods of non-Aryan origin, and therefore they were considered destructive by the Aryans.

Though the non-Vedic gods and the modes of their worship were taken over by the dominant classical tradition, one can still find some grumbling remarks against them in later works also. In some of these works the Pāśupatas, and the Pañcarātras are considered outside the Aryan tradition. The Vṛddha-Harīta Smṛti recommends that the householder should not enter the places of the Śaiva, Bauddha, Skanda and Śākta cults.[3] Medhatithi[4] on Manu says: "Pāncarātras, Nirgranthas, and Pāśupatas are outside the pale of Vedic othordoxy". The Kūrma Purāṇa says that the various Śāstras opposed to the Vedas and Smṛtis that are popular among people such as Kāpāla, Bhairava, Yāmla, Vāma and Arhata were for deluding the world and are based on ignorance.[5] And yet, since many centuries from now the classical Hindu tradition has fully integrated and absorbed gods like Śiva, Śakti (Mother goddess in various forms), Vināyaka (Gaṇeśa) etc. Indeed, the Phallus, the worship of which the Vedic Aryans strongly detested, occupies the place of pride in the sanctum sanctorum at Kashi Visvanātha (Banaras), the holiest centre of Hindu pilgraimage.

Any one familiar with a living folk tradition cannot fail to recognise the folk character of the Gṛhya Sūtras. This is true both of the form and the content. Just like the folk songs, the Sūtras have blank places (indicated as N. N. in the quotations from Sūtras given below) to allow the introduction of the proper names of concerned persons. This is only one example. In true folk style, the Gṛhya Sūtras depict the hopes and anxieties of the ordinary householder. They reveal their daily chores, family relationships and life of women. The householder in the Gṛhya Sūtra is concerned primarily with the day to day problems of setting up and running a small household. The requirements of colonization of vast areas did not permit the hundling together of a large number of kinsfolk in large households. In fact the rituals prescribed in these aphorisms do not presume the presence of any other adult except the husband and the wife. Strikingly enough, it is the husband who is supposed to act as the midwife when his wife delivers; and he has also to act as the priest-cum- magician and the performer of the child-birth rituals apart from running a variety of errands. Many other elements found in these aphorisms seem to represent the stage when the folk tradition of the Āryans had not yet been transformed into the elite stratum of culture of a great civilization.

The elemental sentiments of pain and pleasure, love and conflict are brought out beautifully by the Gṛhya Sūtras in the long prayers recited during the various rituals and rites. These prayers are sweet in their content and simple in style. An analysis of these prayers can give us a richer understanding of the world of two thousand years ago. The prayers of the householder are the songs of peace. By that time the indigenous inhabitants do not seem to have remained a serious threat. Some of them had taken shelter in the dense forests and hills, while others accepted the life of Śūdra in the social hierarchy. The struggle with them no longer dominated the scene. The Vedas, which preceded the Sūtras are replete with feelings of hostility against the indigenous, and the Smṛtis which came later show great concern for maintaining the racial purity, patriarchy, and cultural heritage of the Aryans. The Gṛhya Sūtra perhaps mark the period when the Aryans were trying to come to terms with the indigenous people, but were not yet afraid of being swamped and absorbed by them.

In this period people started combining agriculture with cattle breeding and tending. The plough drawn by bullocks was used for tilling the fields. The *yava* or barley and the *brīhi,* probably a wild variety of rice, were the chief crops. But the cattle were still constituted the most important form of wealth. Big herds of cows, horses, goats and sheep were reared. These supplied milk and meat for food and skins for making dresses. The hides and skins were also used as mats. Bullocks and horses were used for pulling carts and chariots. Dog was personified by their pastoral forefatheres as the divine bitch, Saramā, of the hero-god Indra. But by the time of the Gṛhya Sūtras it was degraded to such an extent that the diseases of children were given the form of dog demons. This was most probably a consequence of the anagonistic interaction of the Indian branch of the Aryans with the Iranians, as we shall see in the next chapter.

The Sūtras throw interesting light on the emerging patterns of basic social relationships between man and woman on the one hand, and between different classes on the other. These relationships were later institutionalized and sanctified as God given. But the Sūtras give us an inkling into the era when they were taking shape.

The relationship between man and woman seems to have been deeply influenced by the fact that the Aryan settler had often to take a non-Aryan indigenous woman as his wife. This was unavoidable as there were not enough women of his stock to go round. But he considered her inferior and was suspicious of her. In the Sūtras the wife is supposed to bring some evil elements with her, which can harm her husband, his forthcoming progeny, cattle, house and fame. He also doubts her integrity. Sensing these dangers, the husband performs prayers to divert these elements towards his wife's earlier lover or spouse. This indicates that wives did not belong to the same stock as their husbands. In Ṛgveda itself we get such references. The word *Vadhū* was used for a bride as well as a slavegirl.[6] We also get the statement of a general principle : 'When a Brāhmaṇa takes the hand of a girl though she be married, she becomes his wife'.[7] Though this mode of acquiring a wife may have ended by the time of Gṛhya Sūtras she is still suspected to be destructive for her husband's family and unfaithful towards him. However, he does not fight with his rival physically like his Vedic ancestor but satisfies himself by diverting her destructive attributes towards her lover. He lives with the same wife, not even thinking of deserting as provided in the Smṛtis. This indicates that the demand for absolute chastity from woman which hardened later was not so strong at that time. This may perhaps be related to the scarcity of women among the Aryans.

It is quite probable that the low position of woman in traditional Indian society owes a good deal to the fact that in the period of settlement the Aryans took wives from the indigenous people whom they considered low. Later on this relationship crystallized. The wife no more belonged to an alien stock and the husband was not suspicious of her on that score, but she herself had internalized the values of male superiority and of considering her husband as her lord. To inspire whole-hearted devotion in his bride he shows her the Dhruva or firm star (polar star) : "Dhruva art thou, I see thee Dhruva (firm). Dhruva (firm) be thou to me, O thriving one."[8]

The husband prays to the gods for whole-hearted devotion of his wife. He recites this verse during the marriage ceremony : "When thou wanderest far away with thy heart to various regions of the world like wind, may the gold-winged Vaikarana (the great eagle) grant that thy heart may dwell with me, N. N."[9] The wife being an outsider in the husband's house may bring some evil elements with her. The husband sensing this danger, diverts it by his straightforward prayer. On the fourth day before the consummation of conjugal relationship, the husband makes offerings of cooked food in the fire for Agni or the fire-god, Vāyu or the wind-god, Sūrya or the sun-god.

> Agni, Thou art expiation of gods.
> What substance dwells in her that brings death to her husband;
> Drive that away from her.
> Vāyu, Thou art expiation of the gods.
> What substance dwells in her that brings sonlessness;
> Drive that away from her.
> Sūrya, Thou art the expiation of the gods.
> What substance dwells in her that brings destruction to the cattle,
> Drive that away from her.[10]

Similarly, he offers oblations to Candra, the moon, and Gandharva, respectively to expiate the substances which dwell in her that bring destruction to the house and fame. Each time after he has sacrificed, he pours the remainder of the oblations into the water-pot, and out of that pot he sprinkles her head with the words : "The evil substance which dwells in thee that brings death to thy husband, death to thy children, death to cattle, destruction to the house, destruction to fame, that I change into one that brings death to thy paramour. Thus live with me to old age, N. N."

The householder of the Gṛhya Sūtra is full of ambition and optimism. He is a practical man; having potentiality of overcoming various individual problems through magical acts. While taking Madhuparka (curds with honey and clarified butter) he sits down with the verse: "I am the highest one among my people; as the Sun is among the thunder-bolts. Here I tread on whosoever infests me." And with the feet, he treads on the bundle of grass. Obviously, the old militant spirit of crushing one's enemies has by now taken the form of symbolic action.

While entering courts of justice, the judges first pray to the personified court: "Court, Thou that belongest to the Angiras? Trouble art thou by name, Vehemence art thou by name, Thus be adoration to thee." He then enters the court with the words : "(May) the court and the assembly, the two daughters of Prajāpati (protect me). May one who does not know me, be below me. May (all) people be considerate in what they say." He should whisper while entering : "Superior (to my adversaries) I have come hither, brilliant, not to be contradicted. The lord of this assembly is a man insuperable in his power."

When he thinks that any person is angry with him, he addresses him (silently) with the verse: "The destroying power of wrath and anger that dwells here on thy forehead, that the chaste, wise gods may take away. heaven am I and I am earth; we both take away thy anger; the she-mule cannot bring forth offspring, N.N."

When he thinks that this person will do evil to him, he addresses him with the words: "I take away the speech from thy mouth, I take away the speech in thy heart. Wheresoever thy speech dwells, thence I take it away. What I say, is true. Fall down, oh inferior to me."[11]

The folk nature of rituals found in the Gṛhya Sūtra is well brought out in the aphorisms dealing with ceremonies connected with child-birth. The householder, who is a cattle breeder and a farmer, eagerly wants more sons. For securing many longlived sons, a number of rituals are prescribed which appear to be magical acts. Performance of so many rituals indicates that having a living son must have been quite difficult at that time. During the marriage ritual, the husband puts a boy of good birth on both sides of his bride's lap. Through this act, it has been asserted that she will certainly become the mother of male children.[12] It is ordained that after the marriage the couple should sleep for three nights on the ground and serve the nuptial fire in evening and morning. On the fourth day the first pre-natal ritual, Garbhādhāna or securing conception, is performed. The wife offers the oblation in the fire with sacred verses, *mantras*. She prays to the gods in pairs : "Let the two men Mitra and Varuna, let the two men Asvins both, let the man Indra and also Agni make a man grow in me. Svāhā."[13]

In this prayer the manliness of gods is asserted so that a male child be born. The husband prays : "May a male embryo enter the womb, as an arrow (enters) the quiver; may a man be born here, a son after ten months." He further says that the gods may give girls to other women, but a son must be bestowed on him. he addresses his wife :

> Be a well-breading cow and produce a son from the auspicious sperm.
> Prajāpati has created him, Savitar has shaped him.
> Imparting birth of females to other (woman),
> May he put here a man.[14]

Infantile mortality must have been a great threat. To avoid this the bridegroom prays god Agni during marriage rituals to release the offspring of his wife from the fetter of death, so that he may enjoy a long happy life together with his son and wife:

> May Agni come hither, the first of the gods.
>
> May he release the offspring of this wife from the fetter of death.
>
> May this king Varuna grant that this wife does not weep
>
> Over distress (falling to her lot) through (the death of) her sons. Svāhā.

May Agni Gārhapatya protect this woman.

May he lead her offspring to old age.

With fertile womb may she be the mother of living children.

May she experience delight in her sons. Svāhā.

In the third month of pregnancy, Puṁsavana or securing the birth of a male child, is performed. The wife observes a fast. The husband gives her two beans and a barley grain with a handful of curds of a cow, who has a calf of the same colour. The husband asks : What do you drink? She replies thrice: "Puṁsavana, (generation of a male) Pumsavana, Pumsavana."[15]

The Gṛhya Sūtras of Hiraṇyakeśin say that the husband should give the barley grain in wife's right hand with words: "A begetter are you", and two beans on either side: "Two testicles are you." He pours a drop of curds on these grains with the formula : "Śvāvārātat". The wife eats that and sips water. He touches her belly with the formula, "With my ten fingers I touch thee that thou mayst give birth to a child after ten months."[16] The Jaiminī Gṛhya Sūtra says that after the wife has eaten two beans and a barley grain with a drop of curds, a Nyagrodha shoot together with fruits is fastened by means of two threads, one white and the other red, to her neck for wearing constantly. This is believed to be a sure way of begetting a son.[17] The Sūtras also prescribe putting the Soma stalk or a blade of Kuśa grass or the last shoot of Nyagrodha tree after pounding in the right nostril of the wife.[18] The Pāraskara Gṛhya Sūtra says that if the husband desires a valiant son, he should put the shell of a tortoise with water on the wife's lap with some Mantras (incantations).[19]

In the fourth, sixth or eighth month of pregancy Sīmantonnayana or the parting of hair of the wife is performed during the first pregenancy. The husband cooks Sthālīpāka or a dish of sacrificial food containing sesamum and Mudga beans and sacrifices to Prajāpati. The husband parts her hair upwards with a bunch containing an even number of unripe Udumbara fruits and three pieces of Darbha grass, a porcupine's quill that has three white spots, a stick of Vīratara wood and a full spindle with the words, "Bhūr bhuvaḥ svaha". He ties the bunch to a string of three twisted threads with (the words): "Rich is sap of this tree; like the tree, rich in sap, be thou fruitful." Then lute-players sing songs.[20]

The husband prepares the Sutikālaya or labour room for the wife. He besmears it with various herbs in order to drive away goblins. Then, the wife enters the room. When she is about to deliver, the husband is required to place his hand dripping with water on her head and touch her with the dripping wet hand from the head to the heart downwards with the *mantras*: "As the wind blows, as the ocean trembles, so may thy foetus move, may it come out together with the afterbirth."[21]

When the boy is born, he performs for him the Medhājanana or production of intelligence and *āyuṣya* or the rite for procuring long life, before the navel string is cut off. He makes the new born infant lick honey and ghee with a gold article (gold spoon or ring) thrice, with the recitation of some Vedic formulas. Then near the child's navel or his right ear he murmurs.

> Agni is longlived, through the trees he is longlived;
>
> By that long life I make thee longlived.
>
> Soma is longlived through the herbs he is longlived;
>
> By that long life I make thee longlived.
>
> The Brahman[22] is longlived, through the Brāhmaṇas he is longlived;
>
> By that long life I make thee longlived.
>
> The gods are longlived, through ambrosia (*amṛta*) they are longlived;
>
> By that long life I make thee longlived.

The Ṛṣis are longlived, through their observances they are longlived;

By that long life I make thee longlived.

The fathers are longlived, through the Svadhā[23] oblations they are longlived;

By that long life I make thee longlived.

Then, the father should place five Brāhmaṇas in the five directions and should say to them, "Breathe ye upon this (child)". The Brāhmaṇa to the south should say, "Back-breathing"; the one to the west, "Down-breathing"; the one to the north, "Out-breathing"; the fifth one looking upwards, should say, "On- breathing".

In case the father can not find Brāhmaṇas he may himself do this, going round the child. He recites over the places at which the child is born:

I know, O earth, the heart that dwells in heaven, in the moon.

That I know; may it know me.

May we see a hundred autumns.

May we live a hundred autumns.

May we hear a hundred autumns.[24]

He then touches him and lays an axe on a stone, a piece of gold on that axe and turns them upside down and holds the boy over them with the verse:

Be a stone, be a axe, be imperishable gold.

Thou indeed art the self called son.

Thus live a hundred autumns.

In all these prayers the father performs rituals which are symbolic. The forceful movements of ocean and wind are represented by the movement of the wet hand so that the infant may come out with the after-birth. By the same ritual he ensures a long life for the infant by remembering the longlived gods.

Breathing round the infant is again a part of the same magical ritual, adding more breaths into his life. He prays to the earth for his long life. He suggests to his son to be imperishable like stone, axe and gold.

The father washes the infant with lukewarm water. He washes his wife's right breast and gives it to the child with a verse addressed to the right breast: "O breast you swell up for his life, glory, renown, splendor and strength." Similarly, he washes and addresses the left breast.[25]

For a secure confinement, the father puts down a pot of water near his wife's head with the verse, "O waters, you watch with the gods. As you watch with the gods, so do watch over this mother who is confined, and her child."

He also establishes the *sūtikāgni* or the fire of confinement at the southern side of the door to ward off various evil spirits. He pronounces the names of various demons and goblins and throws mustard seeds mixed with rice chaff into that fire in the morning and evening twilight, until the mother gets up from child-bed:

> May Śaṇḍa and Marka, Upavīra, Śauṇḍikeya, Ulūkhala, Malimulca, Droṇāsa, and Cyavana vanish hence. Svāhā.
>
> May Ālikhat, Vilikhat, Animiṣa, Kimvadanta, Upasruti, Haryakṣa, Kumbhin, Śatru, Pātrapāṇi Nṛmani, Hantrimukha, Sarṣaparuṇa vanish hence. Svāhā.
>
> Keśini, Śvalomini, Bajaboja Upakāśinī go away, vanish hence. Svāhā.
>
> Wearing variegated garments, the servants of Kubera, sent by the king of demons, all of one common origin, walk through the village wishing (to harm) those who are unprotected. Svāha.
>
> Kill them. Bind them; thus says this messenger of Brahman.
>
> Agni has encompassed them.

Indra knows them;

Bṛhaspati knows them;

I, the Brāhmaṇa, know them who seize (men), who have prominent teeth, rugged hair, hanging breasts. Svāhā.

The night-walkers, wearing ornaments on their breasts, with lances in their hands, drinking out of skulls. Svāhā.[26]

Their father Uccaihsarvyakaraṇaka (walks) at their head; their mother walks in the rear, seeking Vidhura in the village. Svāhā.

(Their) sister, the night-walker, looks at the family through the crenice (Sandhi) of the door, she who wakes the sleeping (child), whose mind is turned on the wife that has become the mother. Svāhā.

O god with the black path, burn the lungs, hearts and the liver of these female demons, burn their eyes.[27]

In the fifth or sixth month after the birth of the son, the ritual of Annaprāśana or feeding the child with solid food is performed. The Gṛhya Sūtras prescribe a variety of fowls and fish as the baby's first food for infusing different qualities in the son. If the father wishes for the child fluency of speech, he should feed him with the flesh of the Bhārdvāji bird; if the abundance of nourishment is desired the flesh of partridge should be given. If he wants swiftness in the child, he should be fed on fish. In case he wants long life for the child, the flesh of the bird Kṛkaṣā is to be given. If he wishes holy lustre in the child, the father should feed the child on flesh of the bird Āti. In case the father wants all these qualities, he should feed the child with all these things.[28]

The similarity in the features of son and father strengthen the bonds of love with the son. When the father returns from a journey and sees his son, he whispers. "From limb thou art produced; out of the heart thou art born. Thou indeed art the self called son; so live a hundred autumns". He then kisses his head with the words, "With the Himkāra of Prajāpati, which gives thousandfold life, I kiss thee, N.N. Live a hundred autumns". He kisses him thrice with the words, "With the Himkāra of the cows". In his right ear he murmurs, "Bestow on us, O bountiful, onward-pressing Indra, plentiful rich treasures. Give us a hundred autumns to live; give us many heroes, oh strong-jawed Indra". In the left ear he murmurs, "Indra, bestow on us the best treasures, insight of mind, happiness, increase of wealth, health of our bodies, sweetness of speech, and our days may be good days".

It is remarkable that in the Gṛhya Sūtras it is the husband who has to act both as the midwife and the priest during his wife's delivery. This strongly suggests that an ordinary household in that period had no other adult member besides the couple. Thus the joint family consisting of more than two generations and several married couples, which is often regarded as the characteristic institution of the traditional Indian social structure is conspicuous by its absence. This is understandable. When the Aryans were colonizing the vast areas they had conquered, they had to be mobile; and the large joint family did not suit these conditions. That institution acquired its pivotal position with the establishment of settled plough agriculture.

The Indian caste system, which has been in existence for more than two thousand years, also owes a great deal to the clash of races. But for a long time now the lower castes, a majority of whom seem to be derived from the non-Aryan stock, have been accepting the superiority of the upper castes as God given, and the service of the latter as their sacred duty. This situation had not been institutionalized during the Sūtra period. The Aryan householder had to try hard to find servants from amongst the indigenous and it was not easy to retain them. They were captured and forced to work for their masters. They often ran away from the unpleasant job. Sūtras prescribed a magical rite, *Utulaparimehaḥ*, for a servant who habitually runs away. The master had to discharge his urine into the horn of a living animal, and had to walk three times round him, turning his left side towards him, and sprinkle (the urine) round him, with the verse : "From the mountain (on which thou art born), from thy mother, from they sister, from thy parents and thy brothers, from thy friends, I sever thee Run-away-servant, I have made water round thee. Having been watered round, where wilt thou go." In case the servant ran away, his master established a fire and performed sacrifice with the formula: "May the stumbler stumble round thee, may he tie thee with Indra's fetter, loosen thee for me, and may he lead another one up to (me)". It is asserted that after this ritual the servant quietly remains in his master's house.[29]

Thus, the Gṛhya Sūtras seem to provide rare glimpses into the twilight zone of the growth of Indian civilization. They reveal how the folk tradition of a conquering people was raised to the status of the elite tradition of culture in the composite civilization. It is obvious though that the conquerors had to take over and absorb a good deal from the culture of the people whom they vanquished, and whom they began by despising wholesale.

The battering of two streams of culture against each other resulted in intricate patterns. The open conflict subsided but it gave birth to a stratified sociocultural structure in which the subjugation of the vanquished people was legitimised and sanctified.

The intricate structure of the immense edifice of the Indian caste system bears testimony to this process. Though the hostility between the invading Aryans and the indigenes ended, it led to the overall supremacy of the former. The low position of woman in the traditional order and the suspicion with which she was looked upon also seems due partly to her extraction from the indigenous peoples. The foundations of this civilization were, however, laid solidly in the sense that both women and the Śūdras accepted their position as natural and god given; and shuddered even to think of revolting against it.

Notes

1. Asvalayana Gṛhya Sūtra IV, 8,32.
2. Mānava Gṛhya Sūtra II, 14.
3. Vṛddha Hārita XI. 143.
4. Medhātithi II. 6.
5. Kūrma Purāṇa I, 12. 161, 162.
6. Ṛg Veda VIII. 19. 36. 37.
7. Atharva Veda 7. 17. 8-9.
8. Śānkhāyana Gṛhya Sūtra, I 17, 3.
9. Pāraskara Gṛhya Sūtra, I 4, 15.
10. Śānkhāyana Gṛhya Sūtra, I. 18, 3. Pāraskara Gṛhya Sūtra I. 11, 2- 4.
11. Paras. G. S. III, 13, 2-6.
12. San. G. S. I, 16, 8.
13. Pāraskara Gṛhya Sūtra, I.9.5.
14. San G.S. I, 19,6.
15. Para. I, 4,11. Asva. G.S. I, 13, 2-4.
16. Hir. G. S. II, I, 2,3-5.
17. Jai G. S. I, 5.
18. San. G. S. I, 20, 3-5, Hir G.S. II, 2,6, Para, G.S. I, 14, 2-4.
19. Para. G. S. I, 14,5.
20. Para, G. S. I, 15, 3-7.
21. Kathaka Gṛhya Sūtra XXXIII, 1-3.
22. The word Brahman refers both to the Vedic aphorisms and the mysterious power inherent in them.
23. Offerings made to forefathers during the Śrāddha cermony.
24. Paras. G. S. 16, 3-18.
25. Hiranakesī Gṛhya Sūtra, II, I, 4, 3-4.
26. This description strongly suggests Kālī, who is now a goddess.
27. Para, G.S. I, 16, 23; Hira G.S. II, I, 3,7.
28. Para. G. S. I, 19, 7-12.
29. Para, G. S. III, 7, 1-4.

XIII

Culture Contact Between Ancient India and Iran: Consequences of Antagonistic Interaction

Many obscure aspects of the growth of Indian civilization in its early phase are illuminated when the traditional Iranian lore contained in the Zend-Avesta and the Pahlavi texts is analysed side by side with the Vedas and Brahmanical literature. Comparative study of the tradition of the two branches of the Aryans fills many gaps that would inevitably remain if we were to confine ourselves only to the Indian tradition.

This is understandable, for the people who composed the Vedas and the Zend-Avesta belonged originally to the same stock and shared a common primeval heritage. The reminiscences of the migration of the Aryan hordes somewhere from the bitterly cold region close to the Arctic are found both in the Ṛgveda and the Zend-Avesta. We find, however, that the memory of this land is quite hazy in the Vedas, while the ancient Iranian texts show not only a more vivid recollection of the original land but also a fairly clear idea of the path of migration. In fact there are clear references in the Zend-Avesta which indicate that the ancient Iranians knew that people belonging to the Aryan stock had gone to many lands.

They were aware that that a branch of Aryans had reached

as far as the basin of the river Gangā. But what is even more remarkable is that the Zend-Avesta records that a brother of their own first ancestor established the kingdom of Rum (Rome), thereby showing that they were conscious that the people who lived in Europe also belonged to the same stock. While the people who had migrated to the Sapta-Sindhu (the northwestern part of the Indian subcontinent) were referred to contemptuously because of the racial and cultural admixture that they had undergone, even the later Pahlavi texts continued to regard the people who lived in what are now known as Afghanistan and Kashmir as their kith and kin.

As we shall see later, the relations between the ancient Indian and Iranian branches of the Aryans were similar to those that often exist between cousins or neighbours. Though they shared a lot with each other, there was perpetual jealousy and animosity between them. So much so that the Devas or Gods of the Indian were "Devas'" or demons for the Iranians; and Ahura or Asura, the supreme god of Iranians became Asura or evil being in India in the course of time.

This rivalry and mutual hatred has found expression in various myths in the two cultures. The Zend-Avesta tells how when Yima reached the land of seven rivers, Haft-Hindu (Sapta-Sindhu in Sanskrit), the region now covering the northwestern portion of the Indian sub-continent, he married a demoness who gave birth to bears and monkeys. This obviously has a reference to the offsprings born of the union between Aryan migrant males and the women of the dark-complexioned and snub-nosed people who were living here from earlier times. There are also references in the Zend-Avesta to Aryans becoming "deformed" as a consequence of their migration to the Indian subcontinent. Among the ancient texts the Śatapatha Brāhmaṇa bears ample evidence to this hatred. Here, too, we find the consciousness of kinship between the Indians and the Iranians and also the existence of mutual hatred. According to the Śatapatha Brāhmaṇa, the Asura (Iranians) and Devas were the two sons of Prajāpati but the Asuras became degraded as a result of the influence of magic and poison.

Some striking characteristics like the worship of fire, the drinking of Soma or Haoma, wearing the sacred thread, and considering the cow a holy animal, are found in common in both the traditions. Such similarities between cultures which had branched off from a common stock are not unexpected.

But more remarkable are the similarities that we find in the pattern of growth of the two tradition. The response of both of these traditions to the rise of Buddhism is comparable in several respects. For a time Buddhism held sway, but later both the traditions threw up strong revivalist movements to combat it. These movements sought to restore the ancient Aryan religion, but in this attempt they were not fully successful. In their fight against Buddhism, both these movements had to seek the support of people who were bearers of non-Aryan traditions. Thus in Iran the Assyrian elements of culture extensively penetrated the revivalist movement and in India the movement of revival had to accept much from the culture of the proto-Austroloid, proto-Mongol, and proto-Mediterranean people who were settled here before the Aryans came.

We find some interesting differences also. In India there was a rigorous oral tradition of ancient Aryan lore. The Vedas are called Śruti or "the listened". In Iran the sacred lore was committed to writing. This had its disadvantages as well as advantages. During foreign invasions, which were frequent, libraries were burnt. Alexander's invasion of Iran is an outstanding example of such destruction. In the existent Iranian texts the loss of substantial portions of ancient sacred texts due to this destruction is lamented again and again. After the invaders had withdrawn, priests had to meet together to reconstruct the texts as much as they could. The ancient Iranian texts are a kind of patchwork rather than smooth wholes as they might have existed originally. As a contrast, in India the ancient Aryan lore was meticulously preserved through rigorous oral tradition which disapproved the alteration even of a single syllable. It may be mentioned, however, that while the original form of the Vedas seems to have been largely preserved, later works which were not considered perfect revelation continued to be reworked through the process of oral tradition.

A basic difference between the cultures of India and Iran stems from the fact that while the Aryan hordes which invaded India encountered earlier settlers who were racially very different from them, the non-Aryan people in ancient Iran did not present such a racial contrast. In India it is this vast racial difference that seems to lie at the root of the Varṇa and caste system. In Ṛgveda there are only two Varṇas primarily, the Aryan and the Kṛṣṇa Varṇa. The latter obviously refers to the pre-Aryan dark complexioned, snubnosed people, who are disparagingly referred to in the Vedas. This great racial difference seems to have brought to the fore the importance of birth. The caste hierarchy is determined strictly by birth. On the other hand, in ancient Iranian society there were no exclusive ranks based on birth. What is even more remarkable, the Iranian society did not develop any servile class comparable to the Śūdras of India who are believed to be born only to serve the people of higher castes.

There is ample evidence that the Aryans of Sapta-Sindhu as mentioned in the Ṛgveda and the Aryans of Iran as mentioned in Zend-Avesta, had a common ethnic origin. While the Aryans of Iran clearly remembered the original land and their migration from that land, Ṛgvedic Aryans do not seem to have as clear a memory of these. The original land of Iranians is referred to as "Airyana Vaejo" in Zend-Avesta.

In Airyana Vaejo, there are ten months of winter and two months of summer. The winter was dire there. "It was cold for waters, cold for earth and cold for the trees".[1] There the sun rises and sets only once in a year.[2] The land was covered with snow. Similar passages are found in Vedic literature also. The Aitareya Brāhmaṇa speaks of a land where the sun never sets.[3] We come across a similar description in the Ṛgveda: "Snow or

Hima has stolen the leaves of the forest."[4] This obviously does not refer to conditions in the plains of India. This description fits in well with the climate in the polar region. The bitterness of winter and the never-setting sun are clearly related to that region. We do not find such a place near Iran. Since the migration from the original land had taken place centuries ago, it was natural for them to forget the proper location of the ancient land.

The first leader of migration, yima or Yama, had to move towards the south to "meet the sun;" this also shows that the original land was situated in the north where the earth is covered with the "thick falling of snow-flakes". In that land of ice, the dog is certainly the greatest friend of man. In Avesta a whole chapter (Fargard XIII) is devoted to the dog. In Ṛgveda too, the first mortal, Yama, and god Indra, have dogs. Later on, however, the dog became a despised animal in India. Perhaps the animosity that developed between India and Iran contributed to this reversal of attitude.

According to Zend-Avesta, in the original land of Aryans a couple produced only two children in forty years, a son and a daughter.[5] The ideal that a couple should have only two children, indicates scarcity of food which must have been a great problem. In later Pahlavi texts the original land is also endowed with the quality that "one loaf sufficed to satisfy the hunger of ten persons". This also suggests that the ancient Aryans faced some sort of a population problem. The Avesta vividly brings it out as the cause of migrations.

Among Indo-Aryan languages, the Lithuanian language is considered to be the most archaic. The polar region is not very far off from Lithuania. In the Śatapatha Brāhmaṇa and Apastambiya Mantrapāṭha we find the word Sālva, denoting a particular people who are considered to posses expert knowledge of performing various sacrifices.[6] The word Sālva is strikingly similar to the word Slav; only the sounds have changed places, which is not uncommon in the evolution of languages.

It appears that hard winter in the original land of Aryans was also a cause of migration. The worship of the sun and fire also indicates this. But the later migrations were certainly due to over-population as is described in the Zend-Avesta: "The earth has become full of flocks and herds, of men and dogs and birds and of red blazing fires, and there is no more room for flocks, herds, and men." Yima, the leader of the migrating Aryans, took a golden ring and a poniard inlaid with gold as the symbol and the instrument of sovereignty from Ahura Mazda. And the great king, fair Yima, the son of Vivanghat, migrated "towards the luminous space southward to meet the sun."[7]

In Śatapatha Brāhmaṇa we have: "Yama hath given the settlement on earth."[8] The Zend-Avesta mentions sixteen settlements. These are situated in central Asia, Iran and the north-western part of the Indian subcontinent. The names of the settlements are not always in proper order. In the Indian sub-continent the first settlement is Cakhra. Cakhra seems to be the land situated at the foot of Hindu-Kush, the site of modern Charikar in Afghanistan. The adjectives "strong" and "holy" are used for this land in Avesta. At this site an old constructed city was excavated during British rule. According to Avesta, the evil custom of burning the dead was introduced by Angra Mainyu or the Satan in this land.[9] It is possible that this custom was prevalent here. Even now it is practised by Hindus in India.

The fourteenth settlement is mentioned as the four-cornered Varena. The adjective "four cornered" suggests that it was a four-cornered hill fort. Probably it is the fort "Aornus," mentioned in the accounts of the campaign of Alexander as a strong hill fort. It corresponds to Sanskrit, "Varaṇa" mentioned by Pāṇinī (c. fifth century B.C.) who also described it as a four-cournered hillfort. It was situated near the junction of the Kabul and Sindhu rivers. Sir Aurel Stein thinks that this mountain citadel was washed away by the Sindhu river later on.[10] At this spot Thraetaona in Avesta or Traitana in Ṛgveda fought with Azis Dahaka or Ahih Dasaka. In the Ṛgveda we find the mention of a warrior named Traitana. Traitana is mentioned as a Dāsa who subjected the composer Dirghatamas to the ordeals of fire, water, and single combat and the latter was protected in all the three ordeals by the Aśvins.[11] It is interesting to note that in both the traditions the adjective "Dahaka" or Dāsa is used for the adversary in a derogatory sense.

In the Avesta we find an interesting reference which shows their consciousness that the Roman culture had the same roots as their own. There is a myth in Avesta that two daughters of Yima who were earlier abducted by Azi (the dragon) were set free and married by Thraetaona and bore him three sons. One of these became the king of rum (Rome) while the other two ruled Iran and Turan.[12]

The Asvins or Nāsatyau of Ṛgveda (Naunghaithya in Zend-Avesta) became fiends in the Iranian tradition while Traitan, who is a hero in the Iranian tradition, is portrayed as a villain in Ṛgveda.

In Zend-Avesta we find that in Varena (northwest of India), "the Angra Mainyu, who is all death, counter-created by his witchcraft abnormal issues in women and the oppression of foreign rulers."[13] It appears that "deformity" in children refers to the offspring born of a union between Aryan and non-Aryan people. In Zend-Avesta it is said that first Yima "took from Daevas both riches and welfare, both fatness and flocks, both wealth and glory", but later on he began to find delight in words of falsehood and untruth, the glory was seen to "flee away from him in the shape of a bird".[14] in the Pahlavi texts we find that "when reason departed from Yima, for the fear of Daevas (the demons), he took a demoness as wife and gave Yimak, his sister, to a demon as wife; and from them have originated the tailed ape and bear."[15] In the Ṛgveda the Dāsas are described as Kṛṣṇa Varṇa[16] or dark coloured, Anāsah[17] or without nose, and Amanuṣya[18] or non-human. In the epic of Rāmāyaṇa, the indigenous tribes are simply called apes and bears though they are faithful friends of the god-hero, Rāma, of this popular epic, who himself is a dark-coloured prince.

These descriptions present an interesting spectacle of similarity and contrast which brings out the cultural processes resulting from racial admixture. The Iranian texts look upon the off-springs of inter-racial unions as beasts—apes and bears. The Ṛgveda, the earliest account of Aryans in India, also regards the non-Aryan people who were subjugated as less than human. It refers despisingly to their snub-nose and dark complexion. But the great epic Rāmāyana, which must have been composed when the Aryans had developed a stable relationship with the non-Aryan inhabitants, pictures apes and bears (referring perhaps to non-Aryan tribes) as the best and respected friends of the god-hero Rāma. The god-hero Rāma is considered an incarnation of lord Viṣṇu. According to Avesta, another evil created by Angra Mainyu for the land of Varena is oppression by foreign rulers. It is a historical fact that the northwestern part of the Indian subcontinent has been the victim of foreign invasions since time immemorial. Oppression is of course involved in any invasion.

It is interesting that in this very text of Zend-Avesta, a class of fiends is called "Varenya Daevas' or those Daevas who live in Varena. The ancient Aryan migrants who had settled in Varena gradually mingled with the local population and lost their racial purity. Their religious practices were also influenced by indigenous culture. Being close neighbours, they developed a kind of rivalry with the Iranians and were turned into fiends in Avesta.[19]

The next settlement is described as the land of seven rivers or haft-Hindu (Sapta-Sindhu in Sanskrit). According to Avesta, in this land too, women gave birth to abnormal issues. This obviously refers to offsprings of inter-racial unions and indicates the disapproval of racial admixture. The land of seven rivers is mentioned as a place having excessive heat.[20] Some names of the fiends are strikingly similar to the names of Aryan tribes which lived in the land of seven rivers. These are Kurugha (Kuruḥ in Sanskrit), Sarastya (Sārasvata in Sanskrit), Durika[21] (Druhyu in Sanskrit). The theme of the famous epic of Mahābharata is the family feud of Kuru princes. The Sarasvatas are the Brāhmaṇas of northwestern India. The Druhyus are one of the militant Aryan people mentioned in the Ṛgveda.

The sixteenth and the last settlement of Aryans is the land made by the floods of the Rangha. This seems to have an obvious reference to the recurring floods of the river Gaṅgā.[22] The basin of the Gaṅgā has always fascinated those who viewed it for the first time. In the Ṛgveda the large-heartendess of a chief of the Paṇis is compared to the vastness of the basin of the Gaṅgā. Even in modern times the Europeans were struck by the vast expanse of the plains of the Gaṅgā. In Avesta, the Rangha is the river "whose shores lie afar," and which flows in distant lands.[23] Zarathuśtra blesses king Viśtasp that he might have strength enough to reach the shores of Rangha. This suggests that the river was difficult to reach, which further confirms its identification with the river Gaṅgā.

The Zend-Avesta says that in this plain "headless" people reside. This is an expression of antagonism towards these people. It reflects a low estimate of their intelligence. It is also possible that this may have reference to the republics which had no monarchs. It is a historical fact that Gaṇas, or republican states, existed in northern India in ancient times, even before the birth of Buddha.[24]

The early Aryans were cattle-breeders. Their illustrious mythical leader, Yima or Yama, bears the title of the Great Shepherd. He was the first man and the first king to receive the law from the supreme God Ahura Mazda,[25] or Asura Medha in Sanskrit. The adoption of the name Ahura Mazda seems to be the result of the profound influence of the powerful Assyrians on the Aryan tradition. King Assurbanipal (700 B.C.) established Assura Mazas as the supreme god along with seven good angels and seven bad spirits. This god became popular among the masses of Iran, and became Ahura Mazda of Avesta, the sacred book of Iranian Aryans.

In the Indian tradition too, the word "Asura" seems to have

its origin in the Assyrian influence. According to Arrian, the Indians living between the rivers Sindhu and Kabul (Cophen) "were in ancient times subjected to the Assyrians, the Medes, and finally, to the Persians under Cyrus to whom they pay the tribute he imposed upon them."[26]

In the Ṛgveda, "Asura" is used as an epithet for many gods. But this word does not denote any particular god. Obviously the term was borrowed from the Assyrians. Often the word Asura has been used as an epithet of Varuṇa. The ancient Aryan god Varuṇa is the supreme guardian of the cosmic order, or Ṛta. Varuṇa is the Ṛgvedic transformation of the old Slav god "Peruna". We find in Ṛgveda:

"With bending down, oblations, sacrifices,
O Varuṇa, we deprecate their anger;
Wise Asura, thou king of wide dominion,
Loosen the bonds of sins committed by us".[27]

In the course of time, however, the meaning of "Asura" underwent a change in India and a study of the transformation in its denotation and connotation is extremely interesting. From an epithet for the highest gods like Varuṇa, Agni, Soma etc., it came to be employed in a derogatory sense in some parts of the Ṛgveda itself. This change may have been brought about because of the animosity that developed between the Aryans in India and those in Iran. The transition is singularly remarkable. One hymn of the Ṛgveda uses "Asura" both in good and bad senses.[28]

By the time of the Śatapatha Brāhmaṇa, the word Asura came to be used only for demons. What is even more interesting, in the Upanishads an antonym of this word was coined to designate gods. This was done simply by interpreting the opening letter "A" of the word Asura as the negative prefix. By dropping this letter "A" the word "Sura' was derived which became the most common word for "God".

In the Aitareya Brāhmaṇa we find a myth in which it is said that "Indra has slain Aururmaghas". The word Arurmaghas seems to be the corrupt form of Ahura Mazda. In the Kauṣītaki Upaniṣad the word acquired another form, "Arunmukhas".[29] In a myth, Indra boasts that he delivered the Arunmukhas to the wolves. The commentator, Samkarananda, adds a curious remark to the effect that the skulls of the Arunmukhas were turned into a thorny tree named Karīra.

In the Śatapatha Brāhmaṇa, the Devas (gods) and the Asuras (demons) seem to come from the same stock but they are depicted continually fighting with each other. However, in the myths of Śatapatha Brāhmaṇa, these fights are carried on through contending sacrifices. There is bitter rivalry, and abuse is freely exchanged. The Devas and Asuras, armed with various elaborate sacrifices, rites and rituals, seek to vanquish each other. In one myth it is said that between these two people stood the Gāyatrī. It is asserted that "Gāyatrī was the same as this earth, and this earth indeed lay between them. ... Agni acted as messenger for the gods and an Asura-Rākṣas named Saharaksas, for the Asuras."[30]

In the passage of Śatapatha Brāhmaṇa the words "Gāyatrī stood between them" indicate that both the peoples belonged to the same cultural tradition. Both the Devas and Asuras are described to be the progeny of Prajāpati, the progenitor. This is a strong indicator that both the people had a common ancestory.

The name of the messenger of Asuras, Saharaksas, reminds us of Cyrus, the famous Persian ruler. Cyrus conquered the land between Iran and India. Greek records support this identification. "According to Ctesias (Fragment 37, 2d. Gilmore), Cyrus died of a wound inflicted by an Indian, in a battle which the Indians were fighting on the side of Derbikes whom they supplied with elephants". Radha Kumud Mookerji thinks that these Derbikes might have been a frontier tribe.[31] The word "Derbikes" may, however, be the Greek version of the Sanskrit word "Devaḥ".

This mythical battle between Devas and Asuras seems to be

an expression of the continuously strained relationship between the two branches of Aryans. We find, in the Taittirīya Samhitā, that "the defeated gods were reduced to the position of Viś or common people of Asuras."[32] The word Viś stands for commoners in the Iranian tradition also. The Sapta-Sindhu or Haft-Hindu is mentioned as a province of Iran in the inscriptions of the illustrious Persian king Darius,[33] or Darayavauśa (Dharayavasu in Sanskrit).

In Zend-Avesta Yima is depicted as the guardian and protector of mankind. In the original land of Aryans, Ahura Mazda warned Yima that fatal winters were going to occur; therefore, to save mankind from this winters he must make a Var, or enclosure, about two Hathra, or two miles, long on every side.[34]

The law of Mazda was brought by a bird called Karshipta (one having stretched wings) in the Vara of Yima. This mythical bird lives in heaven. It recited the Avesta in the language of birds. James Darmester thinks that this bird is an incarnation of lightning. The swiftness of lightning is similar to swiftness of the bird. Thunder was considered the voice of God speaking from heaven, a revelation. In the Talavakara Upaniṣad we find a similar expression, which supports the explanation given by James Darmester. It says : "The knowledge flashes forth in the lightning and now vanishes again".[35] A striking parallel is found in the Ṛgveda too. In the Ṛgveda a bird of golden wings, the envoy of Varuṇa, hastens to the home of Yama.[36] Varuṇa is the supreme lord who is the upholder of law, the Ṛgvedic counterpart of Ahura Mazda.

There are many similarities between Zend-Avesta and Ṛgveda. Yima, the son of Vivanghavant, was the first mortal who prepared the Haoma or Soma for the incarnate world. In the Ṛgveda, Vivasvan is the morning sun personified. He is the father of Yama. With him lives Soma.[37]

The Var of Yima is pictured as the ideal place to live. Zend Avesta affirms : "In the reign of Yima swift motion was there, neither cold nor heat, there was neither age nor envy made by Daevas or demons."[38] Similarly the Ṛgvedic poet aspires to live in the realm of Yama :

> "Make me immortal in that realm where dwells the king Vivasvan's son (Yama).
>
> Where there is the secret shrine of heaven, where those waters are young and fresh".

Like Yima of Zend-Avesta, Yama is also described as the leader of the Aryans who migrated from the original land.

> "Honour the king with thine oblations, Yama,
>
> Vivasvan's son, who gathers men together,
>
> Who travelled to the lofty heights above us,
>
> Who searches out and shows the path to many.
>
> Yama first found for us a place to dwell in;
>
> This pasture never can be taken from us.
>
> Men born on earth tread their own paths,
>
> That lead them whither our ancient Fathers have departed."[39]

Both in Zend Avesta and Ṛgveda,[40] Yima or Yama is described as the leader of the Aryan migration from the original land, and the lord of the dead. In both the traditions he is described as the first mortal who shows the souls the path to heaven, the abode of the blessed.

In Ṛgveda, Yama keeps two dogs who show the path to the departed souls. These dogs are of dark colour and have four eyes. The mother of these dogs is the she-dog of Indra named Saramā. The Ṛgvedic poet describes them vividly :

> Run and outsped the two dogs,
>
> Sarama's offspring, brindle, four-eyed, upon thy happy pathway.
>
> Draw night then to the gracious-minded fathers where they rejoice in company with Yama.

And those two dogs of thine, Yama, the watchers,

Four-eyed who look on men and guard the pathway

Entrust this man, O King, to their protection, and

with prosperity and health endow him.

Dark-hued, insatiate, with distended nostrils, Yama's

two envoys roam among the people.

May they restore to us a fair existence here and today, that we may see the sunlight.[41]

Among the Parsis (descendents of Iranians who migrated to India) there is a custom that a four-eyed dog (having two spots above the eyes) is shown the dead body before its disposal.

We find much glorification of the dog in Zend-Avesta. In the original land, which was perhaps in the polar region, the dog must have been essential for the survival of man. This glorification seems to be a vestige of that ancient tradition. In Ṛgveda, though the dog is not praised to any comparable extent, we do find that the gods Indra and Yama keep dogs.

In Zend-Avesta a whole Fargard (chapter) is devoted to the dog. It is declared that the dog possesses the character of eight persons. Among the characters enumerated are those of the priest, the warrior and the husbandman. These are the three ranks of ancient Iranians. The ancient Iranians' veneration for dogs was so pervasive that even beaver, fox, hedge-hog and tortoise are conceived as dogs. But in post-Vedic India the dog was reduced to a despised position. In the Pāraskara Gṛhya Sūtra diseases of the newborn male child are personified in the dog. In the ritual for warding off these diseases they are addressed as the dog.[42] Looking at a dog is considered as an evil omen. A student who has taken a bath after studentship should avoid seeing dogs for three nights. Anyone who touches a dog should take a bath with his clothes on. The food seen by a dog is unfit for eating.[43] This may well be a result of persistent antagonism that the ancient Indians had against the Iranians who considered the dog holy.

In Zend-Avesta the priest is called Athravan. Yima is described as the first priest. In the Ṛgveda, too, Atharvan is the first fire-priest. The mention of Yama is also significant.[44] There are other parallels too in Ṛgveda and Avesta. Ṛta, the universal eternal, physical and moral order of Ṛgveda is found in Avesta as Rata, the good, or the order made by Mazda to regulate the worlds.[45]

Mitra of Ṛgveda has the same attributes as the Mithra of Avesta. The largest Yast (chapter) of Avesta is dedicated to Mithra who is the god of light or sun. Light symbolized the truth. Mithra is the god of truth. Mithra is ever vigilant, watching every deviance of mankind. Similarly in the Ṛgveda it is declared :

> Mitra, when speaking, stirreth men to work :
>
> Mitra sustaineth both the earth and heaven.
>
> Mitra beholdeth men with eyes that never close.
>
> To Mitra bring oblation with clarified butter.[46]

In Avesta, Mithra is also the lord of pastures and the chief of Assemblies. The attribute of being the "chief of assemblies" is obviously related to the conception of the upholder of law. "We sacrifice unto Mithra, the lord of wide pastures who speaks the truth the chief in assemblies with a thousand ears, well-shapen, with ten thousand eyes, high with full knowledge, strong, sleepless and ever awake"[47] Mithra also punishes those who deviate from the right path. Due to ardent antagonism against those Aryans who had settled in India, the Iranian Mithra is described as "one who breaks the skulls of the Daevas."[48]

In Ṛgveda, Juhu is mentioned as the deserted wife of Bṛhaspati who was restored to him by gods.[49] Perhaps this Juhu is Jahī of Avesta. Jahī is originally a god's bride who gave herself to the demon and became the demoness of unlawful love and unchastity. The courtesan is her incarnation.[50] In a similar way, Angirases, in Ṛgveda, are described as a race of higher beings, between gods and men. They are the first sacrificers whose ritual is considered as ideal. But their Iranian version, Angra Mainyu is the Satan of Avesta who always creates evil things.

In Avesta the genius of earth is named Spenta Armaiti. In Ṛgveda also we find a similar name "Armati" for the genius of the earth.[51]

Predictably the worship of fire is a common feature found in the sacred books of both the traditions. There are a number of similar words related to fire sacrifice. These similar words indicate that common ritual practices were prevalent in the two branches of Aryans. For instance the sacrificer is Zaotar in Avesta and Hotarah in Sanskrit; the sacrifice is Yasna is Avesta and Yajna in Sanskrit; the hymn is Manthra in Avesta and Mantra in Sanskrit; the oblation is Azwti in Avesta and Ahuti is Sanskrit. The Fire-priest is called Athrvan in Avesta and Atharvan in Sanskrit. In Avesta the name of the Fire-god is derived from it. Atharvan is one who has the fire. The fire became Athra and later on the word was corrupted to Atar. The Dṛṣṭārah of Mantras (or the perceivers of hymns) of Ṛgveda are Dasturs (priests) in Avesta. In both the traditions a great deal of stress is laid on the maintenance of the sacred fire. The Zend-Avesta and Pahlavi texts maintain that failure to do so results in drought, the diminishing of milk in cows, barrenness and abortions in women and acute scarcity of male offsprings.[52] These Iranian texts prescribe maintenance of fire for protection of the pregnant woman from demons. It has also to be kept up for three days after the birth of a son.[53] Fire is a must in India too in confinement and childbirth. Taking oath in the presence of fire and water seems to be an ancient Indo-Iranian custom. The Zend-Avesta prescribes that an oath should be taken before water and blazing fire. Even today marriage among Hindus must be solemnized in the presence of a water-filled jar and blazing fire. Oath-taking is an essential feature of marriage. The bride and bridegroom take an oath to live as husband and wife in the presence of fire and water.

The H(a)oma or Soma was the sacred drink of both the branches of Indo-Iranian Aryans. According to Avesta the H(a)oma grows on high mountains whose "snow peaks" remain ever white. It has tremendous healing power. It gives vigour. When people take it mixed with milk, it makes them prosperious. It is described in Avesta as being of many varieties.[54] It appears that H(a)oma was a kind of shrub which could grow on lofty mountains as well as in the valleys.[55]

In Rgveda, also, the Soma is described as the "king of the forest"[56] who is the "dweller of the hills".[57] The Soma-juice is also taken together with milk.[58]

The H(a)oma or Soma has been variously identified by different scholars. But it seems that atleast by the time the Aryans had reached Iran and India it was the plant now known as Bhaṅga in India (Indian hemp) that was used as H(a)oma or Soma. It grows as a shrub which when ground and taken, preferably with milk, produces euphoria and fantasies. In Avesta, Trita is described as the third person who prepared H(a)oma for the corporeal world.[59] In Ṛgveda also it is said that Trita refined Soma.[60] In Zend-Avesta there are "thirtythree lords of ritual order". In the Ṛgveda also thritythree gods are mentioned.[61]

In appears that the ancient Aryans who had settled in Iran used to take beef, and later on this practice was disapproved. In Zend-Avesta it is declared that if a householder fattens a cow for beef, he receives the curse of the cow. The cow curses : "Childless be thou, shorn of offspring, illfamed, and slander-followed,who gives me fodder but does not use me (for milk), but fattenest me for wife or children, and for thy niggard selfish meal."[62]

In India too the early Aryans relished beef, but later on it was entirely forbidden. The Gṛhya Sūtras mark the stage of transition. Here in the ritual of Madhuparka the householder offers a cow to the guest and gives him a butcher's knife to sacrifice it, but at the same time implores him to let the cow live if he so decides.[63]

The cow is considered to be sacred by the Hindus even to this day. The urine of the cow is believed to have medicinal properties. Besides this, it is an important ingredient for purificatory rites. The Smrtis prescribe drinking of Gomūtra (urine of the cow) for expiation of grave sins. Similarly, the Zend-Avesta, and also Pahlavi texts, extol the medicinal and purificatory properties of Gomez (bovine urine). According to Zend-Avesta three cups of bovine urine have to be administered for three days to a woman who bears a stillborn child to get rid of the pollution.[64] Such a woman is believed to be polluted because she had become a living grave. The urine is given to wash over the grave within her womb. The Pahlavi texts also allude to the use of cow-dung as fuel. It is used as fuel in India to the present day. The value of the cow depends also on its dung in both the cultures.

Giving a sacred cord to the boy at the initiation ceremony is a common sacrament of Iranian and Indian Aryans. In this ceremony the boy or the teenager is given the sacred girdle and initiated into the elite community. While initiating the student according to Gobhila Gṛhya-Sūtras, the teacher touches his navel with the word "Ahura".[65] This seems to be a clear Iranian influence. "Ahura" is the actual word which the Iranian use for the supreme God.

Despite these numerous similarities, in the course of time relations of animosity seem to have developed between the Indian and Iranian branches of Aryans. The Ṛgvedic gods came to be considered as evil spirits by the Iranians. This is true of Indra, who is mentioned by the same name both in the Ṛgveda and Avesta; Surya of Ṛgveda who is Sauru in Avesta; and Nasatyau of Ṛgveda who is Naunghaithya in Avesta. It is declared in Avesta that all these fiends are to be driven away from the house with the words : "I drive away Indra, I drive away

Sauru, I drive away the Deava Naunghaithya from this house, from this borough, from this town, from this land."[66]

The Avesta does not recognise the Indian Aryans as full human beings. It is recommended in Avesta that a surgeon should first perform surgery on three Daevas (Indians); only if he treats them successfully should he operate on Iranians.[67]

Unlike other ancient civilizations, the ancient Iranian society as portrayed in the Zend-Avesta did not have a distinct servile class, though the word Śudra, the generic name of the Indian servile class, seems to be of Iranian origin. Probably it is derived from the Persian word Khurd which means "small". The Kurdas are the people who have been fighting with the Iranians since ancient times.

We find the mention of three classes in Avesta. The first one is of Athravans or priests; the second one is that of warriors, and the third one is that of agriculturalists. Zarathuśtra blesses king Viśtasp thus: "May ten sons be born of you. In three of them mayest thou be an Athravan. In three of them mayest thou be warrior. In three of them mayest thou be tiller of the land. And may one be like thyself, Vitśtap."[68]

In the Pahlavi texts, we find mention of four classes. These are those of priests, warriors, husbandsmen and artizans.[69] The first rank consists of judges and those learned in religion. The second rank is that of warriors. They keep watch over the cities and destroy the enemy, thus performing both police and military functions. The third rank consists of writers and, secondarily, cultivators and the other urban people. The traders, artisans and shop-keepers form the fourth rank.[70] Preiesthood is the most important profession in ancient Iran. According to James Darmester only the son of a priest could be a priest; anybody whose father was not a priest could not be a priest. But the blessings of Zararthuśtra to the king Vistasp do not seem to confirm the hypothesis of James Darmester.[71] In these blessings Zarathuśtra says that the king should beget ten sons of body and three of them may be Athravans or priests.

From these blessings it becomes quite clear that a son of a king may follow the profession of a priest if he so chooses. It is possible that during ancient times the profession of priest was not hereditary, but later on it became hereditary, as in India. However, while the priestly castes in India became perfectly endogamous, in Iran the priests continued to take brides from other ranks. This, in a way, can be considered the continuance of hypergamy, which was also permitted in India for a long time.

The Pahlavi texts enumerate certain vices of priests. These are heresy, covetousness, negligence, usuriousness, attention to trifles and unbelief in religion.[72] The Śatapatha Brāhmaṇa also describes Asuras as usurers who declare Vedas to be magic. In a myth it is also asserted that the Asuras lack sacrificial knowledge.

Gods and Asuras are the progeny of Prajāpati. Both came in a sacrifice and aspired for the Vāk or Speech. But "being a woman she went to gods, who had well-trimmed houses. The gods cut her off from the Asuras and enveloped her completely in the sacrificial fire. The Asuras, therefore, lack the sacrificial knowledge."[73]

It is not certain that these ranks were hereditary. It seems that people of higher ranks could take the professions of lower ranks, but naturally it would be difficult for the people of lower ranks to climb. However these ranks were not exclusive. There is a provision that if a son is born of a maidservant he should be given the status of the son of the master. However, female children, born of a maidservant were not recognized as his daughters.[74] Comparable provisions are found in the traditional law books, such as the Nārada Smṛti of India.

In ancient Iran, the people whom the Aryans subjugated were racially not very different from the victorious Aryans. Therefore the ranks did not get crystallized as castes, as happened in India. In India the castes became hereditary as well as endogamous units. In Avesta, when the Aryans entered the Indian sub-continent and took a "demoness" as wife, the issues born of the union became "deformed", The proto-Australoid people who lived in the Indian subcontinent were racially very different from the invading Aryans.

In Ṛgveda we find the story of Yama and his sister Yamī, a counterpart of the ancient Iranian myth of Yima in a different form. In this story, Yamī, the sister of Yama, offers herself as wife to her brother Yama. It appears that in the beginning the Aryans married indigenous proto-Australoid women, but when they found that the children born of these unions had a dark-complexion and were snub-nosed they avoided such marriages. This avoidance seems to have found expression in the myth of Yama and Yami in the Ṛgveda. Perhaps such scruples crystallized into the codes of endogamy which characterize the Indian caste system. In Ṛgveda the word Varṇa means colour. The two Varṇas are Arya Varṇa and Kṛṣṇa Varṇa. These indicate two different racial groups. According to Hindu mythology and sacred law books, all the numerous castes have emerged as a result of hypergamous and hypogamous unions among persons of different Varṇas. This is not entirely true. Many invading hordes and indigenous tribes turned into distinct castes and became integral parts of the caste hierarchy. However, the studies of anthropologists like D.N. Majumdar indicate[75] that even today the order of castes in the basin of the rivers Gaṅgā and Yamunā, which is regarded as the cradle of Hindu civilization, shows a remarkable correlation with the amount of Nordic traits in its members.

The people of Iran were exposed to various influences. The Assyrians were their closest neighbours. The traces of Assyrian religion can be seen clearly in Avesta. The Assyrian religion seems to have been superimposed on the ancient Aryan religion. Zarathuśtra, the reformer of Iran, wanted to revive and revitalize the ancient fire-worship. But as the Assyrian religion was popular among the masses, the revival of the ancient Aryan religion in its pure form was not possible. It is the Assura Mazas of Assyrians which came into the Avestan religion along with seven good angels and seven bad spirits. Zarthuśtra had to accommodate it. But he succeeded in overthrowing the influences of Buddhism and the transformed, Indianized, Aryan religion, at least in its manifest form. Buddhism was established by Aśoka in the north-west of the Indian subcontinent also. In the Zend-Avesta, Zarathuśtra is described as the "first priest" who took the turning of the wheel from the hands of the Daevas.[76] As is well known, the wheel (Dhamma Chakka) is the central symbol of Buddhism.

The words "Buddha" and "Deva" both came to be employed for fiends in the Iranian tradition. In the Avesta "Buiti, the Daeva" occurs as a fiend. It is called "unseen death" and "hell born".[77] Even the name of Gautama (the Buddha) occurs in Zend-Avesta. The ideal son, who is born by the grace of glorious gods Mithra and others, defeats Gaotema or Gautama (presumably the Buddhists) in disputation. "Through their brightness and glory a man is born who is a chief in assemblies and meetings, who listens well to the (holy) words, whom wisdom holds dear, and who returns a victor from discussions with Gaotema, the heretic"[78] In a Pahlavi text the "Daeva Bud" is called "Secret-moving pestilence, the deceiver"[79]. It is also said in the same Pahlavi text that these Buddhist preached the "nature of sacred beings to mankind but mankind fully understood that they are not sacred beings but Daevas"[80] or demons. At another place in pahlavi texts it is declared, "The demon 'But is he whom they worship among the Hindus, and who lives in idols, as one worships the horse as an idol".[81] This is a clear reference to Buddhists of India. The worship of the horse probably refers to the horse-sacrifice or Aśvamedha-Yajña, which a mighty king in ancient India aspired to perform as a token of his supremacy over other rulers. In the Śatapatha Brāhmaṇa we find a myth in which Asuras, the wicked enemy of gods, held the horse of the gods in the horse-sacrifice. But the horse, who is a "thunderbolt", killed the four-eyed dog under his feet.[82] This is obviously a symbolic representation of the trouncing of Iranians by the Indian warriors.

From time to time Iranians sought to revive their ancient religion, demolished the idol-temples and established the sacred fire on the river Veh or Sindhu and restored the empire of Iran. Zarathuśtra is described as the priest of Kabul who, during the reign of king Viśtasp, "established the fire at the shining mountain in Kabul".[83]

The movement for the revitalization of the original Aryans faith in ancient Iran and India bear remarkable similarities. In India as well as in Iran these revivalist movements were aimed at undoing the pervasive influence of Buddhism. The Manusmṛti, the most sacred law book of Hinduism, owes its predominance to the fact that it laid the normative foundations of the traditional Hindu society of Brahmanical revival against Buddhism. However, no revivalist movement ever succeeds in reviving a bygone age. The Iranian religion and norms of the revivalist era borrowed heavily from the Assyrian tradition; and in India the Brahmanical revivalist movement had to take over many prevailing non-Aryan religious and institutional elements in order to enlist the support of the wider masses in its fight against Buddhism.

It appears that the people of Kashmir, Iran, and Kangdez (Kundez valley is situated in Afghanistan) shared the same religion and culture. In the Pahlavi texts it is laid down that the people living in these places are mutually connected and equally meritorious.[84] It is interesting to note that the land of Sapta-Sindhu is not mentioned as one where people of the same religion are living. Perhaps the people of Sapta-Sindhu were following the transformed Indo-Aryan religion, and were therefore ignored by the Iranians.

Like most ancient Aryan civilizations, in Iran also the family was predominantly partiarchal. The head of the family, usually the father or the eldest male, wielded considerable authority. The position of the wife was subordinate to her husband. A woman needed guardianship of a man in discharging her duties. He could be her husband or son, or, failing these, her father.

According to the ancient Iranian tradition, in cases where the husband died prematurely, and the son was too young to head the family, the father of the wife would assume the family guardianship. From this provision it is clear that in Iran, at least during the revivalist era, the partiarchal values were not as strong as in traditional India. Unlike India, where the eldest male member of the late husband's family assumes the guardianship of the family, in Iran it was to the relatives of the wife that this responsibility was assigned. After the father of the wife, her eldest brother is declared to be the guardian of the sister's family.[85] This custom of appointing a guardian from the wife's family seems to be of non-Aryan, probably of Assyrian origin.

It is also provided that the family guardian—that is the father or brother of the widow—should be given ample remunenation for food, clothing, medicine and shelter.[86] Unlike India, where taking money from daughter or younger sister is taboo, in Iran this was not considered improper. It must have been an established usage of the country and was therefore included in the law books.

There are remarkable similarities between the ancient civilizations of Iran and India as regards the status of the woman. In both civilizations there is no salvation for the woman who is not married. According to the Pahlavi texts the man could have lineage in the future existence by reciting Avesta but the woman could have no such lineage without offspring.[87] According to the Hindu sacred law books, the unmarried woman cannot attain salvation because without marriage she remains unsanctified; marriage is the only full sacrament for her while for a man there are other sacraments also. A woman was not recognized as a witness in either civilization; though litigation between husband and wife is permitted in Iran,[88] but not in India.

Both in ancient India and Iran the son has been given great importance in the family. The daughter has been assigned a lower position than the son. In the later Pahlavi texts, the father is called the fire and his son is the lamp-light.[89] A person who has a son is considered more privileged than the one who has none. It is believed that a sonless person cannot attain heaven.[90] A sonless person cannot cross the "bridge of the heaven". The word *pur* or son means *pul* or bridge through which the father goes to heaven. A person who has no son is called "one having severed bridge". He cannot attain heaven though he has performed many meritorious deeds. At the gate of the Cinvad bridge, while taking account of his deeds, every archangel would question him as to whether or not he has left any substitute for himself in the world. Where the reply is in the negative, his soul will have to remain in the place full of anguish and grief.[91] In the Chāndogya Upaniṣad, self or the Ultimate Reality is called Setu or bridge, from which all evil-doers are turned back.[92]

In the Indian tradition also, the importance of a son is emphasized. A son is necessary for the spiritual welfare of man. A man is saved from the hell, named "*put*", from the very sight of his son's face, according to Bṛhaspati.[93] In fact the Sanskrit word for son Putra is etymologically interpreted as "one who saves his father from the hell named "*put*." A sonless person is considered miserable and inauspicious. He can never gain heaven or salvation.[94]

Both the traditions prescribe a low age of marriage for girls. The Pahlavi texts ordain that a daughter must be given in marriage before she is fifteen, lest she is exposed to paramours and the father incurs sin.[95] In the traditional Indian law books the maximum age of marriage is even lower. It is twelve years. A father who does not give away his daughter in marriage before this age incurs sin. Both the traditions bear witness to the prevalence of bride price. Marriage between cross-cousins is preferred both in the Iranian tradition and Ṛgveda. But in later times it was looked upon with disfavour in northern India.

However, in matters of inheritance and ownership of property, the woman of ancient India was in a position of disadvantage as compared to the woman in ancient Iran. In ancient Iran the property of a sonless person could go to his wife and daughters. But the Mitākṣarā system of law which prevailed over most of India did not permit the wife or the daughter to inherit property. It had to go to the paternal kin, unless a person adopted his daughter's son as his own son. The difference between the position of women in ancient Iran and India may have something to do with the influence of the Assyrian civilization on the former. This influence is also visible in the conception of life after death in ancient Iran. Besides the idea that the dead proceed to live with the departed ancestors, which is found in common in the Zend-Avesta and Ṛgveda, we also find in later Iranian works the conception of a "Day of Judgement" on which the souls of the dead rise up.[96]

The interaction between the ancient Iranian and Indian cultures presents an interesting spectacle. Though in both the traditions there is distinct consciousness of a common descent and close kinship with each other, the animosity and jealousy between them leads to the transformation of the gods of one into the demons of the other. And this attitude is mutual and raciprocal. Because of significant differences of race and culture in the people that they encountered, the two branches of Aryans developed different kinds of social stratification and other aspects of social structure. Even so, both the traditions of culture responded to a challenge in a remarkably similar manner. Both of them threw up strong revivalist movements to combat Buddhism which had almost entirely swamped them. These revivalist movements in both the traditions took over non-Aryan cultural elements on a large scale in order to win the support of the larger masses in their fight against Buddhism. Such processes throw interesting light on certain common modes of response which cultural traditions tend to make when faced with a challenge to their existence. The side-by-side analysis of the source material of the two cultural traditions makes intelligible many points that would have remained obscure and appeared meaningless when studied in isolation.

Notes

1. The Zend-Avesta, I, Vendīdād I. 1-4.
2. The Zend-Avesta, I, Vendīdād II. 40.
3. Aitareya Brāhmaṇa, III. 4-6.
4. Ṛgveda, X. 68. 10.
5. Zend-Avesta, I, Vendīdād II. 41.
6. Śatapatha Brāhmaṇa, X, 4.1.10, Āpastambiya Manta Patha, II, 10.12.
7. Zend-Avesta, I, Vendīdād II. 79.
8. Śatapatha Brāhmaṇa, VII. I. I. 3.
9. Zend-Avesta, I, Vendīdād I.17-18.
10. Smith, Vincent A, Early history of India, 3rd edition, pp. 56-58.
11. Ṛgveda, I, CLVII. 4-6; Zend-Avesta II Aban yast IX.34.
12. Zend-Avesta, I, Vendīdād II. Aban yast IX. 34. Fn. 2.
13. Zend-Avesta, I, Vendīdād I.17.
14. Zend-Avesta, II, Zamyād yaśt VII. 31-34.
15. Pahlvi Texts, I. Bundahiṣ, XXIII.
16. Ṛgveda, II. 20.7.
17. Ṛgveda,V. 29.10.
18. Ṛgveda, X. 22.8
19. Zend-Avesta, I, Vendīdād X.14.
20. Zend-Avesta, I, Vendīdād I. 19.
21. The Zend-Avesta, I, Vendīdād XXII 21.
22. Zend-Avesta, I, Vendīdād I.20.
23. Zend-Avesta, II, XXIII. 4; XXIV. 2.
24. Mahaparinibbana-Sutta, VI. 62.
25. Zend-Avesta, I, Vendīdād II. 2.
26. Indica, I. 1.3.
27. Ṛgveda, I. XXIV. 14
28. Ṛgveda, X, 124-5.
29. Aitareya Brāhmaṇa, VII. 27; Kausītaki Upanisad, III. 1.

30. Śatapatha Brāhmaṇa, I. 4.1.34.
31. Radha Kumud Mookerji "Foreign invasions" in The History of Culture of Indian People ed. By R.C. Majumdar and others, Bombay, Bharatiya Vidya Bhavan, 1968 (4th ed.), Vol. II; p. 39.
32. Taittiriya Saṁhita, II. 37.1.
33. There are two inscriptions of Darius which mentioned haft-Hindu as a part of King Darius's Domain. These are at Persepolis (c. 518-515 B.C.) and at Naksha-i-Rustam (c. 515 B.C.)
34. This enclosure was thus a square. It is not impossible that the planning of neighbourhoods in "squares", as found in many European cities and Indian towns like Jaipur, has its roots in the distant past when the Aryans had not yet branched off.
35. The Zend-Avesta, I, Vendīdād II. 31-41; Talavakāra Upaniṣad, IV. 4.
36. Ṛgveda, X, CXXIII. 6.
37. Ṛgveda, XI. XXVI. 4.
38. The Zend-Avesta, III, Yaśna IX. 4-5.
39. Ṛgveda, IX. CXIII. 89.
40. Ṛgveda, XXIV. 1-2.
41. Ṛgveda, X.IXV. 10-12.
42. Pāraskara Gṛhya Sūtra, I.16.24.
43. Śatapatha Brāhmaṇa, I.I.31; Pāraskara, Gṛhya Sūtra, II. 8.3. Apastamba Dharma Sūtra, I. 515-16. I. 5.16.30.
44. Ṛgveda, I. LXXXIII.5.
45. Zend-Avesta, I, Vendīdād XI.X.19.
46. Ṛgveda, III. LIX. 1.
47. The Zend-Avesta, II, Mihir Yaśt. 7.
48. Zend-Avesta, II, Mihir Yaśt. 25.
49. Ṛgveda, X. CIX. 2-7.
50. Zend-Avesta, I, Vendīdād XVIII. 62.
51. Ṛgveda, X. XCII.5.
52. Pahlavi Texts, III. Sad Dar XI.6.
53. Pahlavi Texts, IV. Dinkard, VIII. XXXVIII. 6-7.
54. Zend-Avesta, I, Vendīdād IV. 46.

55. The Zend-Avesta, III, Yaśna X.II-17.
56. Ṛgveda, IX. V.10.
57. Ṛgveda, IX. LXII.15.
58. Ṛgveda IX. 2.
59. Zend-Avesta, III, Yaśna IX.9.
60. Ṛgveda, IX. XXXIV.4.
61. Zend-Avesta, III, Yasna I.10.
62. Zend-Avesta, III, Yasana XI. 1.
63. Cf. Shrirama Indradeva, "Genesis of Indian Civilization : The Evidence of Gṛhya Sūtra" Diogenes, no. 84, pp. 25-40.
64. Zend-Avesta, I. Vendīdād V. 51.
65. Gobhila Gṛhya Sūtra, II. 10.20.
66. Zend-Avesta, I. Vendīdād. Fargard X. 9.
67. Zend-Avesta, I. Vendīdād VI. 37-39.
68. Zend-Avesta, II. XXIII.5.
69. Pahlavi Texts, IV. Dinkard IX. Xl. VII. 21. p. 308.
70. Pahlavi Texts, IV. II. The Rivāyat of Kamah Bahrah. 12. p. 425.
71. Zend-Avesta, I. Introduction 47.
72. Pahlavi Texts, III. LIX, 7.
73. Śatapatha Brāhmaṇa, XIII. 4.3. 11; III. 2.1.19.
74. Pahlavi Texts, I. Shatyast La-Shayst. XII. 14.
75. D. N. Majumdar, Races and Cultures of India, Lucknow: Universal publishers, n.d. pp. 36-37, 52,59.
76. Zend-Avesta, II. XIII. XXIV. 89.
77. Zend-Avesta, I. XIX. I.1.
78. Zend-Avesta, II. Yasts and Sirozahs. 16.
79. Pahlavi Texts, V. Dinkard VII. 37.
80. Pahlavi Texts, V. Dinkard VII. 46.
81. Pahlavi Texts, I. Bandahis XXVIII. 34.
82. Śatapatha Brahmaṇa, XIII. 11.
83. Pahlavi Texts, I. Bundahis XVII. 6.
84. Pahlavi Texts, III. Sad Dar X. 7.

85. Pahlavi Texts, II. Dadistan-i-Dinik LVI. 7.
86. Pahlavi Texts, II. Dadistan-i-Dinik LVI. 8.
87. Pahlavi Texts, I. Shāyast La-Shāyast. X. 19.
88. Pahlavi Texts, IV. XX. 87.
89. Pahlavi Texts, IV. Dinkard VIII-XXXI.21.
90. Zend-Avesta, I. Vendīdād IV. 47.
91. Pahlavi Texts, III. Sad Dar XVII. 4-7.
92. Chāndogya Upaniṣad, VIII. 4.1.
93. Bṛhaspati Smṛti, XXVI.81.
94. Bṛhaspati, Saṅskāra Kāṇḍa, I.58.
95. Pahlavi Texts, IV. Dinkard VIII.XX.95.
96. Pahlavi Texts, IV. Dinkard IX. XXXXVII. 10.

Index